KEYS FOR LITERACY INSTRUCTION IN THE ELEMENTARY GRADES

DEBRA COFFEY
KENNESAW STATE UNIVERSITY

ELAINE ROBERTS
UNIVERSITY OF WEST GEORGIA

Kendall Hunt

publishing company

Cover image © Shutterstock, Inc.

Kendall Hunt
publishing company

www.kendallhunt.com
Send all inquiries to:
4050 Westmark Drive
Dubuque, IA 52004-1840

Printed in the United States of America
10 9 8 7 6 5 4 3 2 1

PROLOGUE

Golden Keys

A bunch of golden keys is mine,
To make each day with gladness shine.

"Good morning," is the golden key
That unlocks each new day for me.

When at the table,"If You Please,"
I take from off my bunch of keys.

When friends give anything to me
I use the little "Thank you," key.

I say, "Excuse me," or, "I'm sorry," too
When by mistake some harm I do.

On a golden ring these keys I'll bind;
This is its motto—"Be ye kind."

Hearts, like doors, open with ease
To very, very little keys.

I'll often use each golden key,
And so a happy child I'll be.

Dedication to My Mother, Ruby Brock

My mother inspired me to teach, and she shares keys for living in creative ways. "A Bunch of Golden Keys" was displayed in her classroom, and she used the accompanying poem to encourage students in her first grade classes to live happy, meaningful lives. Mother grows lovely roses in her garden, and she inspires beautiful qualities in students. She cherishes memories, such as the days she designed lesson plans for successful early reading experiences, and her first graders looked up from their books with enthusiasm saying, "We're reading!" She is a remarkable cheerleader and a loving mother. I am grateful for her marvelous impact on many lives!

—Debra Coffey

Dedication to My Mother, Helene Roberts

My mother is my inspiration! She is a loving mother, small in stature yet feisty, wise, and famous for creating phrases about the joys for living such as, never worry unnecessarily . . . . "What can you do about it?" She was raised listening to the classics from her twin aunts. Mother enjoys gardening, winning at cards, dancing, listening to music, sewing, homemaking, and reading everything in the newspaper from front to back cover. Although she has passed, I think of her daily.

ACKNOWLEDGEMENTS

We appreciate our mentors Drs. William G. Brozo, Eileen Carr, Peter Dewitz, Harry Morgan, and Katherine Wiesendanger. We would like to extend our appreciation for the inspiration of Dr. Irene Gaskins whose expertise, scholarship, research, and passionate practice of researched-based literacy instruction included time to assist us with shaping part of the book. We are grateful for the contributions of our colleagues, David Anderson, Pam Henry, Dr. Laura Staal, Dr. Feland Meadows, Dr. Stephanie McAndrews, and Dr. Stacy Delacruz who enthusiastically shared their talents.

We value our dedicated students and teachers from kindergarten through graduate school who have contributed to the content ideas of the book. We extend special thanks to Rachel Royal, Julia Buff, and Rob Allen.

We are grateful for the exceptional photographs for the book crafted by Tyler Davis.

Meriting a heartfelt thank you are our families, especially our husbands, Dr. Gary Wenzel and James Coffey, and children Lauren Tompkins, Stephen Patti, and Jill Jacoby, who encouraged us to persevere with the message of the book to improve literacy instruction for all.

We sincerely appreciate the efficiency and dedication of Sarah Flynn and Katie Wendler from Kendall Hunt Publishing. Their thoughtfulness inspired us throughout the writing process.

Image © Shutterstock, Inc.

—Elaine Roberts

CONTENTS

MEET THE AUTHORS

Dr. Debra J. Coffey is an associate professor of Literacy and Language Instruction in the Department of Elementary and Early Childhood Education in the Bagwell College of Education at Kennesaw State University. During regional, national, and international conferences, she shares innovations from teaching experiences across the spectrum from preschool to the university level. She has written widely about literacy strategies, and she co-authored the book *Unlocking the Power of Language: Research-Based Strategies for Language Development.* As an academic lead coach, mentor, and co-advisor for student organizations, she conducts outreach programs and literacy projects for partnership schools in Nigeria, Belize, Costa Rica, Mexico, and Ecuador.

Dr. Elaine Roberts, PH.D., is an associate professor of Reading Education at the University of West Georgia in the College of Education Department of Clinical and Professional Studies, Area of Language and Literacy. She was a leader in the development of the Reading Endorsement for the state of Georgia and has written articles in peer reviewed journals as well as presented at numerous conferences, state-wide, regionally, nationally and internationally. Her main areas of interest include critical literacy, word recognition and comprehension, and literacy progress monitoring across the content areas. She was a university reading clinic supervisor and has taught first and fourth grade and high school. She enjoys working as a literacy consultant.

Image © Shutterstock, Inc.

Keys for Effective Teaching

Chapter 1 explores the characteristics of effective teachers and resources to enhance active literacy exploration in the elementary classroom and beyond. Consider what you know about effective teaching. Before you read the chapter, answer the first two questions about what you know and what you want to explore about effective literacy instruction. Then answer the last two questions after reading this chapter and discussing ideas and insights with friends.

TABLE 1.1

K	E	Y	S
What do you **know** about effective literacy instruction? What does it mean to be an effective teacher?	What do you want to **explore** about effective literacy instruction?	What are you **yearning** to learn after reading and discussing the chapter?	How will you **satisfy** your curiosity? What ideas will you apply to your teaching after reading this chapter?

Effective Literacy Instruction

Effective teachers use balanced, integrated instruction to enhance children's achievement in literacy. Children develop positive attitudes toward reading and writing when they are provided with engaging classroom libraries and digital resources. They benefit from numerous reading and writing opportunities in centers that integrate various subjects. These opportunities help to nurture their interest in books and inspire them to grow as readers.

Frances Hodgson Burnett's book *The Secret Garden* (1911/2009) described a young girl named Mary who exemplified the qualities of an effective teacher after she overcame her own challenges. Mary's life changed drastically after her parents died and she moved to England. As she learned to deal with her own challenges, Mary began to grow and understand life from a new perspective. Her life started changing after she found the hidden key to a secret garden. She explored the garden and became interested in growing plants to restore the garden. This interest intensified when she made a new friend named Dillon and met her cousin, Collin. When Mary discovered that Collin could not walk and was missing the beauty of nature, she teamed with Dillon to awaken Collin's enjoyment of life. Mary pursued this quest with diligence and patience. As she nurtured plants in the garden they started growing, and Collin became fascinated with the emerging life all around him. When these remarkable changes became a way of life, Collin enjoyed the beauty of the garden, and he learned to walk. When his father returned, he was amazed to see the changes in Collin. Then Collin told his father that Mary and the garden made all the difference.

Effective teachers demonstrate many of the characteristics that Mary exemplified as she carefully nurtured plants in the garden and helped Collin to enjoy life. These teachers show patience and perseverance as they differentiate instruction and plan programs that match the needs and interests of students. Teachers who practice differentiated instruction understand students' readiness and literacy skills, their mastery of reading strategies across the content areas, and preferred styles of learning. Through this tender-loving care they often see remarkable changes in the classroom.

Three Keys for Effective Literacy Instruction

Effective teachers help children to master strategies and skills for enjoyment of reading. They read marvelous books that capture students' imaginations and help them to become aware of **conventions of print** (knowledge of words, spaces between words, sentences, and reading left to right). Effective teachers help students develop **auditory and visual discrimination** as well as **automaticity** (recognizing words quickly). They give children opportunities to enjoy learning story grammar with theme and character analysis while they connect comprehension strategies and critical thinking skills with engaging discussions of literature.

Effective teachers model literacy skills and strategies during class sessions, and they often use mini-lessons to share concepts. Afflerbach, Pearson, and Paris (2008) suggested that strategies are goal directed and lead to reading skill. For example, a teacher models how to use the reading strategy of making text to self connections for comprehension of a narrative text. The teacher models, "This reminds me of when I was . . . ." The students then practice using the strategy to make text-to-self connections in order to understand a narrative story. With practice, the students automatically use text-to-self connections independently during reading as an unconscious acquired reading skill.

Teachers guide students as they practice strategies as a large group, in small groups, and then independently. After they initially teach these strategies, they reinforce them in context to help students understand literacy skills for authentic reading and writing purposes. They often use computer activities to reinforce these skills and strategies across the content areas.

Effective teachers collaborate to design beneficial instruction, and their discussions typically revolve around the development of literacy skills that connect to individual student needs. Since they realize that students will be reading at various levels and have different literacy skills, they collaborate with other teachers to meet students' needs. Their successful collaboration, when grounded in research, will lead to a creative vision of literacy learning (National Council of Teachers of English, 2002).

The National Institute of Child Health and Human Development (NICHD, 1997) emphasizes the following key principles of effective literacy teaching (*www.nrrf.org/synthesis_research.htm*):

- Begin teaching phonemic awareness at an early age.
- Use interesting stories to develop oral language and comprehension.
- Teach children explicitly what single sound a given letter or letter combination makes.
- Teach frequent, highly regular sound–spelling relationships systematically.
- Model and teach students how to decode words. Use decodable texts for children to practice the sound–spelling relationships they learn in context.

Components of Language and Literacy

As teachers nurture literacy development, students become **strategic learners** and transfer skills and strategies during reading and writing experiences. Effective teachers help students develop the ability to use word recognition, fluency, and comprehension strategies independently. They design literacy lessons that help students to convey their ideas clearly when writing and sharing literature in the classroom. Awareness of the components of literacy helps teachers to nurture literacy development more effectively.

TABLE 1.2 Components of Literacy: Reading, Writing, Listening, Speaking, and Viewing.

Listening	Speaking
Multifaceted opportunities for listening to stories and enjoying story elements enhance literacy development.	When the classroom is an engaging literacy environment, students have opportunities to communicate their insights.
Reading	**Writing**
Effective teachers provide enjoyable books for pleasant, meaningful reading experiences.	Effective teachers help students to capture imaginative ideas as they write.
Viewing/Media Literacy Effective teachers provide student choice and motivation viewing of multimedia to extend comprehension and engage students in reflective reader response.	

Listening

Language and listening skills are necessary for interacting with others on a personal level at home and at school. Socioeconomic status (SES) and level of education influence the quality of oral language and listening skills (Huttenlocker et al.2002; National Institute for Literacy, 2008). Language and listening skills are enhanced when there are in-depth conversations, as well as listening and learning opportunities at home and at school. Hart and Risling (1995) found that by age three, children from educated caretakers were likely to come across 30 million words whereas children in welfare families were exposed to approximately10 million words. When students enter school with different literacy experiences, they make discoveries as they listen to teachers and other students and learn to interpret media. Since good listening skills are required in order to interact and comprehend text critically, teachers can model listening strategies and have students share experiences to practice how to be good listeners when they are **engaged in oral reading and writing activities**.

There are motivating ways to enrich students' listening and oral language development. Research by Gaab and colleagues (2005) suggests that children's interest in sounds and melody develops the brain for listening and language skills. Songs like "Old McDonald" and nursery rhymes engage students' attention. The website *www.burnsparentsmartblog.spot.com* has multiple resources for speech and language development. The website includes a blog about the importance of using melody to learn easy speech sounds like *m, k,* and *l*. By building interest in sounds and melodies, young children learn to enjoy listening for predictable patterns and sounds in words.

Resnick and Snow (2009) state that "children need both 'air time' opportunities and 'ear time'—the attention of fluent, responsive adults to develop oral language skills" (p. 6). When teachers and parents use read-alouds, think-alouds, and sing-alouds to share their thinking for making meaning, they expose students to listening and speaking skills. When effective teachers use repetition of "catchy phrases," figurative language, and sounds of words, they involve children in interactive listening and speaking. These experiences benefit all students and help them develop cultural understanding of each other while they learn together.

Speaking

Integrating the skills of listening, reading, writing, and speaking is essential for effective communication. Gonzalez (2001) summed up the importance of language when he stated, "Children's ties to a heritage and thus to an identity, whatever it may be, are brought about through the heart and mind, and language is the building block of both" (p. 71). Thus, authentic conversations are reciprocal because they enrich all students' understanding and comprehension during discussions about texts. Culturally responsive teachers help students expand their speaking skills by becoming mini philosophers. They guide students when building background knowledge about topics they will discuss, are generous with praise and encouragement, and offer positive suggestions to develop meaningful conversations. They use small groups, peer conferences, and shared reading and writing as opportunities to model and have students practice how to share opinions and appreciate others' interpretations of reading and writing materials beginning at early ages. Teachers can model how to question using new vocabulary and higher-level questions, share methods for discussing topics of interest, and model how to agree and disagree gracefully. Role playing, puppet shows, and drama combined with physical movement to music and singing about learning motivate student oral language development.

English language learners benefit from interaction with English speakers, and this interaction is often mutually beneficial. English language learners need comprehension skills to comfortably access the types of texts they encounter in regular classrooms (Valdez, 1994). This helps them (1) explore language and vocabulary, (2) find main ideas and details, and (3) communicate with other children in regular classroom settings. Linguistically diverse children bring speaking skills, such as code-switching (ability to make use of two languages to understand texts) and shared reading and writing interpretations, to create a rich literacy environment. For example, teachers can encourage students to compare and contrast bilingual words using a Venn diagram as a word wall. Words with cognates (similar spellings of words) are written in the center circle, and words with different features are written in their own circle, as presented in Figure 1.1. Using labels, picture cards with words on the reverse side of the picture, role playing of stories in students' home language and English can also be encouraged.

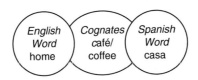

FIGURE 1.1

Quality language and literacy instruction is necessary to improve communication skills for all (Franquiz, 2003). These quality conversations and shared learning expand existing knowledge for all concerned. Students need to share their languages and have opportunities to read materials in a variety of languages that are easily accessible in classrooms. As a result, students' **decoding skills, vocabulary, and comprehension skills** are developed along with cultural appreciation of each other.

Reading and Writing

Collaborative sharing opportunities, such as discussions and listening activities during book clubs, can be enhanced by extensions of reading and writing. Students build background knowledge through positive experiences with text on the Internet, computer games, videos, instant messaging, and virtual field trips. Discussions about interpreting images found in texts, rap music, and hard copies of students' writing shared at home and school often motivate students to read and write. Reading and writing need to be emphasized at home and school to provide choices and multiple learning opportunities for children. Choice allows an expansion of reading and writing comprehension skills in innovative ways. Encouraging critical thinking during multiple reading and writing activities expands listening and speaking skills.

Critical thinking skills help students explore meaning-making as they integrate literacy skills across the content areas. Student-centered learning allows them to bring personal interpretations to literacy learning as they critique what they view, discuss, read, and write. When students have meaningful conversations about topics that interest them and listen to others, they learn to view themselves as knowledgeable interpreters of information. Multiple literacies reinforce two elements of thinking, according to Cope and Kalantzis (2000). They are (1) the importance of cultural and linguistic diversity and (2) the numerous avenues for retrieving text information and comprehending (i.e., digital and hard copies of text). Teachers need to model and help students learn to ask higher-level questions during reading and writing discussions, such as book clubs. Sociocultural discussions and interactions during book clubs and similar activities help students to refine their thinking and extend comprehension when reading and writing independently across the curriculum.

Media Literacy

Students today are in constant interaction with media. Media literacy is the application of critical thinking and responding to the messages of print and electronic media (Luke, 2000; Summers, 2000). It helps students encompass the skills and knowledge needed to question, analyze, interpret, and evaluate the messages of the mass media (i.e., television, the Internet, and films). Effective teachers guide students to:

- Think about the impact of media literacy on their viewing, listening, reading, writing, and speaking skills.
- Interpret and analyze the message of the author and understand how it impacts their impressions and others' impressions.
- Consider how the visuals and audios influence their thinking.
- Understand the values and opinions expressed and how they impact their thinking.

When media is used to reinforce literacy strategies and skills, teachers provide choices of follow-up activities to extend the media learning. These activities may include media research projects, reader response, and student monitoring of learning. When a website is used for a specific reading strategy, such as use of a phonics website game to reinforce knowledge about vowels for word recognition, the students should understand the purpose of the game and what was learned. Then they should be given opportunities to implement the strategy during authentic reading and writing experiences. Media literacy can be useful as a student resource for organizing what was learned, and it inspires creative methods to categorize and synthesize new information for long-term learning across the content areas (Leu, 2000; Jenkins, 2006). Jenkins, 2006, p. 259 suggested that media educators help young people "to think of themselves as cultural producers and participants and not simply as consumers, critical or otherwise."

Literacy Theory and Research

Research in the field of literacy shapes the way we integrate assessment, instruction, and learning. The essence of literacy instruction is comprehension. Literacy theories emphasize the importance of activating background knowledge for effective comprehension.

Building Background Knowledge: Schema Theory

Students bring personal experiences to the reading and writing experience. The mental ideas and concepts they hold about events, objects, and situations are schema (Wade, 1990). Schema theorists emphasize that students need to activate their background knowledge and make predictions before, during, and after reading. Anderson and Pearson (1984) noted that schema integrates a number of simultaneous cues and concepts into an orderly representation. This extensive network of thought patterns coordinates with four cueing systems for comprehension of text (Adams, 1990; Goodman, 1996): (1) syntactic (language patterns, grammar structure, and order), (2) semantic (meaning through text/illustrations), (3) graphophonic (letter-sound relationships, phonics), and (4) pragmatic (function and sociocultural aspects of language).

Students benefit when schemata are networked in relationships by categorizing information. For example, it enhances the understanding of English language learners when headings are written on word walls in students' primary language and the English language. On a word wall column headings such as "Plants" could have subcategories of "daisies, spikes, and cone flowers." Students can add what they know to the subcategories and build new schema as they assimilate information.

Reader Response Theory

Literacy researcher Louise Rosenblatt (1994) emphasized the importance of reader response theory. She stressed that reading is more than an interaction but rather a transaction between the reader and the text. Students need to be aware of the purposes for reading and appreciate the unique interpretations shared by students. Students can learn to appreciate each other's interpretations and selections of particular parts of text that appeal more to one individual than another. Through conversations new meaning can be reconstructed as the students share cultural responses to the literature. Rosenblatt stressed the importance of including a variety of types of multicultural literature to help students build authentic knowledge about others and value cultural pluralism in our society.

Literacy researchers explore the cultural perspectives that relate to readers' efferent (reading for information) and aesthetic (reading for enjoyment) stances that are used to construct knowledge during collaborative learning exchanges. Galda and Beach (2001) noted that "in constructing texts as cultural worlds, readers are learning to interpret characters' actions within larger frameworks of worlds constituted by cultural forces." They stated that it is important for the reader to "move beyond a focus on individual characters to a consideration of the systems that shape the characters" and consider "how lives reflect social forces" (p. 67). Furthermore, Galda and Beach discuss the importance of teachers allowing "discourses of freedom" to help students share their beliefs while interpreting characters' actions and feelings. They emphasize that teachers should go beyond inferring characters' actions and beliefs to interpretations that involve social practices. The social practices involve construction of beliefs about identities, inclusion/exclusion of others' beliefs, building relationships, influencing others' beliefs, development of groups as communities, dealing with conflicts, and sharing knowledge to construct new understandings of how characters represent cultures. These discussions help students to build and reconstruct background knowledge for comprehension.

Social Constructivist Theory and Critical Literacy

Teachers who practice diverse social constructivist theory provide shared cultural and social contexts for reading and writing experiences during literacy learning. They search for methods to discover how students are motivated to create and analyze interpretations of text in relation to their prior knowledge. They emphasize critical literacy when they (1) use effective questions; (2) teach students to question information before, during, and after reading; and (3) encourage discussions about cultural responsiveness. These teachers scaffold literacy learning and help students to use effective comprehension strategies independently to increase background knowledge. In addition, they engage students in interactive discussions to recognize, analyze, reconstruct, and write about interpretations of text across the content areas.

When teachers focus on critical literacy, they help students make meaning of texts "as process of construction . . . textual meaning is understood in the context of social, historic, and power relations, not solely as the product of intention of an author . . . and a means to social transformation" (Cervetti, Pardales, & Damico, 2001, p. 5). Effective teachers integrate these diverse social constructivist and critical literacy approaches to generate student enthusiasm for literacy learning:

- Multiple, ongoing authentic assessments to determine students' prior knowledge before, during, and after literacy learning
- Scaffolding learning to make appropriate adaptations for teaching and individual learning
- Time for student reflection about effective use of reading comprehension strategies
- Self-assessment, self-questioning, and shared learning to develop students' critical and analytical responses to literature
- Reading and thinking aloud to model and teach students how to build background knowledge together by teaching them how to select effective comprehension strategies and use them during reading and writing to expand their critical literacy
- Culturally sensitive interactions to develop curiosity and reconstruction of meaning
- Incorporate student interest, choice, inquiry, and discovery to perpetuate student talents among diverse groups and a variety of language opportunities
- Integration of literacy multimedia projects to extend background knowledge and higher-level thinking about cultural implications of text
- Literacy experiences related to the arts, such as drama and music, that authentically represent all cultures

Interactive Reading Theory

Rumelhart's (1980) model of interactive reading theory features knowledge of semantic knowledge for meaning-making with word recognition, vocabulary, and comprehension strategies during reading and writing experiences. Rumelhart's model was reconstructed by McIntryre and Pressley (1996). They integrated Rumelhart's model of learning within a balanced and integrated approach for responsive literacy activities across the curriculum. Routman (1991) also stressed responsive and integrated literacy learning. She emphasized the importance of reading and writing aloud, guided and shared reading, and independent reading and writing to extend prior knowledge and build background knowledge.

These models for interactive reading focus on (1) integrating the teaching of reading and language arts, (2) student choice, (3) high-level conversations and questioning, (4) scaffolding of learning, and (5) independent student effort and improvement. They emphasize the importance of activating reader response across content areas, using authentic literature, and providing instruction to improve writing.

Integrating Engaging Literacy Instruction

Literacy instruction should not be limited to a block of time for reading and language arts assessment and instruction separate from other content areas. An integrated approach to literacy assessment, teaching, and learning synthesizes purposeful instruction in all content areas rather than isolating reading instruction from the balance of the curriculum (Graves, Graves, & Dewitz, 2011; Guthrie et al., 2001; Vaca & Vaca, 2002). It involves effective teacher organization and management, flexible grouping, teacher modeling, and student implementation of effective reading strategies across all content areas. Teachers further motivate and engage students with diverse needs in literacy learning through the use of interactive digital resources.

Integrating literacy and technology across the content areas is motivating. The International Society for Technology Education (ISTE) standards for teachers address the importance of facilitating and engaging students in creative literacy learning through use of digital tools and resources. These creative ideas may be accessed on the ISTE website at *www.iste.org.*

Integration of learning involves effective inclusion of special education students into general education classrooms. "The true essence of inclusion is based on the premise that all individuals with disabilities have a right to be included in naturally occurring settings and activities with their neighborhood peers, siblings, and friends" (Erwin, 1993, p. 1; Larkin, 2001). Inclusion is beneficial when student-centered, curriculum-based instruction is combined with modification to meet students' learning styles and needs. Student collaboration and productive peer tutoring engages all students. When students with disabilities face challenges in general classroom settings, the success of inclusion may be enhanced by the decisions and team efforts of classroom teachers, content-area teachers, reading specialists, special education teachers, speech therapists, counselors, and ELL teachers.

Teaching effective literacy strategies across the content areas is essential for comprehension, the foundation for reading and writing. Researchers emphasize the importance of helping students to understand the purpose for reading—making meaning—during reading and writing in all subject areas (Allington, 2003; Allington & Johnston, 2002; Cunningham & Allington, 1994; Duke, 2000; Gaskins; Ehri, 1998; Pearson & Raphael, 1999; Pressley, 1999; Pressley, Allington, Wharton-McDonald, Block, & Morrow, 2001). Effective teachers equip their classrooms with a multitude of authentic texts from a variety of genres. They provide extensive time for students to discuss and interpret narrative and informational texts, making personal connections to learning through writing. High-interest multimedia texts help students learn authors' styles of writing and provide keys for searching for meaning. Instruction, therefore, should include teaching students to use self-monitoring strategies to make meaning during reading and writing. These strategies include rereading, self-correcting, and using other effective comprehension, fluency, and word recognition strategies. These strategies help learners build confidence and literacy skills across the content areas.

Effective Teaching Strategies

According to Allington (2003) and Pressley et al. (2001), effective teachers integrate multiple literacies by:

- Providing a substantial amount of time daily for reading and writing across the content areas
- Giving students free choice for book selections with multiple copies of authentic texts of various genres
- Encouraging students to use high-level conversations and questioning
- Developing skills for building background knowledge and scaffolding of student learning
- Allowing students to independently demonstrate the ability to use literacy skills and strategies while they transfer this knowledge to all content areas
- Valuing student effort and improvement to guide literacy assessment and learning rather than solely depending on standardized test results to foster motivation
- Providing opportunities for student projects with rubrics and student portfolios with self-monitored learning opportunities

Student Choice

Allington (2003) emphasized that teachers should provide books on appropriate reading levels during self-selected reading sessions. Each student should have opportunities to read at an independent level during self-selected reading, with appropriate selection of texts and options for reader response. For example, students may work together in small heterogeneous groups to discover and design research projects using leveled texts available in the classroom, on the Internet, and from interviews. Student-centered teaching provides opportunities for students to choose texts and methods to acquire information. Thus, students learn to value each other's choices, conversations, and extend their own literacy learning methods and explorations during reader response.

Sharing cultural experiences during research projects opens opportunities for inquiry learning through discussions based on international magazines, websites, pictures, catalogues, flash cards, bilingual graphic organizers, and videos about curriculum-based topics. This student-centered approach increases reading fluency and comprehension as students choose texts and acquire information collaboratively. During this collaborative research students develop new interests and learn to value each other's choices and opinions.

Providing numerous books about topics of interest and allowing selection of subtopics of choice for curriculum-based learning motivates students to be engaged in literacy learning across the content areas. Interest inventories assist teachers when they are selecting books of interest for students that read at different reading levels. High-interest, low-reading level books are an essential resource for students who are below grade level. They can be used to teach reading strategies and motivate students to advance to higher-level books. Creating books for students about topics of interest are a way to motivate students. Series books are another popular student choice, suggested on the website *Kidsreads.com*. Series books include *Amelia Bedelia* by Peggy and Herman Parish, the Boxcar series by Gertrude Warner, and the Chet Gecko Mysteries by Bruce Hale.

High-Level Conversations and Questioning

Self-efficacy skills help students to view themselves as successful participants who engage in literature conversations and extend literacy learning to higher levels of thinking (Alvermann, 2002; Guthrie & Wigfield, 2000; McCrudden et al., 2005). Self-efficiacy is a belief in your ability to succeed. Teachers who model and discuss **self-efficacy** skills build the confidence that is critical during social reading and writing interactions. As a consequence, students learn to enhance their discussions and develop questioning skills at higher levels of thinking. These experiences help students to generate "how" and "why" questions during conversations about texts and extend meaning-making. These experiences help students to realize their capabilities as literacy learners.

Strategies, such as Reciprocal Questioning (ReQuest; Manzo, 1969), help students to become comfortable with debating and sharing opinions. During the ReQuest strategy students experience the teacher role by formulating their own lists of questions. Then the teacher and peers answer the students' questions. These experiences help students generate "how," "why," "who," "what," and "where" questions during conversations about texts. Students become confident mini-philosophers when they learn to develop higher-level questions that include "Explain why. . ." or "What is the meaning of. . .?" or "How does this affect me?"

Scaffolding Learning

Learning to read is a complex instructional process. It involves social, cognitive, and emotional factors (Adams, 1990; Lipson & Wixson, 1997). It is essential that students learn effective reading strategies to construct meaning and recognize words automatically, or they will fall behind. Ivey, Bauman, and Jarrard (2000) found that second- and sixth-grade students became skillful, strategic readers and writers when a balanced, integrated approach was used that emphasized **scaffolding of learning**. To scaffold literacy learning, teachers (1) model a reading goal; (2) support students as they focus on, practice, and learn the goal through peer interactions; and (3) provide opportunities for students to use the learning goal independently.

Numerous models (e.g., Larkin, 2001; Vygotsky, 1976; Bruner, 1975) have been developed for scaffolding instruction for students with diverse needs through integration of assessment and instruction. For example, a teacher models a word recognition strategy. Then students use the strategy to pronounce unfamiliar words. Next, students listen as the teacher reads aloud and talks about use of the strategy. Finally, they use the strategy during independent reading across the content areas. Effective teachers observe and take notes as students respond to texts, listening to see if they use meaning-making and self-regulating strategies successfully during reading and writing.

English language learners especially benefit from scaffolding academic learning. Bradley and Bradley (2004, p. 1) identified three types of scaffolding that are effective for English language learners. They are (1) simplifying language by shortening selections, speaking in the present tense, and avoiding idioms; (2) asking for completion before expecting generation of ideas as students choose answers from a list or complete a partially finished outline or paragraph; and (3) using visuals, such as graphic organizers and charts. English language learners need to tie new information to their prior experiences and self-monitor learning. Active involvement during scaffolded theme-centered literacy lessons should include reading strategies and student choice. The strategies should be reinforced before, during, and after reading and writing responses. Teachers need to have newspapers, trade books, magazines, reference materials, and Internet resources for students. E-pals can enhance communication.

Independent Student Effort and Improvement

Allington (2003) found that students' motivation is tied to improvement in reading and writing across the content areas. He emphasized that teachers should look beyond using standardized test results to plan instruction. He highlighted the importance of (1) providing opportunities for student inquiry projects, (2) self-monitoring of learning, (3) teacher- and/or student-developed rubrics, and (4) literacy artifacts in student portfolios to motivate students to understand and expand their literacy learning. According to Allington, teachers who designed instruction using a teacher and student accountability model reported a "greater sense of personal professional responsibility for student outcomes. In other words, these teachers accepted the professional responsibility for developing high levels of reading proficiency but insisted on the autonomy to act on their expertise" (p. 12).

Effective teachers motivate students to use strategies and develop the skills they need to become successful readers and life-long learners. Throughout this book we explore strategies, activities, and literature for beneficial literacy instruction. We will consider the most effective ways to nurture students just as Mary carefully provided the right amount of water, nutrients, and sunshine for plants in *The Secret Garden*.

Photograph by Tyler Davis.

These picture shows that Elaine Roberts provides just the right amount of water and sunlight for the plants in her lovely garden.

Keys for Literacy Instruction and Assessment of Literacy Development

Chapter 2 features an overview of literacy development and instructional strategies. This chapter explores concepts of print, phonemic awareness, phonics, spelling, and the alphabetic principle. Consider what you know about literacy instruction and assessment. Before you read the chapter, answer the first two questions about what you know and what you want to know about literacy instruction and assessment. Then answer the last two questions after reading this chapter and discussing ideas and insights with friends.

TABLE 2.1

K	E	Y	S
What do you **know** about literacy instruction and assessment?	What do you want to **explore** about literacy instruction and assessment?	What do you **yearn** to learn after reading and discussing the chapter?	How will you **satisfy** your curiosity? What ideas will you apply to your teaching after reading this chapter?

Literacy Development

Teachers who understand the framework of literacy development are more prepared to nurture children and promote maximum growth and development. This process is like tending a garden and making sure each plant receives all it needs for maximum growth. Even if a gardener knows what is needed to nurture plants, it may be challenging to find just the right combination for maximum growth. Just as a gardener needs to provide the right elements for development during certain stages of growth, teachers need to provide developmentally appropriate instruction. When we seek to nurture a child's reading development, we need to use an effective research-based approach that promotes engagement and understanding. It is important to consider what children know and what they need to know at any stage of development in order to provide meaningful instruction. Mary found the key to the secret garden, and it unlocked immense joy. Experiences in the garden revived enthusiasm for life and had a transformative effect on Mary and Collin. As we consider the reading and writing process, it is important to discover the keys that unlock the power of language so children will experience the joys of learning. How can we teach reading effectively?

Development of Emergent Readers

Early emergent readers benefit from activities to promote **phonemic awareness** (the ability to blend, segment, substitute, and delete sounds) and **letter-sound knowledge** (Gaskins, Ehri, Cress, O'Hara, & Donnelly, 1996/97). The English alphabet represents approximately 44 phonemes (sounds). Effective teachers design instructional opportunities for children to learn alternative ways to spell and read rather than simply learning through memorization or sounding out words letter-by-letter. Students need systematic instruction for the development of strategy knowledge in **word recognition** (pronunciation of words/phonics/decoding), **vocabulary** (understanding the meaning of words), **comprehension** (understanding what is read), and **fluency** (smoothness and expression in reading). Systematic instruction is most effective in the context of quality literature that promotes reading enjoyment. Quality literature motivates students to personally connect to texts they read or enjoy during read-aloud sessions.

Figure 2.1 provides a profile of this development. While considering these developmental stages, look for components that should be integrated into literacy instruction and learning.

Students in elementary grades need to understand how spelling cultivates knowledge of the alphabetic system. Ehri (1998) emphasized that in addition to learning the spellings of specific words, spelling instruction should cultivate students' knowledge of the alphabetic system. This should include **graphophonic correspondences** (how letters symbolize sounds in the pronunciation of words) and knowledge of consolidated units, including root words, affixes (prefixes and suffixes), and families of related words. The more students understand about the alphabetic system, the more they will retain information about individual words and spelling patterns (Metsala & Ehri, 1998).

Read-alouds enhance students' enjoyment of books because students typically understand what is read to them more easily than what they discern when they initially begin to read independently (Cunningham & Allington, 2010; Curtis, 1980). When students' read independently in the early years they focus on many processes that become automatic in later years. Read alouds help students to enter the world of reading and enjoy books as they develop word recognition skills. This helps them to decode words automatically and enhances their ability to read for meaning (Adams, 1990; Ehri & Robbins, 1992; Share & Stanovich, 1995). Reading to children provides them with new experiences and develops their background knowledge. By integrating literacy experiences in science, math, and social studies, teachers can promote an even greater depth of understanding. Skill and strategy development can be infused naturally through these integrated opportunities to connect children's learning experiences with texts. This must happen intentionally and often. It is essential for teachers to provide enjoyable reading experiences as they identify what children know in order to take them to the next level of understanding.

Nurturing Literacy Development

Social and cultural experiences are linked to literacy progress for students. They need to have knowledge of the alphabetic system and develop literacy skills related to phonological knowledge, which is the ability to recognize and understand sounds in language and produce the sounds in words. Students need phonemic awareness, especially for blending and segmenting sounds.

Effective emergent literacy instruction highlights auditory vocabulary development, comprehension, phonemic awareness, and phonics in developmentally appropriate ways. During effective literacy instruction these components are integrated during enjoyable reading and writing activities. Students need to be involved in high-interest activities that increase their oral language, ability to manipulate sounds in words (phonemic awareness), and ability to understand letter-sound relationships (alphabetic principle).

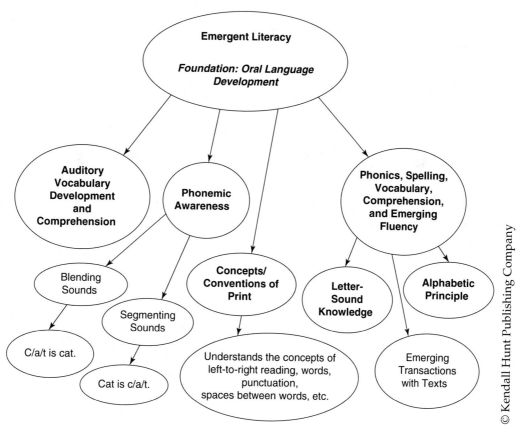

© Kendall Hunt Publishing Company

FIGURE 2.1   Web of Emergent Literacy Instruction

Students need to develop **morphological knowledge**. When students develop morphological knowledge, they become aware of the roles affixes (i.e., prefixes and suffixes) and root words play in decoding and understanding the meanings of words in context.

Lexical development begins with conceptual information about one-word utterances and expands into recognition of hundreds of words during early literacy development (Vygotsky, 1986). These words are stored in lexical memory as references to help children pronounce unfamiliar words with similar subunits. For instance, recognition of the word "cat" helps a student to read the word "hat." Recognition of the word "prefer" helps a student to read the word "prepay." Vygotsky emphasized that children should learn to use words as functional tools to help them comprehend text. Word recognition, therefore, can be thought of as the foundation for comprehension.

Modeling and Scaffolding Emergent Literacy Instruction

Effective emergent literacy instruction helps children to thrive and enjoy the learning process. Responsive teachers plant the seeds for learning, nurture children, and inspire successful achievement through delightful literacy experiences.

Concepts of Print

Emergent readers need to understand **concepts of print**. Thus, they need to recognize the front and back of the book, understand that reading follows in a left-to-right progression in the English language, realize there are spaces between words, and note the differences between words and sentences. An informal assessment for concepts of print includes the necessary literacy concepts for emergent readers. An excellent resource is Marie Clay's *Observation Survey of Early Literacy Achievement* (1993).

Informal concept of print assessments for word knowledge includes the **voice-pointing procedure** (Gillett & Temple, 2000). First, children memorize a selection of text even if they cannot read it, such as "Twinkle, Twinkle, Little Star." The teacher reads the selection to the child aloud and points to each line as read. Then the child recites the lines, pointing to each word. Next, the teacher reads selected words aloud and has the child point to them. Finally, the teacher uses word cards to test word recognition.

Phonemic Awareness and Phonological Awareness

Yopp and Singer developed a test of phonemic awareness titled the *Yopp-Singer Test of Phonemic Segmentation* to determine childrens' ability to segment and blend sounds. Researchers Yopp and Yopp (2000) define phonemic awareness as the "awareness that the speech stream consists of a sequence of sounds—specifically **phonemes**, the smallest unit of sound that conveys meaning and makes a difference in communication. It is the phoneme that determines the difference between the words 'dog' and 'hog,' 'look' and 'lick'. . . these differences influence meaning" (p. 130). Students are phonemically aware if they can recognize the speech stream as a sequence of small sounds and can manipulate sounds in words. **Phonological awareness** refers to the individual's awareness of the sound structure of spoken words. Levels of sound structure for phonological awareness include (1) phonemes, (2) syllables, and (3) onsets and rimes.

Phonemic awareness is a subset of phonological awareness. **Phonological awareness** is an awareness that spoken language consists of any size unit of sound. It is the ability to identify and manipulate the sounds of language (Adams, 1990). Students who have phonological awareness can clap to indicate that they hear individual sounds in words and also clap when they recognize individual words in sentences or individual syllables in words. These students are also aware that there are sometimes small words and syllables in words. Thus, rhyming and separating syllables are a part of phonological awareness. Phonological awareness instruction helps students pronounce words and lays the foundation for the ability to read and comprehend text. These skills need to be reinforced during rich literature activities that focus on meaning, oral language development, and writing to spark students' interest and enjoyment of reading (Moats, 2000). One of the most common causes of early reading problems is weakness in phonological features of language, a close relationship between a child's phonemic awareness, ability to manipulate sounds, and reading success. It is crucial, therefore, to assess phonemic awareness skills because this ability may be causally related to early word reading skills (Adams, 1990; Lundberg, Frost, & Peterson, 1988; Wagner et al., 1997; Yopp & Yopp, 2000).

Phonemic Awareness

Students in kindergarten and first and second grade need to develop oral language, phonemic awareness, understanding of concepts of print, and letter–sound relationship knowledge as they listen to teachers read aloud. This helps them to make meaning of print. Teachers **scaffold instruction** when they model the skill, use guided practice while students try the skill, allow time for students to discuss and practice the skill with others, and have students show how they use the skill independently (i.e., pre-post assessments, projects, sharing related reading and writing activities).

Students with excellent phonemic awareness skills can blend, segment, delete, and substitute sounds in words. For example, when students can rhyme words (i.e., bed-fed) they can manipulate some sounds. They need to develop the ability to **delete** and **substitute initial sounds** in words (i.e., the "b" sound in "bed" can be deleted and substituted with the "f" sound to create the new word "fed"). By modeling and providing students with opportunities to rhyme words, teachers can help extend the learning to deleting and substituting initial sounds. When students can combine several sounds they have the ability to **blend sounds** (i.e., b/e/d or b/ed to say "bed"). When students can **segment sounds** they have the ability to manipulate parts of the sounds in words (i.e., "bed" becomes the phonemes b/e/d). These essential phonemic awareness tasks and activities help students learn to manipulate sounds in words.

Levels of Phonemic Awareness

When children participate in sound manipulation tasks, they acquire phonemic awareness. Children who have reading disabilities frequently lack phonemic awareness skill. It is essential to provide phonemic awareness activities during word study, reading, and writing experiences in kindergarten and first grade and in upper grades when necessary.

There are varying levels of phonemic awareness (Adams,1990; Wagner, Torgesen, Laughon, Simmons, & Rashotte, 1993; Yopp & Yopp, 2000). According to Adams (1990), the following levels indicate easy to difficult tasks for developing phonemic awareness skill:

- Children remember **rhyming** words rather than nonrhyming words. For example, children can repeat and remember nursery rhymes.
- Children can select the **odd word** as in a series of words such as "cat," "hat," and "bed." "Bed" is the odd word recognized by the student. Students learn to make sound comparisons.
- Children can **blend** sounds to form words. For example, children can blend the sounds in b/e/d to say the word "bed."
- Children can **segment** a word into sounds. For example, children can segment the word "bed" into the sounds b/e/d. (*The Yopp-Singer Test for Phoneme Segmentation* identifies their ability to segment sounds.)
- Children can **delete** individual initial sounds from words. For example, children can delete the "b" sound from the word "bed" and say "ed." Finally, children can delete the final sounds from words. For example, they can delete the final "d" sound in the word "red" and say "re."
- The more advanced levels of phonemic awareness, such as segmenting words into sounds, are more predictive of reading ability than easier levels, such as recognizing rhymes (Nation & Hulme, 1997).

Students need **auditory discrimination**, the ability to hear similarities and differences in phonemes within words in order to become phonetically aware. Students can identify phonemes by matching initial sounds to pictures. Ask students to identify whether the picture of a "cat," "bat," or "mouse" starts with the same sound as "b" in "bed." Teachers can scaffold learning by modeling and encouraging discussions about how, for example, the word "cat" has three sounds (phonemes) c/a/t. These activities help young students realize that words are made up of distinct sounds. Teacher read-alouds, poetry, student discussions about sounds in words, tongue twisters, songs, invented writing, and games help students manipulate sounds.

An Activity to Promote Phonemic Awareness

Phonemic awareness is the ability to manipulate and play with sounds by blending, segmenting, deleting, and substituting sounds in words. Singing rhyming lyrics helps children play with the sounds. To understand the meaning of phonemic awareness the following poem demonstrates the concept:

BOX 2.1

Sing the sounds of the segmented letters:

c-a-t is cat (**blending sounds**),
cat is c-a-t (**segmenting sounds**),
The "cat" was "at" (**deleting the sound** "c" from "cat") the house of the "rat"
(**substituting the sound** "r" for "c" with "at") and sang "rat tat tat" (**substituting
sounds**) to the mouse!
Put it all together and sing:
The cat was at the house
of the rat and sang
rat tat tat to the mouse.

The vignette in the next section includes activities to help children build phonemic awareness and provides an example of a literacy case study instructional plan.

Phonemic Awareness in the Classroom—A Vignette

A first-grade teacher, Michael Adams, had a student, Richard (pseudonyms), who was having difficulty learning to read. In January Michael administered the *Yopp-Singer Test for Phonemic Segmentation, Roberts' Phonemic Awareness Test,* and the *Bradley and Bryant Oddity Test* to determine if Richard knew how to manipulate sounds in words. The results indicated that Richard had problems with rhyming, segmenting, and blending sounds in words. His lack of phonemic awareness skills (ability to manipulate sounds) was interfering with his ability to read successfully at the first-grade level. After Michael analyzed the test results, he decided to develop lessons based on research and International Reading Association (IRA) standards for individualized instruction with Richard. The lessons focused on manipulating and blending sounds together in enjoyable activities. First, Michael modeled and talked about the purpose of blending tasks to develop phonemic awareness through the use of the song, "The Farmer and the Dell." Next, he asked Richard to pay attention and clap when he heard the rhyming sounds in the song, especially when he heard "at" in the words, "cat," "hat," and "rat."

The Farmer in the Dell (Modified)

The farmer in the dell
The farmer in the dell
Hi-ho, the derry-o
The farmer in the dell.

The farmer takes a c/at
The farmer takes a c/at
Hi-ho the derry-o
The farmer takes a c/at.

The c/at takes a r/at
The c/at takes a r/at
Hi-ho the derry-o
The farmer takes a r/at.

The r/at stands alone
The r/at stands alone
Hi-ho, the Derry-o
The r/at stands alone.

Link to music and lyrics at *www.kididdles.com/mouseum/f001.html*.

The Matthew Effect and Language Development

Some students, like Andy (pseudonym), have gaps in early literacy learning and immense problems catching up without individual help from educators and caretakers. Stanovich (1986) explains how these students frequently suffer from the "Matthew effect." The Matthew effect states that students who do well continue to do well while those who fall behind tend to stay behind their peers because they are often placed in low-ability groups based on one formal assessment (i.e., standardized test). These students repeatedly begin each year below grade level due to this placement. Reducing the Matthew effect involves identification of individual strengths and needs, multiple authentic assessments that guide instruction, and flexible grouping practices for learning successfully.

Early interventions for oral language development, phonemic awareness, the alphabetic principle, and concepts of print are crucial. Research states that once students fall behind they need intensive assistance to overcome barriers to literacy learning (Allington & McGill-Frazen, 1994; Purcell-Gates, McIntyre, & Freppon, 1995; Torgesen, 1998). Table 2.2 provides a record of Andy's progress as activities for phonemic awareness and phonics were used to help him increase his ability to blend, delete, and substitute sounds.

TABLE 2.2   Student Portfolio Sheet for Language Development

Name: Andy			
Date	**Phonemic Awareness Task**	**Activity Used**	**Follow-Up**
12/5	Blending sounds	"at" words in "The Farmer and the Dell"	Told a story using onset-rime ("at" words as in "cat")
12/12	Blending sounds	"at" and "un" words in "The Farmer and the Dell"	Used Elkonin box activity
12/19	Blending sounds, deleting and substituting initial sounds	"at," "un," and "ide" words using deleting and substituting sounds game	Created a poem to music using the words created during the activity

Literacy Instruction

Emergent literacy for beginning readers focuses on teaching oral language as well as phonemic awareness. Assessment of language development typically focuses on the ability to pronounce sounds and words to communicate appropriately. Language development is shaped by language practices at home and at school. Lack of opportunity to develop a rich vocabulary as well as language difficulties related to speech problems may create challenges with language development. For example, a student with speech problems might say "flute" to represent the word "fruit." Teachers need to collaborate with speech therapists to assess student language skills and plan instruction.

In other instances, students may have problems with language that require clinical interventions (Owens, 1995). The problems could include omitting word endings, immature vocabulary, problems comprehending concepts, difficulty with phonemic awareness, and comprehension of new words and difficulty using language socially. Once the students are assessed, individual lesson plans and reflective portfolios can be created to develop oral language during reading and writing activities.

Phonemic Awareness and Phonics

Phonemic Awareness is the ability to manipulate sounds and does not require letter recognition. **Phonics**, on the other hand, includes both letter-sound knowledge and the ability to blend sounds represented by letters in words. For example, the letter or symbol "b" represents the sounds in the words "boy," "bring," and "barn." Since English letters do not always represent one sound, this can be a difficult task during early literacy learning.

TABLE 2.3 Comparison of Phonemic Awareness and Phonics Instruction

Phonemic Awareness	Phonics
Sound/speech based	Letter-sound and letter pattern knowledge in words
Auditory, focusing on speech sounds	Visual and auditory
Example of instruction and learning: blending, segmenting, deleting, and substituting sounds in words	Example of instruction and learning: blends, digraphs, and diphthongs
Reinforce during oral chants, read-alouds, games, and various oral activities	Reinforce during reading and writing activities involving letters and sounds

Examples of Assessments to Differentiate between Phonemic Awareness and Phonics

- ### Example Question from Phonemic Awareness Assessment (Roberts, 2012)

The Phonemic Awareness Assessment uses small disks to represent sounds in words.

Directions: Students say the phonemes (sounds) in the target words for the number of disks presented. If they are unable to say the sounds, the administrator of the test can show them a picture of the target word as a visual cue (if a visual cue is used, indicate in test margin with a "v"). Record their responses. **Ask:** "What are the sounds (i.e., <u>phonemes</u>) in the targeted word? Show the number of sounds in the words by moving the appropriate number of disks.

For example: "What are the sounds in the word 'run'? Answer: The student orally makes the sounds r — u — n and moves a disk to represent each phoneme.

- ### Example Questions from a Phonics Test

What is the diphthong in the word "toy"? It is *oy*. What happens to the vowel sounds? The "oy" in "toy" makes one unique sound rather than two individual vowel sounds.

Weaver (1996) emphasized the delicate balance between reading and writing instruction. Frequently, too much time is spent on instruction without an integration of oral language skills, phonemic awareness tasks, and enjoyable reading and writing activities (Moats, 2000; Pressley, 1998). It is important for students to contextualize their learning in order to realize the connections between the content of various subjects and their interests.

Phonics Instruction

Phonics instruction focuses on connections between sounds and letters. Word recognition, phonics, and decoding are interchangeable terms. Harris and Hodges (1995) defined word recognition as "the process of determining the pronunciation and some degree of meaning of an unknown word" (pp. 282–283). Frequently, pronunciation of a word leads to recognition of the word's meaning unless the reader is not familiar with the word. When less-skilled readers seek to read a passage, their comprehension is often dependent on word recognition skills (Sawyer, 1991; Stanovich, 1991). **Phonics** emphasizes the relationship between phonemes (sounds of language) and graphemes (letters and spelling that represent the sounds in written language). Understanding this process helps students to use the phoneme-grapheme relationship to recognize familiar words and decode unfamiliar words. Effective phonics instruction helps students learn about spelling patterns and morphology (Moats, 1998).

To introduce the sound-to-spellings of words during reading and writing lessons, the teacher should have the children read words relating to the letter-sounds they have taught. For example, if some students are learning about the letters *m*, *a*, and *s*, they should read words such as: "am," "Sam," and "mass." The words can be rearranged to create sentences, and they should be identified in the context of interesting stories to increase comprehension. This meaning-making process is enhanced when teachers read aloud to the students and help them create meaning. **Decodable texts** are often used because these texts are composed of words that include the letter-sound spelling correspondences that the students have learned and sight words that have been taught. Students increase their command of the English language when phonics instruction is paired with sight word recognition in meaningful contexts.

a) Using authentic stories and poetry for read-alouds during word study, guided reading, reader response, writing, and self-selected reading time develops comprehension. These experiences also enhance phonemic awareness, letter-sound knowledge, and concepts of print instruction (Cunningham & Allington, 2010; Mason, Herman, & Au, 1991; Fisher, Flood, Lapp, & Frey, 2004). This is particularly true during the early stages of reading acquisition because students' oral language and listening comprehension is usually higher than their silent reading comprehension.

TABLE 2.4 The 54 Most Common Sound-Letter Relationships

a	as in *sat*	a-e	as in *cake*	ai	as in *rain*
ar	as in *car*	au	as in *haul*	aw	as in *lawn*
ay	as in *hay*	b	as in *ball*	c	as in *cat*
ch	as in *chip*	d	as in *duck*	e	*as in net*
ea	as in *beat*	ee	as in *need*	er	as in *fern*
ew	as in *shrewd*	f	as in *fancy*	g	as in *gate*
h	as in *house*	i	as in *sit*	i-e	as in *ride*
igh	as in *light*	ir	as in *first*	j	as in *jump*
k	as in *kite*	kn	as in *know*	l	as in *lamb*
m	as in *mop*	n	as in *nut*	o	as in *octopus*

(continued)

oa	as in *boat*	o-e	as in *pole*	oi	as in *soil*
oo	as in *took*	ou	as in *cloud*	oy	as in *toy*
p	as in *pop*	ph	as in *phone*	qu	as in *queen*
r	as in *rabbit*	s	as in *seal*	sh	as in *shop*
st	as in *stop*	t	as in *top*	th	as in *thank*
u	as in *under*	ue	as in *clue*	u-e	as in *use*
ur	as in *turn*	v	as in *van*	w	as in *well*
wh	as in *what*	y	as in *yellow*	z	as in *zebra*

Another way to enhance letter-sound knowledge is sharing discussions about names. **Name charts** help students find letter-sounds in words that are similar to their names. Research suggests that if students lack phonemic awareness they frequently do not recognize that words are composed of individual sounds and have difficulty with phonics and the alphabetic principle.

The Alphabetic Principle

The alphabetic principle is the term coined when children use their knowledge of letter-sound relationships during reading and writing activities. Understanding letter-sound relationships and acquiring phonemic awareness knowledge provides a basis for fluent word recognition. Letter **fluency** (the ability to easily recognize letters) is enhanced when students receive alphabetic instruction in a multitude of settings (Adams, 1990; Duffelmeyer, 2002; Morrow, 1993). Students benefit from a wide range of activities to enhance their ability to segment and blend sounds in many contexts:

BOX 2.2

SEGMENTING AND BLENDING SOUNDS

Materials: Word cards with pictures on one side and the word on the other side (*cat, bat, hat*), word list with the same words as the word cards
Standards: Segmenting and blending
Strategy: Model, Say, and Talk Strategy

- **Model and Say**, "This says c/a/t=cat (point to each letter as you say the sound-blending activity)

Students Say what was modeled (blending activity).

- **Model and Say**, cat=c/a/t/ (point to each letter as you say the sound-segmenting activity)

Students' Say what was modeled.
Continue this process for the sounds in "bat" and "hat." When using manipulatives, move an object for each sound.

- Use the words and the sounds in songs such as "The Farmer and the Dell."
- Talk about what was learned about the sounds—the sounds can be blended and segmented in words.
- Observe and take notes to determine which students understand blending and segmenting sounds in words.and segmenting sounds in words.
- Students practice this strategy in learning stations and/or on the World Wide Web with and without the teacher.

Discuss how knowing a familiar word such as "cat" can help read an unfamiliar word like "hat." Practice sliding/blending the sounds in words together to pronounce words.

Beyond understanding the most frequent letter-sound relationships, students need to recognize high-frequency words that are found most often in print. High-frequency words, sometimes noted as sight words, are the most frequently occurring words in the English language. High-frequency words such as "I" and "me" should become sight words quickly for students when noted daily in reading and writing activities. Learning to recognize high-frequency words helps children become fluent, confident readers. Using word walls, labeling items in the classroom, and stressing similar spelling patterns in words assists students when learning high-frequency words (Cunningham & Allington, 2010; Cunningham, 1995; Ehri, 1983; Fox, 2003). Students should be encouraged to add words to word walls and proclaim high-frequency words they encounter in their reading and writing activities across the content areas.

There is a rich resource of alphabet-related activities observed in kindergarten classrooms daily that enhance letter-sound knowledge. For example, including literature, writing, and the Internet extends fluency for phonemic awareness, letter-sound relationships, concepts of print, and most importantly comprehension of text. Students of all ages should be read to frequently and also have time to experiment with print and letter-sound relationships when reading and writing independently. There are numerous alphabet books that help children learn the alphabetic principle by connecting letters to sounds within story formats. Duffelmeyer et al. (2002) suggests alphabet websites for learning letters of the alphabet in electronic, graphic formats. Internet websites and software should be introduced/modeled by teachers, parents, or reading buddies. Eventually, emergent readers will be able to share what they learn from the Internet independently.

WEBSITES FOR EMERGENT READERS:

www.learningplanet.com/act/abcorder.htm,
http://funschool.com, www.sesameworkshop.org/sesamestreet (Hidden Letters), and *http://library.thinkquest.org/50027/AlphabetSoup/incex.html* (audio-enhanced versions are helpful for vision-impaired and some LD students).

The Morning Message

The **Morning Message** is a great way to expand letter-sound knowledge because it is writing to, by, and with students. Initially, the message can be written in a predictable format for easy reading by all students. For instance, "It is Monday. We are going to_____. It is Tuesday. We are going to   ."

During the morning message, students observe and participate in the authentic usage of capital letters and spaces between words to develop concepts of print. Sight words such as "it" and "is" and letter-sound connections can be emphasized in the context of the message, as in Box 2.3.

BOX 2.3

USING THE MORNING MESSAGE TO BLEND SOUNDS FOR PHONEMIC AWARENESS, IDENTIFY ALPHABETIC PRINCIPLE RELATIONSHIPS, AND EXTEND CONCEPTS OF PRINT KNOWLEDGE

Today is Tuesday, November 8.
It is raining outside.
Heather is 5 years old today.
She is having a birthday party Saturday.
She wants a new bike for her birthday.

The teacher asks the children, "What do you know about this message?" Individually, the children come forward and circle the information they know in the message. For example, Heather circled her name. Stephen circled all the *r*'s that he could find. Rashad pointed to the spaces between words. Tina pointed to the punctuation. These instructional activities increase their knowledge of punctuation as well as their concept of a word, a sentence, and the process of reading left to right (concepts of print).

Some students in the upper grades still need instruction in phonemic awareness (the ability to manipulate sounds in words), as well as word recognition, spelling, vocabulary, fluency, and comprehension strategies. This instruction will depend on the developmental needs of the individual student. Fortunately, it is never too late to integrate literacy assessment and strategy instruction for students who are struggling with word recognition/phonics, spelling, and vocabulary during reading and writing in the content areas.

For example, some older students might use only single-syllable words to express their thoughts during writing rather than trying to spell or include multisyllable words when writing (i.e., they use the word "many" for "multiple"). The students need spelling and/or vocabulary strategies in order to feel comfortable with the writing process.

To help students with challenges in word recognition and comprehension feel more comfortable, teachers can discuss and help students learn to transfer effective reading strategies to reader-response activities like narrative/expository text reading and writing experiences.

Combining phonemic awareness tasks with instruction in oral language activities, letter-sound relationships, concepts of print, word identification strategies, and reading and writing across the content areas benefit emerging readers (Adams, 1991; Stanovich, 1986; Gaskins et al, 1996/97; Yopp & Yopp, 2000, 2002; Weaver et al., 1996). For example:

- During a **science activity** about spiders, teachers can emphasize the "s" sound in the word spider. Then they introduce the book by Eric Carle, *The Very Busy Spider* (1995). They use think-aloud discussions to enhance oral language and comprehension.
- Have the children write a poem about a spider using rhyming words. Emphasize the "s" sound in spider and clap for rhymes while reading the poem.
- Next, cut out the individual words in the poem and scatter them in a spider web.
- Finally, have the children remove the words from the web to fill in the body of a spider with the words in the correct sequence for making meaning of the story.

Stahl's (1997) research findings indicated that teachers should use the alphabet letters and sounds as part of phonemic awareness instruction to help with reading acquisition. He recommends that teachers begin with small sets of sounds. The consonant sound m,s,n,f,z,v can be used more easily than stop-consonant sounds *t, d, b, k* because they are difficult to manipulate. These activities should be included in an integrated approach to teaching that combines reading, writing, and word study with phonemic awareness activities across the content areas. Thus, Stahl notes that combining phonemic awareness with phonics instruction can enhance reading acquisition.

Terminology for Phonics Instruction

Phonics instruction is enhanced when teachers have a thorough understanding of terminology and the structure of words. It is often wise to make sure students understand phonics terminology, rather than just assuming that they have a working knowledge of phonics. Engaging activities give students opportunities to interact with words and explore patterns. Students need to be aware of the characteristics of the consonants and vowels in our alphabet in order to read and analyze words effectively.

Consonants

The **consonants** are *b, c, d, f, g, h, j, k, l, m, n, p, q, r, s, t, v, w, x, y, z*. In consonant blends two or three consonants come together and blend their sounds. Each consonant sound may be heard in a consonant blend.

TABLE 2.5   Consonant Blends

Consonant blends include *bl, br, cl, cr, dr, fl, fr, gl, gr, pl, pr, sc, scr, sk, sl, sm, sn, sp, spl, spr, st, str, sw, tr,* and *tw*							
bl, br	cl, cr	dr	fl, fr	gl, gr	pl, pr	tr, tw	l, r, w
black, brick	clap, crab	drop	flip, friend	glass, grass	play, prose	tree, twin	
Blends beginning with *s*							
sc	sk	sl	sm	sn	sp	st	sw
scale	skate	slate	smile	snail	speak	state	swim
scr	spl	spr	str	c, k, l, m, n, p, r, t, w			
screen	splash	spring	stream				

Table 2.5 shows how teachers can use cards with consonant letters to design a making words activity. Blends on the first two rows may be created by combining cards with the letters *b, c, d, f, g, p,* and *t* with *l, r,* and *w*. Blends with *s* may be created by combining a card with *s* with *c, k, l, m, n, p, r, t,* and *w*.

TABLE 2.6   Consonant Digraphs

Consonant digraphs are two consonants that come together and make a new sound. Consonant digraphs include *ch, ph, sh, th,* and *wh*.				
ch	**ph**	**sh**	**th**	**wh**
cheek	phone	sheet	think	when

VOWELS

TABLE 2.7 Vowels

a	e	i	o	u
apple	elephant	igloo	octopus	umbrella

Vowels may have long or short sounds. You will note that the first letter in each word in Table 2.7 is a vowel, and the vowel sound is short (the vowel sound is little). In diacritical markings, we indicate short vowel sounds with a breve. A breve, like the lower part of a circle, is placed over a letter with a short sound. The letters *y* (as in dry with a long *i* sound) and *w* (as in saw) may also be used as vowels. The long sound of the *y* may be indicated with a macron, or small straight line, over the *y*.

TABLE 2.8 Vowel Digraphs

ai	ay	ea	ee	oa	ue
rain	hay	eat	meet	oats	blue

When we see vowel digraphs, two vowels come together and have one vowel sound as in *ai, ay, ea, ee, oa, ue*. We typically hear the sound of the first vowel in this combination. The term digraph comes from the Greek word *di*, meaning "two," and the word *graph*, meaning "write."

TABLE 2.9 Vowel Diphthongs

au	aw	ew	oi	oo	ou	ow	oy
haul	awl	ewe	soil	book	house	fowl	boy

Vowel diphthongs have a gliding sound. The word *diphthong* comes from the Greek words *di* and *thong*, meaning "tone or sound." Thus, diphthong means two tones. In a diphthong two vowels come together and have a new sound. The most common diphthongs are *ou, ow, oi*, and *oy*. Diphthongs include *au, aw, ew*, and *oo*.

TABLE 2.10 *R-Controlled Vowels*

The letter *r* influences the sound of the vowel in words such as "barn" and "fern." We refer to these as **r-controlled vowels**. (Based on research from the National Institute of Child Health and Human Development Research Program, 1997).

R-Controlled Vowels	
ar as in car apart, arch, are, arm, art, bar, car, cart, chart, dark, dart, far, farm, guitar, jar, lark, mark, park, remark, scar, shark, star, stark, start, tart	**er as in her** fern, her, herd, paper, river, ruler, tiger, water,
ir as in bird bird, chirp, dirt, girl, shirt, thirty	**or as in for** author, corn, for, fort, fork, horn, horse, manor, north, short, stork, storm, word, worm, port
ur as in turn burn, church, churn, curves, disturb, hurdle, hurl, surf. turn, turkey, urn,	

TABLE 2.11 Schwa

Schwa is a mid central vowel sound noted with the "ə" symbol. It makes the "uh" sound as in the words *sofa and away*. In English it is in unstressed positions while it sometimes occurs as a stressed and neutral vowel in other languages.

Whole Word Methods for Phonics Instruction

While whole word methods for phonics instruction can be used to increase students' sight word vocabulary, whole word instruction does not provide the strategy-based learning necessary to analyze unfamiliar words (O'Shaughnessy & Swanson, 2000). Students need to learn strategies for word analysis that help them read independently. Keep in mind that simply learning phonics rules will not suffice because many words break the code (rule). For this reason, we often refer to phonics generalizations rather than rules.

Sight Words

Students need to develop the ability to automatically recognize words in order to increase reading fluency and comprehension. Beginning readers, therefore, need to "acquire a lexicon of sight words by retaining the spellings of individual words in memory as graphophonemic (spelling-to-sound) symbols of their pronunciations" (Ehri, 1997). For example, "fun" contains the phonemes f/u/n and "ball" contains the phonemes b/a/l. Teachers emphasize this by teaching students the word "fun" to help them learn to pronounce the word "sun" and teaching the word "ball" to help them learn to pronounce the word "call."

A **sight word** is a word that is recognized instantly. Sight word lists include the most frequently encountered sight words (Buckingham & Dolch, 1936; Fry & Fountoukidis, 1993). The *Dolch List* contains the 220 most frequently found words in children's books. The *Dolch List* was compiled by Edward Dolch as the most frequently used words in grades K-3. The *Dolch List* was reexamined by Dale Johnson in 1971. The *Dolch List,* modified by William Durr (1973), reordered the words according to frequency of occurrence in more recent books. Presently researchers are evaluating and updating the lists for current books (Bodrova & Leong, 2007). Sight word sentences are also available for helping the students learn the sight words in context rather than solely in isolation.

The *Instant Word List* was compiled by Fry and Fountoukidis. The word lists can be used as assessments to determine sight word knowledge. A reasonable criterion for learning entire word lists is 90% or better at a speed of one word per second (adaptations should be considered and noted for students with processing problems).

Learning Sight Words

Building automaticity requires students to learn sight words and store them in lexical memory as references for other words with the same spelling patterns (i.e., the spelling pattern /ed/ in the word "b<u>ed</u>" helps a student pronounce the word "f<u>ed</u>"). Students need to bond letters to a word's pronunciation held in memory so that the sight of the word activates spoken form and meaning (Ehri, 1995). The sounds are then analyzed and matched to the sounds of the letters in words.

Since **sight words** are words that are recognized automatically (within a second), understandings of orthographic representations of frequently accessed words are achieved before rare words (Share & Stanovich, 1995). Initially, phonemes should be separated from words for instruction and then be combined in contexts of words and subunits in words to make sense of literacy learning. For example, the teacher models and introduces information about the letter "m" by stating, "This letter says mmm." New phonemes (sounds) should be practiced and reviewed briefly and at *teachable moments* daily in isolation and then transferred to context. The letter-sound relationship should be discussed and emphasized in the context of words, stories, and writing experiences.

Cueing Systems

Successful readers employ cueing systems to help them integrate word recognition and comprehension strategies naturally when reading. They self-monitor word recognition, vocabulary, and comprehension as they read and write across the content areas. Adams stressed the need for effective literacy instruction that includes semantic clues, syntactic clues, and graphophonic clues. The cueing system should be emphasized and connected during word study, writing, and reading experiences, and supported by technology. Adams (1990) stated that the cueing system is essential to help students understand meaning when reading and writing. Poorly developed word recognition skills are debilitating and can cause reading difficulties (Adams, 1990; Ehri, 1998; Perfetti, 1985; Share & Stanovich, 1995).

Semantic clues help students determine meaning from context. Semantics focus on the meaning of a story or the nuances of particular words. For example, an upper-class person who is "desperate" for an ice cream cone has a quite different perspective than a child of poverty who is "desperate" for a morsel of food.

Syntactic clues help students to understand what is happening in a sentence in order to comprehend it fully. Children should have knowledge concerning **syntactical development**, an understanding of the sequential order and structure in language, as they continue through the elementary grades. When they explore syntax, students begin to understand the impact of the sequential order and structure of language. For instance, a student may say, "I have a kitten that is black, and it is soft." Then class activities relating to syntax help the student understand that this statement can also be rearranged to read, "I have a soft, black kitten."

Syntax is sentence construction in terms of the order of words and parts of speech (i.e., noun, verb, adjective, etc.). Students need to understand what is happening in a sentence to comprehend fully. For instance, the subject of a sentence tells who is doing something. The verb tells what is being done or describes a certain state of being. For example, "Johnny hits the ball to Carrie" provides a

Image © mexrix, 2012. Shutterstock, Inc.

picture of what Johnny is doing. This can provide a visual representation about what is happening in the sentence. Students need to learn how to transfer this information about what is happening to elements of the story, such as setting, plot, and characters. These connections help them to create new knowledge by linking unfamiliar concepts to familiar concepts. An understanding of syntax is vital for reading success. Students need instruction about interpreting syntactic clues by discussing the impact of word order and grammar on the meaning of the story. Words like "first," "next," and "finally" make stories easier to comprehend. Syntax relates to the "boundaries between clauses and phrases and the clarity of the meaningful relations between them" (Adams, 1990, p. 155).

Graphophonic clues involve an understanding of the spelling-speech correspondence or the ability to pronounce words by looking for familiar patterns. For instance, the words "tell" and "sell" have the same "ell" pattern. Adams stressed that **graphophonemic knowledge** is necessary for literacy development.

Adams (1990) stated that students need to possess an understanding of the **cueing systems** (semantic clues, syntactic clues, and graphophonic clues) to make meaning during reading and writing. This reaffirms the need for an integrated approach to literacy instruction and learning that includes word study, comprehension of texts, and purposeful writing skills.

Goodman (1996) and Rhodes and Shanklin (1993) discussed the importance of the **pragmatic cueing system,** which emphasizes the function and the sociocultural aspects of language. Students use the pragmatic cueing system to interpret dialectical variations of language and other social conventions of language usage.

During the early stages of literacy development teachers who are familiar with developmental stages, terminology, and instructional methodology nurture learning by using the most effective strategies in the context of quality literature. As teachers plant seeds they see gradual growth and development. Careful planning and attention to details throughout this process often yield remarkable results, just as Mary planted seeds and provided just the right water, soil, and sunshine for plant growth in *The Secret Garden*

Image © Sergej Khakimullin, 2012. Shutterstock, Inc.

Keys for Word Building and Authentic Assessment

Chapter 3 highlights a combination of research-based phonics approaches to help students experience the excitement of becoming word detectives who use words in meaningful contexts (Gaskins, 2005; Gaskins et al., 1996/97; Ehri, Satlow, & Gaskins, 2009). Consider what you know about instruction for word building and assessment of literacy development. Before you read the chapter, answer the first two questions about what you know and what you want to explore about word building strategies. Then answer the last two questions after reading this chapter and discussing these ideas with friends.

TABLE 3.1

K	E	Y	S
What do you **know** about instruction for word building and assessment?	What do you want to **explore** in relation to instruction for word building and assessment?	What do you **yearn** to learn after reading and discussing the chapter?	How will you **satisfy** your curiosity? What ideas will you apply to your teaching?

Combining Research-Based Phonics Approaches for Effective Decoding and Spelling Instruction: Teaching Children the Excitement of Becoming Word Detectives

The research of Gaskins et al. (1996/97; Gaskins, 2005) and Ehri (2004; Ehri et al., 2009) helps teachers understand the importance of student engagement and direct explanation of research-based phonics, and comprehension strategies. Students are encouraged to apply the strategies across the curriculum. It is a joy for teachers to experience the children's excitement of discovering how to decode (pronounce) and spell words and use them in meaningful contexts as word detectives. Ehri et al. (2001) also stresses the importance of guided practice in spelling during phonics instruction.

Gaskins (2005) and Ehri et al. (2009) found students benefit from the combination of two research-based approaches to phonics and spelling instruction: 1) the ability to decode and spell unfamiliar words by segmenting words into phonemes and blending them to form a word (grapho-phoneme knowledge) and 2) the ability to decode by analogy with key words.

When children listen to stories read by parents, they hear the small units of separate sounds in words, **phonemes**. These experiences help them develop phonemic awareness and notice letter-sound correspondences, the **alphabetic principle**. They enjoy playing with the rhyming sounds in words heard in nursery rhymes such as *Hey Diddle Diddle the Cat and the Fiddle*. They notice the changes in the initial phonemes of the rhyming words *Diddle* and *Fiddle*. They learn to segment small units of sounds in words and blend them together to form words. Skill in decoding and spelling depends on these **grapho-phonemic** foundations (Ehri, 2004). Juel and Minden-Cupp's (2000) research found that using small phoneme-size units and larger units such as onset- and rime/spelling patterns is most effective for decoding words. The **analogy strategy with key words** includes chunking sounds in words into larger units of onset-rime (spelling patterns) and blending them together to pronounce the words.

The analogy strategy with key words can be an effective tool to enhance students' phonics and spelling skills. Using familiar words to pronounce and compare unfamiliar words is defined as **decoding by analogy with key words**. Students learn to chunk words into onset and spelling patterns. In the word "car" the "c" is the onset and "ar" is the spelling pattern (or rime). An **onset** is the initial consonant(s) that precedes the vowel in the syllable of a word, and a **rime/spelling pattern** is the vowel and the rest of the letters in the syllable. For example, "car" becomes the key word to help the reader pronounce the unfamiliar words "far" and "jar" with the same spelling pattern "ar." These types of rhyming words are often referred to as word families. When knowledge of letter-sound correspondences and segmenting and blending subunits of sounds in words is combined with decoding by analogy with key words, the learning process extends beyond the word family concept to explicit phonics and spelling instruction. The learning is reinforced during reading and writing and enhanced with comprehension strategy instruction.

The **analogy strategy with key words** helps students understand how the onset and spelling patterns in familiar words assists them to decode unfamiliar words with the same spelling pattern to increase phonics, spelling, and comprehension skills. The onsets in syllables are the initial consonants and the spelling patterns in syllables are underlined in the following words: r<u>ide</u>, h<u>ide</u>, s<u>ide</u>; c<u>at</u>, h<u>at</u>, b<u>at</u>, ch<u>at</u>; d<u>ear</u>, cl<u>ear</u>, t<u>ear</u>. Students who learn to chunk words by syllables and discover onsets and spelling patterns in the syllables use effective decoding strategies. The syllables and spelling patterns in the word "responsible" are designated below. Note that the syllable breaks are followed by a slash (/) and spelling patterns are underlined for consistency:

r<u>e</u>/ sp<u>on</u> / s<u>i</u> / ble

Looking closely at the word "responsible" helps teachers and students determine syllables as well as recognize onsets and spelling patterns to decode words. To teach the analogy strategy with key words, students can begin by learning how to chunk a word by holding a hand under their chin to note when the chin drops between syllables. The teacher and students discuss where and why the syllables begin and end. They discuss how to identify prefixes and suffixes. Next, the students underline the spelling patterns in the syllables and compare the spelling patterns to other words with the same spelling patterns. Key words are selected for the spelling patterns and displayed on word walls as references. During reading and spelling, words with the same spelling patterns as the key words can be noted with sticky notes and used for reader responses.

Recognizing common spelling patterns in words helps students create word families to decode words with similar spelling patterns and increases their lexicon of sight words. The 37 common rimes/spelling patterns and related key words assist students to become familiar with approximately 500 words. Many of the spelling patterns are found in familiar nursery rhymes. Finger plays and rhythmic activities reinforce students' ability to use the analogy strategy. During the activities they might say, "If I know 'dog' I know 'hog,'" to decode a word with the 'og' spelling pattern. Interactive word walls help teachers to make the transfer of this knowledge explicit as they refer to the word wall words and emphasize the spelling patterns during reading, spelling and writing for comprehension.

There is a great deal of research based on the effectiveness of the analogy strategy with key words (Adams, 1990; Cunningham, 2000; Gaskins et al., 1996/97; Gaskins, 2005; Ehri et al., 2009; Fox, 2003; Moustafa, 1997; Pressley, Gaskins, Solic, & Collins, 2006). The analogy strategy with key words assisted many of the students (K-adult) who attended the university reading clinic where Elaine supervised student progress through the phrases of sight word learning (Ehri, 1995). She was pleased with the students' progress due to tutoring in the analogy strategy with key words, especially in cases where word recognition problems interfered with comprehension. Many of the students with phonics, spelling, and comprehension problems reacted positively to instruction. At the clinic the students were trained to use the analogy strategy within an integrated approach to literacy learning. It was evident that students needed **explicit**, **direct**, and **systematic instruction** in phonics and spelling to increase comprehension. Essentially, the clinical experience reinforced phonics and spelling research that students need to:

- Recognize the small subunits of sounds in words (phonemes)
- Use sound – letter matching
- Segment and blend sounds together to pronounce words
- Recognize the larger subunits of onsets and spelling patterns in words
- Understand phonics generalizations
- Recognize patterns and special features in words (affixes, etc.)
- Use context

(Gaskins et al., 1996/97; Gaskins, 2005; Ehri, 2004; Ehri et al., 2009; Blachman et al., 1999; Torgeson et al, 1999)

The research-based Benchmark School Word Detectives Program (Gaskins et al., 1996/97; Gaskins, 2005; Ehri et al., 2009) includes engaging differentiated instruction. The Beginning Word Detective program for grades 1–3 is divided into phase I, emergent learning skills of phonemic awareness and concept of word and phase II, phonics. Phase II reinforces learning phonics as word detectives, letter-sound matching, spelling and vowel pattern discoveries, analogy strategy using key words for decoding, word solving methods, comprehension monitoring, and word analysis. The Transition Word Detective program reinforces the Beginning program and includes spelling patterns, automaticity of key word recall, phonics generalizations for blends and digraphs and more, high-frequency irregular words, word solving methods, and comprehension monitoring. The program focuses on metacognition (thinking and talking about what you are learning) and includes independent reading for 30 minutes daily with reading logs, written responses to reading, and parent read-alouds.

Word Analysis

When students analyze words using effective strategies they can transfer their phonics skills automatically to reading, spelling, and writing. They are empowered to focus on making meaning during reading. Table 3.2 presents key spelling patterns students need to know. **Key words** are used for each spelling pattern to assist the students when learning how to pronounce words with the same spelling pattern. For example, the key word "cake" is used to help them pronounce the word "rake." Students would say, "If I know cake, then I know rake, take, bake."

TABLE 3.2   Common Rimes/Spelling Patterns
Use Key Words to Teach Students the Spelling Patterns

ack	ail	ain	ake	ame	an	ank
ap	ask	at	ate	aw	ay	
eat	ell	est	ice	ick	ide	ight
ill	ine	ing	ip	ir	ock	
oke	op	ore	uck	ug	ump	unk

Interactive Word Walls

Interactive word walls are used and referred to for extending knowledge about learning, including literacy strategies. For example, when using the analogy strategy the key words can be placed on an **interactive vowel word wall** as a reference for decoding unfamiliar words with the same spelling patterns.

TABLE 3.3   Vowel Word Wall Examples Using Key Words for the Analogy Strategy

a	e	i	o	u	y
cat	tent	pig	form	up	cry
cake	bed	bike	*cow	drum	
whale	sleep	smile	look	glue	
game	beach	wish			
*car					
Star key words on the word wall that do not have the long or short vowel sound (i.e., *r*-controlled words such as "car"). Note that the spelling patterns are underlined in the words.					

Notice that the interactive word wall has columns labeled with vowels to help students understand spelling patterns since they begin with vowels. For example, if students have confusion decoding long and short vowel sounds in the word "attached" they can easily find the word wall word "cat" with the "at" spelling pattern to help them correctly identify the first syllable spelling pattern "at" with a short /a/ in the word "attached." The word can then be read in context to determine if it makes sense to the student. The second syllable of the word "at/tach/ed" is /tach/. The vowel word wall might contain the key word "batch" since few words contain the spelling pattern /ach/. The word "batch" found under vowel column "a" of the word wall will help the student determine the short "a" sound to decode "ach" in the word "attached." The word should be used in a sentence to determine the correct sound of the vowel and to help with meaning. Another example for using the vowel word wall for the spelling pattern "ed" in the word "red" is found under the vowel column "e." This placement helps students to decode the spelling pattern "ed" in similar words with different onsets such as "fed" and "bed." This draws attention to the short vowel sound of /e/. When the word is used in context, the student can determine if the word sounds right. If it does not sound correct the student should be taught to switch vowel sounds.

Displaying a key word for each common spelling pattern on a word wall helps students understand the subunits in words for successful decoding and spelling. Thus, the most common spelling patterns should be taught to children and added to a word wall. Interactive word walls invite multisensory experiences and are used as a reference for the analogy strategy and other word recognition strategies. (Refer to Table 3.2 for common rimes/spelling patterns students need to learn.) The goal is for students to transfer the key words on the word wall to their long-term memory to help them read unfamiliar words with the same spelling patterns without referring to the word wall.

Students use interactive word walls to play related word building games and include the words in their reading and writing. The vowel word wall may be used effectively in combination with a typical word wall. The words on a typical word wall are usually placed alphabetically. This type of word wall is an asset in any classroom. It gives a reference point for spelling and provides a visual connection with vocabulary that is easy to access. An interactive word wall featuring the vowels takes word analysis to the next level. This word wall is designed to make students more aware of vowel patterns, onsets, and spelling patterns.

Word Walls as Authentic Assessments for Word Recognition

Teachers and students can use **word walls as assessments** by taking observation notes to determine if the students can pronounce the words and whether they transfer the spelling patterns from the familiar words on the word walls to unfamiliar words with the same spelling patterns that they encounter during shared reading and writing. Portable word walls can be created for individual students who need extra assistance. File folders and digital resources can be used as portable walls.

Word Walls for ELL Students

Word walls with a focus on spelling patterns help ELL students because spelling patterns are sometimes more easily remembered than isolated vowel sounds. For example, teachers can add English and Spanish words to a word wall and share how pronouncing Spanish words is different than pronouncing English words. English word decoding includes chunking by onset-rime/spelling patterns while Spanish word decoding includes vowels with the onset (i.e., English c/at; Spanish ca/t). Individual word walls can also be created online with English and Spanish words. Pictures can be included and then hidden when students store the words in lexical memory.

Word wall words can be used in upper grades and can be derived from multisyllabic words (i.e., "aft /er" could be used as a key word for the word "graft/ing"; "cow" could be used as a key word for the word "how/ling"). Words can be starred (*) that do not have short or long vowel sounds. For example, note that "cow" has the "ow" spelling pattern. Students should learn to recognize how "w" affects the vowel "o." They should be able to create and refer to key words from parts of larger words.

TABLE 3.4 Interactive Word Wall Stressing Long and Short Vowels

Long a	Short a	Long e	Short e	Long i	Short i	Long o	Short o	Long u	Short u	y with long sound of i
cake	cat	sleep	bed	bike	wish	boat	hot	un/it	up	cry
whale	aft/er	each	elf	bite		goat	not			
plus			press							

The interactive word wall can be created from syllables found in multisyllabic words such as re/press/i-ble. It is also helpful to create entry slips about word wall use so that students can personalize their word analysis. Julia, an excellent teacher, uses entry slips for her classroom word wall, as exhibited in Table 3.5

TABLE 3.5   Julia's Word Wall Entry Slip

Name:	**Date:**
Word Wall Word:	
Meaning:	
Sentence:	
I like this word because:	

It is important for ELL students to use word walls interactively and discover sight words within context. When pronouncing words, teachers and students should use gestures and facial expressions to indicate meaning. Recently, Elaine was visiting an ELL teacher and students. She asked the students what they thought of their word wall. They told her it helped them decode and spell words during reading and writing activities.

Phonics Generalizations

Word building is enhanced when students are aware of phonics generalizations for word analysis. We refer to phonics generalizations rather than phonics rules because of the variations that may occur in relation to certain contexts.

TABLE 3.6   Phonics Generalizations

Generalization	Example
When a word begins with "wr," the *w* is silent.	write
When "ght" is seen in a word, the "gh" is silent.	light
When a word begins with "kn" the *k* is silent.	know
When the letter *c* is followed by *o* or *a*, the sound of k is heard.	camp
If the only vowel letter is at the end of a word, the vowel sound is usually long.	he
When *a* is followed by *r* and the final *e*, we expect to hear the sound as in care.	dare
The first vowel is usually long and the second vowel is silent in the digraphs *ai, ea,* and *oa*. Some say, "When two vowels go walking, the first one does the talking."	rain bead boat
When *y* is the final letter in a word, it usually has a vowel sound.	dry
When *y* is preceded by a consonant in a one-syllable word, the *y* usually has the long sound of *i*.	by my
In words of two or more syllables, the *y* usually has the long sound of *e*.	baby
The vowel pair "ow" may have the long *o* sound as in "low," or we may hear the "ow" sound of a diphthong as in "owl."	bow owl
Consonants *g* and *c* make hard and soft sounds.	soft *c* – city hard *c* – cut soft *g* – general hard *g* – gold

Vowel and Consonant Patterns for Word Analysis

Word building is facilitated when students recognize vowel patterns (C = consonant, V = Vowel). Here are some common vowel patterns:

- **CVC** – In the consonant–vowel–consonant pattern, the vowel sound is short, as in "him," "leg," "sod," and "cut." Consonants used in this pattern may be blends or digraphs, as in duck and crab. Students can find words with the CVC pattern as in "top," and use them creatively in their writing. Words with CVC patterns give emergent writers effective tools for the writing process.
- **CVCC** – The consonant–vowel–consonant–consonant pattern occurs in words like "desk."
- **CVCe** – When an *e* is added to the end of a CVC combination, the vowel in the middle represents a long vowel sound. Some say the final *e* is silent, and others say it is powerful because it makes the vowel sound long. The word "ride" follows this pattern.
- **CV** – When there is a single vowel at the end of a word or syllable, the vowel is long. This pattern applies to words that have no consonant at the beginning, such as the word "able." The words "he," "she," "be," and "by" follow this pattern.
- **CVVC** – When two vowels are adjacent to the middle of the word or syllable, the first vowel is long and the second vowel is silent. All CVVC words contain vowel digraphs; however, not all vowel digraphs fit the pattern. In the word "boat" the *o* sound is long, but in the word "coin" the *o* sound is not long.
- **Letters *c, q,* and *x* represent sounds from other letters.** For instance, *c* has the sound of *s* or *k*. We hear the *k* sound in "cat." The letter *q* is followed by *u* and makes the *kw* or *k* sound as in "queen." The letter *x* has the *eks, egz,* or *z* sound as in "exit."

TABLE 3.7   A Word Wall for Math

Upper-grades teacher Rob Allen created the following word wall for word recognition and comprehension in math.					
Short vowel if syllable ends in a consonant	**Long vowel silent *e***	**R- controlled vowels**	**Consonant digraph**	**Diphthong**	**Consonant plus *le-le* does not stand alone in a syllable**
ax<u>es</u>	<u>li</u>ne	w<u>or</u>ds	gra<u>ph</u>	p<u>oi</u>nt	tri/an/<u>gle</u>
pl<u>us</u>	ac<u>u</u>t<u>e</u>	int<u>eg</u>ers	<u>sh</u>ift	r<u>ou</u>nd	mul/ti/<u>ple</u>
conv<u>ex</u>	<u>pla</u>ne	v<u>er</u>tex	<u>ph</u>ase	th<u>ou</u>sand	di/vis/i/<u>ble</u>
loc<u>us</u>	m<u>o</u>d<u>e</u>	s<u>ur</u>face	<u>sh</u>ell	j<u>oi</u>nt	var/i/a/<u>ble</u>

Extending Morphological Knowledge

Word analysis helps students to enhance their understanding of words. A **morpheme** is the smallest meaning unit. It is a distinctive collection of phonemes with no smaller meaningful parts. For example, the word "play" consists of one morpheme, but the word "player" has two morphemes. Morphology is the study of word parts that include affixes (i.e. prefixes and suffixes), compound words, and contractions. Chunking words into these subunits helps students pronounce words, spell them more accurately, understand the definitions of words, and comprehend texts (Nagy, Anderson, Schommer, Scott, & Stallman, 1989; Fox, 2003).

Familiarity with terminology helps students to analyze words more effectively. When students recognize root words they can extend their word knowledge by adding prefixes and suffixes to make new words. These terms are important for word analysis:

- A **prefix** is a syllable attached to the beginning of a word. Prefixes such as *pre-*, *non-*, and *re-* often change the meaning of the root word.
- A **suffix** is the chunk at the end of a root word, such as *-ing*, *-ment*, *-ed*, or *-ly*. These structural clues help students decode words, especially in the upper grades (Nagy, Diakidoy, & Anderson, 1993).

Students need to recognize root words and look for prefixes and suffixes that are added to root words. They learn to discern words more effectively while reading if they are taught procedures for discerning how some words are chunked into subunits, including prefixes and suffixes. Teachers need to model ways to discern how prefixes and suffixes affect meanings of words and encourage students to recognize and use suffixes and prefixes in their reading and writing. The following poem includes the suffixes *-ly* (meaning in the manner of), *-ish* (meaning having the nature of), and *ing* (which changes the tense of the verb and is an inflectional ending, as in "love" and "loving"). Students can write their own poems and notice how suffixes affect spelling, as in this example:

BOX 3.1

MY LOVELY KITTEN

My lovely kitten
Is lively and cuddly
Childish and wildish
My loving and lovely kitten!
Author Unknown

Students like to create poems and play games like prefix and suffix rummy. They can play cards with root words, prefixes, and suffixes. During this game they score a point when they create real words. The words can then be used to write stories about content-related topics.

Recognizing and Making Compound Words

Compound words are two or more words that are combined, as in "baseball." Students enjoy sorting and combining words to create compound words. Many activities with compound words can be designed using books by Jan Brett. She provides many delightful activities for word play on her website, *www.janbrett.com*.

Recognizing and Using Contractions

Contractions are shortened forms of words. In contractions one or more letters are replaced with an apostrophe (i.e., "shouldn't" for "should not"). They have the same meaning, although the form is shortened. Contractions are typically used in casual writing rather than formal writing. The following story helps students enjoy reading and writing contractions.

Example of a Student's Story with Contractions

Why You Shouldn't Run Backwards

Last week I learned a lesson. I was playing a game with a friend. You run forward for one minute and backwards for one minute. You repeat this for 10 minutes. I was doing well until I ran into a bike when I was running backwards. I didn't realize that my friend came by to watch the game. Fortunately, I only bruised my knee. I won't be running backwards again without being more careful!

Analyzing Contractions

When students write their own stories with contractions, they can read them to the class. While they are reading, the class can clap whenever they hear a contraction. They could also have another student read the story and write the paper without contractions (i.e., "should not" for "shouldn't") in a more formal format. When this story is read to the class, they might discuss the difference in the tone of the paper without contractions, noting that the message is the same with or without contractions.

Teachers need to allow time for students to play and learn about words. It is amazing how many learning standards can be met during creative literacy play for all levels. It is important that students develop morphological knowledge as they advance through school. Students should begin to understand the importance of learning about prefixes, roots, and suffixes in the early grades. It is critical to help students monitor their learning when they encounter less frequent words in their reading and writing (Arnoff, 1994; Coady, 1994).

Phrases of Sight Word Learning

Research suggests that children progress through phases in acquiring sight word learning to increase word recognition (Ehri, 1991; Gaskins et al., 1996/1997). Ehri (1995) developed the following phases:

- **Prealphabetic Phase-logographic Phase** – Students depend on visual cues and environmental print to decode (pronounce) words. For example, a student would recognize the word "McDonald's" when it is visible with the golden arches of the McDonald's building.
- **Partial Alphabetic Phase** – Students have some phonemic awareness, letter-sound knowledge, and remember sight words by remembering one or a few salient letters in words that correspond to sounds in pronunciations. They can use invented spellings of words. Usually there is confusion about using correct spelling patterns in words. This creates uncertainty about vowel sounds. For example, "bed" could be spelled "bad."
- **Full Alphabetic Phase** – Students have developed phonemic awareness, letter-sound knowledge, and read sight words by remembering their spellings as letter-analyzed forms bonded to their pronunciations. For example, "ship" could be spelled "sip" or "ship."
- **Consolidated Phase** – Students have an understanding of: spelling knowledge for most words and use conventional spellings of words (orthographic knowledge), special features in words such as prefixes and suffixes (morphological knowledge), the importance of using analogies to decode words (aware of subunits in words called onsets and rimes/spelling patterns), and developing a large sight vocabulary (a bank of sight words stored in lexical memory to help them decode and spell unfamiliar words with the same spelling patterns).

Sight Word Phases and Spelling

Teachers assess and determine students' word recognition phases in order to plan effective instruction and help students progress to the next phase. The instruction should emphasize students' development of independent use of strategies for successful word recognition, spelling, and comprehension. When strategies are used independently and effectively the students proceed to the next phase of sight word learning. Table 3.8 presents the Roberts' Spelling and Word Recognition Guide for Miscue Analysis. Miscue analysis is an assessment of students' ability to decode and spell words. Miscues indicate students' deviations from the text when reading and spelling. For example, a student might decode or spell the word "ship" as "sip." The guide indicates the similarities in spelling and word recognition. Teachers can use this tool to analyze students' strengths and needs to plan instruction. Some students have difficulties at the Letter Name Stage for spelling and the Partial Alphabetic sight word recognition phase. These students can benefit from recognizing small subunits of sounds in words and then larger subunits of sounds of onsets and spelling patterns used in the analogy strategy with key words. Students frequently use the wrong vowel in the spelling pattern when trying to decode and spell words. This could be because they have difficulty remembering individual vowel sounds and benefit from instruction that focuses on breaking words into onsets and spelling patterns. For example, they might mistakenly use the spelling pattern /ad/ rather than /ed/ for the word "bed."

TABLE 3.8 Roberts' Spelling and Word Recognition Guide for Miscue Analysis: Aligning Spelling and Word Recognition Skills to Guide Instruction

Ehri's Sight Word Recognition Phase	Bear et al. Spelling Stages	Example
Prealphabetic (visual cues)	Emergent	bed = b
Partial alphabetic (phonetic cues)	Letter name	bed = bad
Full alphabetic (distinct spellings)	Within word pattern	ship = sip, ship
Consolidated (chunks of letters symbolized as blends of sounds)	Syllable and affixes	popping = popping, pleasure = plesour, pleasure

The spelling and word recognition guide was adapted from Bear, Invernizzi, Templeton, & Johnston (2004); Ehri (1992, 1995, 2002).

Spelling, Decoding, and Writing

Spelling should be understood as a part of writing. Bear et al. (2004) describe five stages of spelling development:

- **Emergent Stage** (0–5 years old) – drawing and scribbling, some use of the first letter of a word. Vowels are often omitted.
- **Letter Name Stage** (5–8 years old) – frequently uses the wrong vowel and vowel patterns
- **Within Word Pattern Stage** (6–10 years old) – uses initial and final consonants, difficulties with vowels in unaccented syllables
- **Syllables and Affixes Stage** (intermediate grades) – syllable juncture stage, includes morphological knowledge
- **Derivational Stage** – (intermediate grades) – identifies word derivatives, such as "opposite" and "opposition"

Spelling activities help students develop spelling skills when they are transferred to reading and writing. For example, young children can select pictures and place them under the correct word. Auditory discrimination activities help students learn to discriminate between letters and their sounds. Word walls can be used to help students check their spellings of words. Cunningham and Hall's *Making Words* (2007) activities help students sort words by vowel patterns, spelling patterns, and affixes. These words are then used to create sentences and stories. Students need to analyze words to determine if they look right when they use them in sentences. This helps them to distinguish whether to use similar-sounding affixes, such as *pre-* or *per-*. The activities help them to discriminate whether affixes such as *pre-* or *-ed* or *pre-* or *-ment* would be used at the beginning or ending of a word. The affixes need to be used during authentic reading and writing activities in order for students to retain them in long-term memory.

Roberts's Spelling and Word Recognition Guide for Miscue Analysis (Table 3.8) was created to assist teachers as they determine the sight word phase and the aligning spelling development stage of individual students for effective lesson planning. The lessons are connected to reading and writing skills across the content areas. "Many studies have shown that struggling readers have particular difficulty learning to spell and are especially resistant to remediation" (Bruck, 1993; Ehri, 1997). Students benefit from instruction for spelling and decoding by segmenting and blending sounds in words, analyzing words, and learning the analogy strategy with key words. The guided instruction will help them move to higher levels of Ehri's sight word phases and Bear et al.'s spelling stages:

- During the partial alphabetic phase/letter name stage, students often experience confusion about vowels. These students frequently benefit from learning the analogy strategy.
- During the full alphabetic phase/within word spelling stage, students are more adept at understand spelling patterns and are developing distinct, conventional spellings of words.
- During the consolidated phase/syllable juncture spelling stage students are knowledgeable about chunking sounds, understanding syllables, and recognizing morphological components (prefixes, roots, suffixes, etc.) to assist them with their spellings of words.

Integrating Phonics and Spelling Activities across the Content Areas

Johnson and Myklebust (1967) suggested a spelling strategy that works from partial recall to total recall of words. For example, the word "typical" can be selected from a list of similar words (i.e., "typical," "tropical," "tyrannical"). The same word could be selected from a list of synonyms (i.e., "typical," "similar," "regular"). The word "typical" could then be used in a story about "A Typical Day in the Life of a Gardener." This would give students opportunities to use the word "typical" in context. *Diary of a Worm* by Doreen Cronin (2003) and other books in this series could be used as model texts for this activity.

Students should integrate the words they are learning across the content areas during reading, spelling, and writing activities. Table 3.9 is designed to help students to monitor their own learning.

TABLE 3.9 Self-Monitoring Reading Strategy Sheet for Student Literacy Portfolios

Name _____ Date _____					
Date	**Words I Know and What I Know about the Spelling Patterns**	**Games Played and Words Learned**	**Prefixes and Suffixes Learned**	**Strategies I Used**	**Words I Need to Learn**

Enhancing Sight Word Knowledge

There are numerous activities online to reinforce the most frequent sight words. Games are suggested such as sight word bingo, selecting sight words, using sight words in sentences, and, most importantly, culturally responsive lessons to relate the words to sentences created by the children about their lives. Students need to apply what they learn during the activities to authentic reading and writing to enhance comprehension.

Adaptations for Sight Word Instruction

- Teachers can incorporate the sight words within the context of sentences written in various languages to help ELL students.
- Teachers should provide a large-print copy of the Dolch Basic Sight Word List or Fry Word List for students with visual problems.
- Teachers can use tape recordings of the sight words with the words in sentences. Encourage students to audiotape sight words in sentences they create. Then have them write the sight words or check them off lists.
- Sign/Word Flash Cards are available through the book *Sign/Word Flash Cards* by Bornstein and Saulnier, 1987. They include actions, verbs, animals, etc., on the cards. There is also an accompanying activities booklet.
- Teachers can have the students use digital resources to write sentences and stories that include the sight words.

Assessing Sight Word Knowledge

- Use running records to determine if students are able to automatically pronounce sight words when reading.
- Check K–3 students' ability to read the sight words at the beginning of the year and at each grading period. Include this information with individual goals, student self-reflection, and artifacts in their portfolios.
- Use the Sight Word Lists and identification of the sight words in context.
- Use pocket charts, music, and singing to reinforce the sight words. Write observation notes while the children participate to determine their knowledge of sight words.
- Send the children on scavenger hunts to find the sight words in literature around the school and at home. Note whether children are able to find this information.
- Use flash card boxes and have the children practice the sight words at home and in school. Ask parents to help evaluate their children's sight word knowledge.
- Use the Internet to find websites for sight word games. For example, *http://createdbyteachers .com/dolchsearchp2.html* for sight word searches or go to *www.kidsdomain.com/games/online.html* for online games for children. Include an activity where children journal about what they learned during the Internet experience about sight words.
- Encourage children to write the sight words using the computer to create stories, books, and games. This application of knowledge can indicate their learning about sight words.

Elaine's Experience as a Literacy Consultant: Using the Analogy Strategy A Vignette

One of Elaine Roberts's favorite success stories focuses on the value of teaching the analogy strategy. "Rashad's" third-grade teacher, Virginia, asked Elaine to help him with phonics strategies because the school's standardized test results and classroom reading indicated that he faced challenges with word recognition and comprehension. As a literacy consultant in the school, which receives Title I funding, Elaine assisted Rashad with reading. Rashad did not qualify for special education services, although his performance in reading was below grade level. The Woodcock-Johnson assessment and Informal Reading Inventory results for oral reading indicated that he was on the pre-primer level for word recognition and comprehension. The Yopp-Singer test of Phonemic Segmentation indicated that he had some phonemic awareness, but he had difficulty segmenting some words.

Virginia was teaching the class the analogy strategy with key words for phonics, spelling, and comprehension. Rashad was known to sit alone quietly and rarely smiled. Initially, Elaine assessed his reading strengths and challenges. After an analysis of the pretests, she taught him the analogy strategy with key words and gave him encouragement over a period of three months from January to March. They met once weekly to have Elaine tutor him and give him additional encouragement as Virginia continued to teach the analogy strategy with key words to Rashad and a small group of students. During their sessions Rashad progressed and began to smile.

Rashad learned to attack unfamiliar words and became excited about his role as a word detective. His joy about his progress overcame the barriers to his happiness as a reader. The following paragraphs describe the process Elaine used to teach him the analogy strategy, beginning with her initial assessments.

Assessments and Tutorial Instruction

Interest Inventory

When Elaine began her sessions with Rashad, she gave him an interest inventory to identify his interests and the books he would like to read. She used this as a guide for selecting meaningful books for their tutorial sessions.

Assessment for Rashad's Spelling Level

Elaine used the Bear Spelling Test from the text, *Words Their Way: Word Study for Phonics, Vocabulary, and Spelling Instruction* by Bear et al. (2002) to identify Rashad's level of spelling development. This spelling inventory is designed to identify students' stages of development from the earliest to the most advanced stages of spelling. The stages include the Emergent, Letter Name, Within Word Pattern, Syllable and Affixes, and Derivational Relations Stages. The test is excellent for students at all grade levels who experience difficulty decoding words and spelling. Rashad scored at the late emergent to letter name stage. Late emergent readers have difficulty determining the vowels and sometimes omit the vowels in syllables in words. When they read a word such as "McDonald's," they often search for environmental clues, such as the golden arches, to decode the word. Rashad was only able to spell the word "bed" out of the list of words. He misspelled "ship," "when," "lump," and "float." Elaine stopped asking him to spell words when he missed four out of five words in a row. The results of this assessment indicated that Rashad needed help understanding that each syllable in a word has a vowel, there are small letter-sound subunits in words, and that spelling patterns such as *ip* in the word "ship" and *ump* in the word "lump" help with spelling and decoding unfamiliar words.

Assessment of Decoding and Comprehension

Since an Informal Reading Inventory is an effective tool to determine a student's ability to decode words and comprehend texts, Elaine chose to use the *Qualitative Reading Inventory (QRI)* by Leslie and Caldwell (2000) to determine Rashad's ability to decode words and comprehend words in context. Rashad scored at the preprimer level on the word list even though he was in the third grade. He was able to decode a narrative text at the preprimer level with pictures for comprehension. Analysis of the test results indicated that Rashad depended on picture clues and guessing for decoding words. He had difficulty comprehending the text because of word recognition problems.

Rashad's Writing Sample

This moring I woke up and loked in the mir and my harr was nupp and my teeth wasint brshed and my shurt was on buckwurds.

As Elaine analyzed Rashad's writing and assessments, she noted that he was at Ehri's Partial Alphabetic Sight Word Phase and the Bear et al. Letter Name Stage for spelling. He needed the analogy strategy with key words to advance to Ehri's Full Alphabetic Phase for word recognition that correlates with the Bear et al. Within Word Pattern Spelling Stage (Table 3.8). He also needed to increase his use of organization, word choice and punctuation skills during writing.

Combining Effective Phonics Strategies: Segmenting and Blending of Phonemes and the Analogy Strategy with Key Words

Elaine reviewed letter-sound correspondences and phonemes in words with Rashad based on his assessment results. For example, she used the Dr. Seuss title, *Cat in the Hat*, to help Rashad listen to similar small units of sounds in words. She taught segmenting of words through songs using phrases such as "c-a-t is cat" and "h-a-t is hat." She explained that when we decode words we chunk the sounds in words and blend them together. Then Elaine used the analogy strategy with key words to help Rashad decode larger chunks in words, onsets and spelling patterns. She modeled how you can learn unfamiliar words by remembering familiar key words with the same spelling patterns. She used words and sentences from his selected books of interest. For example, they noted that the spelling pattern in the word "jump" is *ump*. Elaine knew that Rashad needed to understand that syllables often have an onset—the beginning consonants in a syllable—and a spelling pattern. She knew this would help him to pronounce and spell words more easily. Elaine introduced him to words that had spelling patterns that he could not decode from the books. For example, he had difficulty with the spelling patterns "ide" and "ave" so she taught him the key words "ride" and "cave." Then she used the analogy strategy with key words steps that are outlined in this chapter. They met for five weeks, and she experienced great joy when she saw him begin to smile when she walked into the classroom. After each meeting she wrote a note for him stating that he was a "great reader and speller" or a "great writer."

Elaine guided Rashad to use word analysis as a part of the analogy strategy. For example, for the unfamiliar word "mat" she used the following chart from an article by Gaskins et al. (1996/97): The Talk to Yourself Chart by Gaskins et al. helps students think about their learning as they analyze words with partners and on their own. Students look at words and ask each other how many sounds they hear, how many letters represent the sounds, what is the spelling pattern, and what is your rule about the vowels in the word. This helps students talk and think about their learning and use effective phonics strategies during reading and writing. Sometimes using word analysis was tricky with an unfamiliar word such as "far" because it has an *r* controlled vowel.

TABLE 3.10 Talk to Yourself Chart

1. The word is_____. (mat)
2. Stretch the word. I hear ____sounds. (3 sounds m-a-t)
3. I see _____ (3) letters because_____. (I can hear each letter and the *a* makes the short sound, as in the key word "cat")
4. The spelling pattern is _____. (at)

5. This is what I know about the vowel: _____ (It is short because it makes the short *a* sound).
6. Another word on the word wall with the same vowel sound is_____. (cat)
Important: Elaine always asked him to create his own rule for the vowel and asked if the vowel broke a rule he already knew about. He was able to conclude that if a word has a consonant-vowel-consonant (CVC) it might be a short vowel.

Elaine also used the Talk to Yourself Chart with the key word "car" to enhance Rashad's word analysis of *r* controlled vowels:

TABLE 3.11   Talk to Yourself Chart

1. The word is_____. (car)
2. Stretch the word. I hear ____sounds. (2 sounds, c-ar —*r*-controlled vowel)
3. I see _____ (3) letters because_____. (The vowel *a* has an *r* next to it—*r*-controlled vowel)
4. The spelling pattern is _____. (ar)
5. This is what I know about the vowel: _____ (It is not long or short because it has an *r* n*e*xt to it).
6. Another word on the word wall with the same vowel sound is_____. (chart—*r*-controlled vowel)

Elaine always asked Rashad to create a phonics generalization for the vowel in the word and asked if the vowel broke a rule (or generalization). For example, if you have an *r* next to a vowel, the vowel sound is not long or short. It was important for Rashad to share word analysis with another student to reinforce his learning and to remind him how to decode words when reading in context independently.

Summary of the Analogy Strategy with Key Words Instructional Steps

Elaine used the following steps with Rashad based on research by Gaskins et al. at the Benchmark School:

1. Introduce one to five key words to be used during the week. Begin with sentences with words with the spelling patterns you want to introduce. Emphasize and underline the spelling pattern and create word families with the same spelling pattern. For example, use the key word c*at* for decoding m*at*, s*at*, and h*at*. Do not simply write *cat*, *mat*, *sat*, and *hat*. The key word must be emphasized as the word to help decode the other words in the word family. Place the key word on a colored index card and place the other words in the word family under the key words on white index cards. Use the phrase, "If I know (key word), I know (word family word)." Sometimes you discover words that have different spelling patterns but sound the same, such as *bear* and *bare*. In that case use parentheses around words that have a different spelling pattern and tell the student that they are great word detectives who recognize that some spelling patterns sound alike but are spelled differently. When teaching the analogy strategy the key word is at the top of the word family list of words.

cat	grab

h<u>at</u>   c<u>ab</u>
s<u>at</u>   t<u>ab</u>
m<u>at</u>

2. Use the key words and some related word family words in a Language Experience Story (LEA). Have the student(s) find the words with the same spelling pattern as the key word. Here is an example of an LEA story for the key words c<u>ake</u>, <u>eat</u>, gr<u>ab</u>:

BOX 3.2

One day I was helping my mom b<u>ake</u> a c<u>ake</u>. We had to h<u>eat</u> the oven. Unfortunately, the oven temperature was too high. When the timer went off I decided to take the c<u>ake</u> out of the oven. The pan was so hot that I burned my hand! I had to gr<u>ab</u> a potholder. But worse than that, when I took it out it looked like something from outer space rather than c<u>ake</u>!

---

3. Review the key word or words with the same spelling patterns, analyze the words, and use the Talk to Yourself Chart. Analyze the key words for understanding of phonics generalizations for word recognition and spelling. Ask students to repeat a one-syllable word after you pronounce it, such as "ride." Next, ask the students, "How many sounds do you hear?" Then, write the number of letters representing the sounds in the word. Discuss the number of letters and sounds in the word. For example, ask, "How many sounds do you hear in the word 'ride'?" They might answer "three" sounds. Then write the word "ride" on the board and discuss why the word has four letters but only three sounds. Discuss the vowel(s) in the key words and whether it makes a short or long sound or neither and why. Have them create their own phonics generalization and compare them to phonics generalizations. Does the vowel make or break the phonics rule? Why? They might say the /e/ in the word "ride" is silent so the vowel says its name. Here we explore strategies for word analysis.

Consider the following examples of word analysis:

r i d e   Ride has three sounds but four letters. The spelling pattern is <u>ide</u>.

r i d   The students might make up a rule that the /e/ is silent and it makes the vowel /i/ long. The word does not break the phonics rule.

h o u s e   House has three sounds but five letters. The spelling pattern is <u>ouse</u>.

h ou s   The students might make up a rule that the two vowels /ou/ are not long or short and make the "ow" sound. When two vowels like "ou" come together, they make a new gliding sound, or diphthong.

4. Use the key words in sentences and words with the same spelling patterns in challenging sentences. Challenge the student(s) to find words with the same spelling patterns throughout the week during authentic reading and writing experiences.

5. Apply the learning of the spelling patterns to spelling words and use games such as concentration or dice with onsets on one dice and spelling patterns on another dice. Then create fun stories with the words they created.
6. Create an interactive vowel word wall. Notice that only the key words are used on the word wall in Table 3.4, and the spelling patterns are underlined in the words.
7. Use guided practice with scaffolding of instruction and review, review, review!

Rashad was overjoyed with his success, and he helped Elaine select reading goals to write in his portfolio. These goals were used for conferences with Rashad and his teacher. She looked forward to meeting with Rashad and Virginia weekly. All was well until she learned that his neighborhood had been redistricted and he would be attending another school. We were devastated! Fortunately, Virginia was able to tutor Rashad that summer.

Questions for Discussion: Revisiting the Chapter Vignette with Elaine and Rashad

Since students have difficulties with standardized assessments for different reasons, it is important to provide multiple appropriate assessments and instruction to meet unique needs during small-group instruction and individually (Allington & Johnston, 2001; Place, 2002; Valencia & Riddle-Buly, 2004). Students need unique instructional plans that relate to what they know and need to learn. Valencia and Riddle-Buly (2004) suggest that "teachers need to go beyond the scores on state test by conducting additional diagnostic assessments that will help them identify students' needs. . .(this) requires teachers having a deep understanding of reading processes and instruction, thinking diagnostically, and using the information on an ongoing basis to inform instruction" (p. 528).

BOX 3.3

As you consider what you learned from the vignette about Elaine's tutorial sessions with Rashad, discuss your responses to the following questions:

- How will effective word recognition strategies help students like Rashad who have unique literacy challenges?
- How would you assess and instruct students with phonics and spelling needs?
- How do you know if students use the reading strategies you teach them independently and effectively?
- How would you integrate the word recognition strategies with authentic literature and writing experiences across the content areas?
- How would you document student word recognition, spelling, and comprehension progress in literacy portfolios?

Discuss how a student could benefit from the following combined phonics approaches:

1. Segmenting words into small subunits of sounds and blending them to form a word in order to decode and spell unfamiliar words (grapho-phoneme knowledge).
2. Decoding by analogy with key words.

Activities for Transferring Word Recognition Strategies to Authentic Reading and Writing Experiences for Comprehension

Using Predictable Patterns in Books for the Analogy Strategy

Reading-aloud predictable patterns in books of interest helps reinforce fluency, word recognition, and comprehension (See Appendix A). The Natalie and James Stories in Appendix A can be copied, illustrated, and sent home to help children remember specific spelling patterns as they read and comprehend engaging stories. After reading, the spelling patterns/rimes in the stories can be used to create Language Experience Stories. In addition, the students can search the following websites about jellyfish to find pictures and information for Internet projects:

http://search.gallery.yahoo.com/search/corbis?p=jellyfish
http://discovery.com/area/nature/jellyfish/jellyfish2.html

Using Sentences from Authentic Texts for Strategic Learning

Spelling patterns are reliable indicators of pronunciations, except for sight words that do not rhyme, similar to the words "to" and "so," "who" and "go." Some spelling patterns represent two sounds such as the "oo" in "<u>good</u>" and "<u>food</u>." Students who know the cross-checking strategy are comfortable with these exceptions.

The Cross-Checking Strategy

Students verify whether the word makes sense in a sentence. For example, when checking the pronunciation and meaning of the word "bow," the student reads the following sentence for verification of meaning: *The purple bow was around the cat's neck.* If the word did not make sense the students learn how to switch vowel sounds to help the word make sense in the sentence.

Making Words
(Cunningham & Cunningham, 1992)

Making Words activities provide children of all ages with hands-on opportunities to use letters and make words. They begin with little words and expand until they create bigger words. They sort the words by spelling patterns to help them decode and spell words with the same spelling patterns. For instance, Cunningham suggests using the following letters: *a, d, h, n,* and *s* to sort for "_ad, _an, _and" words that can be transferred to other words with the same spelling patterns. For instance, students add an *s* to "ad" to form the word "sad." When they change the initial letters, "can" becomes "man." Then "band" becomes "hand." Many teachers use the Making Words strategy to reinforce the key word spelling patterns used for the analogy strategy. It is important for students to procure the information about sorting words and transfer it to reading and writing experiences.

We can also begin the Making Words strategy by selecting words from a story to create the activity. For example, when reading the book *The Mitten*, by Jan Brett (1989), we could use the word "mitten" as the source for the letters m-i-t-t-e-n. We could have the students find a one-letter word ("I"), two-letter words ("it"), and three-letter words ("ten"). Then the students could sort words by spelling patterns (ten, men). Finally, the students could find the mystery word (unscramble the letters of "mitten") and create their own story using some words with the emphasized spelling patterns. When working with older students, the teacher could read *Redwall*, by Brian Jaques (1998), and select the word "tapestry." The letters would be t-a-p-e-s-t-r-y. Initially, the students could find a one-letter word ("a"), two-letter words ("as"), three-letter words ("try"), and four-letter words ("tape"). Next, they could sort words with the same spelling pattern ("test," "rest," "pest"; "tape," "ape"). Finally, they could discover the mystery word by unscrambling the letters in tapestry and use "tapestry" and the words with the same spelling patterns to create a story.

Word Sorting Activities
(Johnson & Lehnert, 1984; Bear et al., 2000, 2011)

Students learn the purpose for sorting words by categories and/or spelling patterns, short and long vowels, and other vowel patterns. They can sort words individually and with small groups to help them pronounce words in sentences. This strategy builds sight word vocabulary. For the analogy strategy, model the procedure by identifying a key word card and placing it in the appropriate category. Then have the children pronounce the words and place the words in the appropriate category. The words can be used to write online stories and/or stories sent to e-pals.

BOX 3.4

WORD SORTING ACTIVITY: USING KEY WORDS WITH THE ANALOGY STRATEGY

Model for the whole group then have students work in small, heterogeneous groups.

Key Word Cards and Cards to Sort:

make, cake, stake, bake, rake, take, flake;
run, fun, sun, bun, pun;
bed, Fred, fled, led, red, wed
(The key words are in bold print.)
Challenge words to be added to the word sort and use in sentences:
Encourage students to make challenge word card with some of the same spelling patterns (underlined) as the key words for the activity (i.e., for/s<u>ake</u>, <u>ed</u>/<u>u</u>/ca/tion, <u>ed</u>/<u>it</u>; w<u>ed</u>/ding, f<u>un</u>/ny, <u>un</u>/h<u>ap</u>/p<u>y</u>).

TABLE 3.12   Word Sort Activity to Reinforce Word Analysis Vowel Information Using Spelling Patterns Learned

Name								Date		
Short *a* words	Long *a* words	Short *e* words	Long *e* words	Short *i* words	Long *i* words	Short *o* words	Long *o* words	Short *u* words	Long *u* words	*y* and other vowel sounds

Complete the self-check rubric after selecting words from each column to create a shared story. Begin writing the story by having one student begin the first sentence of the story. Then pass the story beginning to other students to complete the ideas in the story. Have the students revise their story and check their spelling. Ask them to record how many words they corrected and what errors they discovered.

Blending Wheels

Blending Wheels help students to blend beginning consonants and blends (onsets) with the rimes in words. For example, in the center of the wheel write the blend "bl." On the outside of the wheel on a separate piece of tagboard that is attached to the center of the wheel write the following spelling patterns: ack, ock, ed, ind, uff. As the students spin the wheel they read the words by blending the onset and spelling patterns. This game reinforces the analogy strategy.

Webbing Words or Mapping Words provides a visual representation of words.

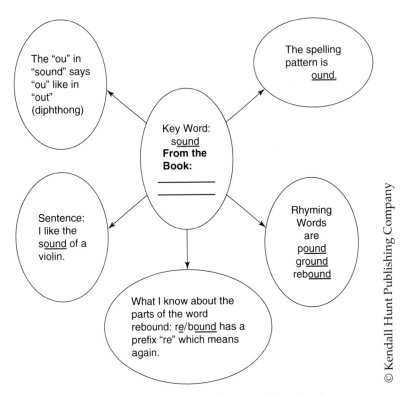

© Kendall Hunt Publishing Company

FIGURE 3.1   Webbing Words for Word Analysis:
What Do I Know About the Word?

Classroom Authentic Assessment

During planning sessions, it is important to consider ways to include authentic assessments to determine students' ability to use strategies and skills. Tables 3.13 and 3.14 may facilitate this process.

TABLE 3.13 My Word Sort Progress for Onset-Rime/Spelling Patterns

Name _____ Date _____

Sort words by the onsets and spelling patterns discovered during the activity:

	Word	Onset	Spelling pattern	Use the word in a sentence.
Word				
Word with the same spelling pattern				
Word with the same spelling pattern and a prefix and/or suffix				

*Vocabulary words with the spelling patterns above may be used in a summary about a favorite topic from any content area.

My Story: _____
_____
_____
_____

TABLE 3.14 Self-Checking Rubric

Name(s) _____ Date _____

Task	Yes	No	Comment
Did I use words that include the spelling patterns I am learning?			
Did I spell the words correctly?			
Do I understand the meaning of the words?			
Do the sentences make sense?			
Does the story make sense?			

Teach students to look for little words within larger words. For example, in the word "em/bed/ded" students can frequently recognize the word "bed." They should also practice recognizing frequent patterns in words such as "em" in "embedded" to help decode words.

Connecting Technology to Word Recognition Learning

Connecting technology to word recognition activities reinforces the skills needed for automaticity. The website *http://funbrain.com/detect/index.html* has puzzles that include words from stories. The websites Spelling Bee the Game http://www.spellingbeethegame.com/ and Game Aquarium-Spelling Games http://www.gamequarium.com/spelling.html motivate students to engage in enjoyable phonics and spelling activities that connect to reading and writing activities. In addition, teachers can create words for puzzles from books or poems.

Electronic or Paper Classification Folders

Electronic or Paper Classification Folders can be used for learning center activities to provide practice for sorting words. The folder might include onset and spelling patterns in words (onsets frequently include blends, digraphs, and clusters), long vowels, short vowels, sight words, and miscellaneous words that do not follow phonics rules.

Conversations about Effective Word Recognition Strategies with Students

It is often challenging to enhance the "I sounded it out" answer from students about decoding words. Encourage students to discuss *how* they sound out and analyze words. Even kindergarten children can explain how they figured out how to pronounce words. Elaine was talking to kindergarten children in a school and asked them how they pronounced the word "sheep." They immediately said, "I sounded it out!" She asked, "How did you sound it out?" At first they could not explain it. Then one of the children pointed to the word in the book (sheep) and said, "I said the 'sh,' and then I said 'eep.'" The child's answer indicated that he knew how to chunk the word "sheep" into the onset, "sh," and the spelling pattern, "eep." It is equally important to recognize and discuss words with different spelling and vowel patterns that share the same sounds, such as the homophones "bear" and "bare." These activities should be connected to authentic reading and writing.

Conversations about how word recognition strategies help with making meaning can be reinforced before, during, and after reading and writing. Chapter 4 emphasizes a variety of ways to enhance vocabulary development and take students to higher levels of word analysis and comprehension.

Image © Dmitriy Shironosov, 2012. Shutterstock, Inc.

Keys for Enhancing Vocabulary Development and Word Analysis

Debra Coffey, Elaine Roberts, Feland Meadows, and Laura Staal

Chapter 4 focuses on ways to enhance vocabulary development and word analysis. Consider what you know and want to explore about vocabulary instruction and word analysis.

TABLE 4.1

K	E	Y	S
What do you **know** about effective vocabulary instruction and word analysis?	What do you want to **explore** about effective vocabulary instruction and word analysis?	What are you **yearning** to learn after reading and discussing the chapter?	How will you **satisfy** your curiosity? What ideas and concepts will you apply to your teaching?

Vocabulary Development

As Mary grew plants in *The Secret Garden*, she divided them into groups in order to meet their needs most effectively. By grouping plants, she made sure they received enough sunlight, water, and nutrients. As students learn vocabulary words, classification activities help them to learn to use them more readily. Chapter 4 emphasizes the value of classification in various aspects of vocabulary development. Extensive vocabulary knowledge (understanding the meaning of words) is highly connected to successful reading comprehension (McKeown et al., 1985, Beck et al. 2002, 2008; Biemiller & Slonim, 2001; Brabham & Villaume, 2002; Celce-Murcia, 1991; Nilsen & Nilsen, 2003; Robinson, 2001 Carr, & Wixson, 1986). Reading and oral language opportunities are highly correlated to vocabulary acquisition. Vocabulary instruction needs to include multiple experiences for students to practice vocabulary words in context and writing. Oral language conversations during reading and writing activities at home and at school help students to acquire new vocabulary. Increasing vocabulary knowledge is essential for reading and listening comprehension (Chall, 1983). Unless students have opportunities to gain vocabulary knowledge in multiple contexts, the gap between known vocabulary and unfamiliar vocabulary widens as students enter the upper grades (Biemiller, 1999; Blachowicz & Fisher, 2010).

Insights for Effective Vocabulary Instruction

Dr. Feland L. Meadows

So, you want to teach reading, right? Of course you do! It is an essential part of what you need to do well if you are going to succeed as a teacher of young children. You have probably read articles by authors that talk about how important it is for children to be able to read. In addition, you have read about dozens of activities that you can use to help children learn to read, but the scope and sequence of those activities is unclear and there doesn't seem to be an integrating principle that will pull them all together into a cohesive whole. You also agree that you must be able to provide children with developmentally appropriate best practices in your teaching of reading.

This part of the chapter presents comprehensible descriptions of developmentally appropriate activities that you will be able to use to help children learn to write and read successfully. These lessons are part of a proven, comprehensive, research-based language and literacy program. Dr. Meadows and his teachers have applied this program successfully on three continents with young children who speak 11 different languages.

Two interesting discoveries have emerged from this work. The first is that you can achieve success when using the strategies with young children, as early as 3, 4, and 5 years of age. So the sooner you start, the better. The second discovery is that the strategies also work with children in the first three grades, but need adaptations for the different levels of development and learning styles of the older children.

Vocabulary Enrichment through Classification

Both children and adults need a ***structured framework*** within which to accommodate new information. Thanks to the millions of sensorial impressions that they have received since they were born and the speech they have heard, young children have acquired significant amounts of vocabulary together with a lot of information. What they have not yet learned, however, is how that information is classified. Three-and 4-year-old children may know that a red apple is different from a red bell pepper, but they do not necessarily know that one is a *fruit* and the other is a *vegetable*. They may recognize a dog and a wolf but do not know that one is classified as *domestic* and the other one as *wild*.

At this stage in a child's development, ***classification*** is the name of the game. Our first responsibility, then, is not to try to fill our children's heads with a lot of randomly selected new vocabulary but rather to help them to classify the knowledge that they already have. In the process, they will also learn new words; however, they will learn them in the context of each classification. That will provide ***comprehensible input***, a valuable educational experience, which helps the learner to *construct* and *integrate* new information into the knowledge base he or she already has.

Classify vegetables by where and how they grow:

1. Grow under the ground as roots (potatoes, onions, and garlic);
2. Grow on the surface of the ground as leaves and crucifers (lettuce, cauliflower, and broccoli);
3. Grow as stalks (celery, asparagus, and mushrooms);
4. Grow on vines (peppers, squash, and eggplant);
5. Grow in pods as legumes (soybeans, peas, and [yes] peanuts);
6. Grow as herbs (cilantro, basil, and oregano); and
7. Grow as grains (wheat, barley, and oats).

Classify fruit by the climate in which it grows: in the tropics, in a temperate climate, and in a cold climate. The classification of fruits by the geographic regions in which they grow will lead easily to a study of geography. You can then identify the tropics of Cancer and Capricorn and then you can relate each fruit to the geographic area on the globe where it grows.

When you introduce fruit from a particular climate to 3, 4, and 5-year-old children, your lesson will be more effective if you present **three real fruits** at a time. This will make the activity multisensory, with real objects that the child can see, feel, and smell. Later, even though the children do not yet know how to read, you can take effective steps toward the abstraction of reading by matching the real fruit to plastic fruit reproductions. Then you can show the child how to match plastic fruit to pictures of the same fruit. Then, as a review and an extension of the new classified information, you can prepare sets of classified matching picture cards of those same fruits, but this time they will have written labels. These activities become important *motives to reading*.

The child recognizes the picture of the fruit and soon will be able to recognize the written word that identifies the name of the fruit just as he or she already recognizes the logo of

Classify domestic animals next by presenting those that live in the home and then those that live on a farm or ranch.

Classify wild animals by the continent on which they live. This will again lead to geography. Your children will learn that many of the same animals live in North America and Europe but there are lions only in Africa and tigers only in Asia. They come together only in a circus or a zoo. They will learn that there are kangaroos only in Australia, polar bears only in the Arctic, and emperor penguins only in the Antarctic.

The most effective way to introduce a new classification and to introduce or review the names of objects within that classification is to present them in groups of three. Use the *Three Period Lesson* developed by Édouard Séguin to help the child identify or learn the names of objects within a particular classification. Here is an example of how you teach this type of lesson.

Tropical Fruit

Materials: Use only three objects at a time. The classification is *Tropical Fruit*, so select three <u>real</u> tropical fruits. Place a banana, a mango, and a pineapple in a basket. Use a rug on the floor to teach the lesson.

Note: Three Period Lesson: Introduce the fruit one at a time in the first period and ask for them in the same order in the second and third periods.

PRESENTATION: Holding the basket with the three fruits, you say to the child, "This is tropical fruit. Please say *tropical fruit.*"

Teaching the Three Period Lesson

First period provides information. You say *This is*.

Take the basket of fruit to the rug and invite the child to kneel or sit next to you to your left if the child is right-handed.

1. Take the banana from the basket; look it over carefully, feel it with both hands, and smell it, inhaling deeply to demonstrate the pleasure of sensing its particular, pungent aroma.
2. Hand the banana to the child and invite him or her to inspect, feel, and smell it the same way.
3. Hold out your hand to receive the banana and place it before the child on the carpet to the child's left.
4. Point to the banana and say, *This is* . . . STOP POINTING and WAIT until the child looks up into your face so that he or she can see your lips when you pronounce *Banana, please say banana*; the child repeats the word.
5. Present *mango* and *pineapple* in the same way, placing them left to right in front of the child on the carpet.

Note: When the information being given is new, the Three Period Lesson is more effective if you repeat all of the steps in the first period before going on to the second period.

Second period allows for recognition: You say, *give me* or *show me.*

1. Change the order in which you place the objects before the child but request them in the original order.
2. Say, *Please give me banana.*
3. The child gives you the banana.
4. Return the banana to the carpet in a different position.
5. Say, *Please give me mango.*
6. The child gives you the mango.
7. Return the mango to the carpet and change the positions of the objects again.
8. Say, *Please give me the pineapple.*
9. The child gives you the pineapple.
10. Return the pineapple to the carpet placing the three objects back to the original positions of the first period.

Note: If the child makes a mistake in the second or third periods, you move seamlessly back to present the first period again, without making any comment.

Third period provides for identification: You say, *What is this?*

1. The objects are now back in the original position of the first period.
2. Point to the banana. Take your hand back. Look into child's face and say, *What is this?*
3. Child answers: *banana.*
4. Use these same three steps to ask about the *mango* and *pineapple.*
5. You say, *Oh, let's say them again: banana, mango, pineapple.* The child says them with you. (Repeat)
6. Review by saying: *Please put the banana in the basket . . . thank you.*

Please put the mango in the basket . . . thank you. Please put the pineapple in the basket . . . thank you!

Phonemic Awareness and Key Words

An effective way to teach phonemic awareness is through key words. The initial letter-sound of each of the key words identifies one of the letters that will later be presented as a symbol with sandpaper letters. The following lessons will help you achieve this goal. The list of research-based key words was developed by the Scottish Rite Children's Hospital Dyslexia Therapy Center in Dallas, Texas. It has been tested with thousands of children who have learning disabilities for over 60 years. Dr. Meadows has also used it successfully with general education children for more than 40 years.

TABLE 4.2

Short Vowels										*Long Vowels*	
						Consonants					
apple	*a*	mitten	*m*	bat	*b*	cup	*c*	fish	*f*	leaf	*l*	apron	*a*
elephant	*e*	nest	*n*	dog	*d*	kite	*k*	house	*h*	valentine *v*	equal	*e*
Indian	*i*			goat	*g*	pig	*p*	sock	*s*	zipper	*z*	iris	*i*
octopus	*o*			rabbit	*r*	queen	*qu*	box	*ks*			opener	*o*
umbrella	*u*			jam	*j*	table	*t*	wagon	*w*			unicorn	*u*
penny	*y*			yarn	*y*							fly	*y*

1ˢᵗ Lesson: Use the *Three Period Lesson* to present **only the names** of three objects from a basket one at a time. Use the following letter presentation order: *cam, led, tis, gon, pur, bkf, vxy, wjq, haz.* This order is based upon the frequency that letters are used in the language. Do not use alphabetical order as it will not be useful to the child until s/he is a reader and can look up words alphabetically in a dictionary. Children learn alphabetic order easily with the a,b,c, song so it is not necessary to invest valuable time "teaching" it in class.

2ⁿᵈ Lesson: Use the *Three Period Lesson* to present **the initial sounds** of three objects from a basket one at a time.

1ˢᵗ Period say: "This is a cup. It begins with *c.* cup. . . *c.* Please say cup. . . *c.*"

2ⁿᵈ Period say: "Please show me the object that begins with *c* . . . thank you."

3ʳᵈ Period say: "What is this? Do the same with apple. . . *a* and mitten. . . *m.*

Materials: A covered basket on the shelf that contains the 26 objects that represent the key word alphabet. Create a smaller basket for the objects that will be used to introduce three objects for the key words one at a time; have children sit on a rug.

Lesson: Use the *Three Period Lesson* to present only the names of three objects from a basket one at a time. Use the following letter presentation order: *cam, led, tis, gon, pur, bkf, vxy, wjq, haz.* This order is based on the frequency of letters in the language. Do not use alphabetical order.

Go to www.montessori-PAMS.org to download the illustrated Key Word Cards shown actual size and reproduce them for use in your classroom.

TABLE 4.3 Pronunciation Guide for the Key Word Phonetic Alphabet

VOWELS	Consonants	STOPPED Consonants & Digraphs		CONTINUANT Consonants & Digraphs		Silent Letters
full voiced	nasal voiced	voiced	unvoiced	unvoiced	voiced	no sound
Short Vowels	mitten *m*	bat *b*	cup *c*	fish *f*	leaf *l*	beat [a]
apple *a*	nest *n*	dog *d*	kite *k*	house *h*	valentine *v*	lamb [b]
elephant *e*	sing *ng*	goat *g*	pig *p*	sock *s*	zipper *z*	scene [c]
Indian *i*		giraffe *g*	queen *qu*	piece *s*	pleasure *zh*	Wednesday [d]
octopus *o*		rabbit *r*	table *t*	ship *sh*		face [e]
umbrella *u*		jam *j*	church *ch*	sugar *sh*		sign [g]
penny *y*		yarn *y*		machine *sh*		gnat [g]
				thread *th*		light [gh]
Long Vowels				box *ks*		hour [h]
apron *a*				whip *wh**		fruit [i]
equal *e*				wagon *w**		knife [k]
iris *i*						talk [l]
opener *o*						Autumn [n]
unicorn *u*						tour [o]
fly *y*						psalm [p]
						often [t]
						four [u]
						wagon [w]*
						wrap [w]*

*The "w" in most English words is silent. It affects the sound of the vowel or consonant, which follows it by the way that you purse your lips before you pronounce the word. It is the vowel or consonant which follows the "w" which gives the sound, if any. For instance: "whisper" has no vowel sound at all and the "w" is completely silent. In "wagon" the "a" is inflected by the pursing of the lips for the "w." In the diphthong "ow", as in "clown", the "w" contributes to the sound of "u" as in the "ou" of "fountain."

*The "w" in most English words is silent. It affects the sound of the vowel or consonant that follows it by the way that you purse your lips before you pronounce the word. It is the vowel or consonant that follows the "w," which gives the sound, if any. For instance, "whisper" has no vowel sound at all and the "w" is completely silent. In "wagon" the "a" is inflected by the pursing of the lips for the "w." In the diphthong "ow," as in "clown," the "w" contributes to the sound of "u," as in the "ou" in "fountain."

Key Word Phonetic Alphabet Cards

Materials: Create a set of 5.5″ ´ 8.5″ cards with colored pictures or drawings of the key words in the center. Each card has letters in its four corners for the particular sound represented: small cursive letter in upper left corner, capital cursive letter in upper right corner; small print letter in lower left corner, capital print letter in lower right corner. Vowel cards have a red border and consonant cards have a blue border.

Lesson: Sit across from the child. Review the names of the key words three at a time using the *Three Period Lesson*. Use **cam, led, tis, gon, pur, bkf, vxy, wjq, haz** presentation order. Do not mention the letters that appear in the corners of the cards.

When pronouncing the sounds of stopped consonants, whether voiced or unvoiced, **you must not add a vowel sound at the end**, as many people do. They say, "This is "buh' or 'cuh" or 'puh'." This introduces sounds that do not occur in the word when its letters are sounded out. Produce the shortened sound of the voiced consonant or the single explosive, unvoiced sound of "c" or "p." An example of a consonant digraph is chair. A vowel digraph example is beat.

I Spy Game with Key Word Objects
Introduction to Initial Letter Sounds

Material: Nine small baskets with three small key word objects in each. Place a small piece of white felt to cover the objects inside each little basket. Write the letters **cam, led, tis, gon, pur, bkf, vxy, wjq, haz** on the white felt covers for the baskets that contain the key word objects that begin with those letters and sounds. Use the same presentation order. This time, you will introduce the initial letter-sounds of the key words.

Note: <u>It is the word that gives us the initial letter sound</u> so that when you show the object you must **always say the word first**, followed by the sound of its initial letter (i.e., *cup – c, apple – a, mitten – m*).

Lesson: Sit opposite the child.

1. Secretly take one object from the little basket and hold it hidden between your hands.
2. <u>Look into your hands</u> and say: *I spy with my little eye an object that begins with c. . . c. . . c.*
3. Slowly expose what is in your hands to the child, saying, *cup – c, cup – c, cup – c, say: cup – c.*
4. Give the cup to the child to inspect. Repeat *cup – c* and encourage the child to say *cup – c* with you while looking at your lips.
5. Let the child give you the cup. Place it in front of the child to his left (your right because you are facing the child).
6. Repeat the procedure for the second and third objects, placing them left to right from the child's perspective.
7. Give the Three Period Lesson with the three key words and their initial letter sounds.

Present the Three Period Lesson

First period: <u>information</u> – *this is . . .*

1. Point to the cup and say, *This is . . .* STOP POINTING and WAIT until child looks up into your face, then say, *cup – c; please say cup – c.* Child repeats.
2. Point to the apple and say, *This is . . .* STOP POINTING and WAIT as above, then say, *apple – a; please say apple – a.* Child repeats.
3. Point to the mitten and say, *This is . . .* STOP POINTING and WAIT as above, then say, *mitten – m; please say mitten – m.* Child repeats.
   (Repeat the First Period)

Second period: <u>recognition</u> – *give me . . .*

1. Change the order in which the objects are placed before the child.
2. Say, *Please give me the object that begins with "c"* (say the sound of "c," not the name).
3. The child gives you the cup.
4. Return the cup to the carpet and change the positions of the objects again.
5. Say, *Please give me the object that begins with "a."* (Make sure you are making the short vowel sound of "a," as in "apple.")
6. The child gives you the apple.
7. Return the apple to the carpet and change the positions of the objects again.
8. Say, *Please give me the object that begins with "m."*
9. The child gives you the mitten. Say *thank you* each time the child does what you request.

Third period: <u>identification</u> – *what does this begin with . . . ?*

1. The objects are now back in the original position of the first period.
2. Point to the cup. Take your hand back. Look into child's face and say, *What does this begin with?*
3. Child answers: **"c," giving the sound.**
4. Point to the apple. Take your hand back. Look into child's face and say, *What does this begin with?*
5. Child answers: **"a."**
6. Point to the mitten. Take your hand back. Look into child's face and say, *What does this begin with?*
7. Child answers: **"m."**
8. Say, *Lets tell the whole story.* Point to each object in turn: *This begins with "c," cup – "c." This begins with "a," apple – "a." This begins with "m," mitten – "m."*
9. Review by saying: *Please put cup – "c" in the basket . . . Please put apple – "a" in the basket . . . Please put mitten – "m" in the basket. Thank you!*

Twelve Games for the Analysis of Sounds

Children who have had some or all of the key words and their sounds presented to them especially enjoy playing these games. Because the children who already recognize the sounds you request will be responding most of the time at first, you can play these games with the entire class. Other children will begin to clue in and will enjoy the games as well.

   1 — Have children think of words that begin with a specific sound. Be sure to say the sound and NOT THE NAME of the letter.
   Who can think of a word that starts with "m"?
   Who can think of a happy word that starts with "l"?
   Who can think of a vegetable that begins with "c"?
   I am thinking of something that begins with "s" . . . and it falls from the sky . . . and it is very cold!

2 — Look surreptitiously at something in the room (a small table) then look quickly away, as if you don't want the children to catch you looking at it.
I'm thinking of something in this room that starts with "t" (look quickly at table) *that starts with "t," can you guess what it is?*
Young children especially love to catch you looking at the object you have chosen.

3 — Give a word and have children identify the initial sound.
What sound does this word begin with . . . ? table.

4 — Have children think of words that end with a specific sound.
Tell me what this word ends with . . . cat.
Tell me what these words end with . . . dog, log, hog.

5 — Have children think of the medial sounds in three-letter words.
What is the medial sound in the word "pot"?
The middle sound in a word is called the medial sound, say "medial sound."
What is the medial sound in the word "cat"?

6 — Identify all of the sounds in a word.
Let's say all the sounds in this word, cat. . . "c," "a," "t."

7 — The Same Sound Game. *Please tell me a word that begins with the same sound as cat.*

8 — First Sound Name Game. Invite children to line up when they hear you say the initial sound of their names.

9 — Shaking Hands. When a child's name is called, he or she goes and shakes the hand of a child whose name begins with the same sound. If there is no one whose name begins with the same sound, he or she may point to or go and get an object that begins with the same sound.

10 — Thumbs Up–Thumbs Down: Announce a sound and give the position in each word where that sound will appear. *The sound is "a" and the place is medial.* The children make a fist with their thumbs up. Recite a list of words with the correct sound and position, then slip in a word that does not follow the pattern. When the children hear the word that is different, they turn their thumbs down.

Example: *Listen to the initial sounds of the words I am going to say. If you hear a "c" at the beginning of each word, give me a thumbs-up. If you hear another sound at the beginning of a word, then give me a thumbs-down. Car, cat, call, come, catch, dog, cab, etc.*

11 — The Quiet Scavenger Hunt: Select two small groups of children. Give each group a sound. Invite them to walk around the room QUIETLY looking for objects that begin with the sound you have given them. After a short while, call them back together. Invite the children to show the objects they have found that begin with the sound they were given. Invite the children to take the objects back to their places.

12 — Going on a Trip: Say: We are going on a trip and we must pack our suitcases. We can only take items that begin with the same sound as the place we are going to visit. We are going to **Hawaii** so we can only take things that begin with **"h," give the sound of the letter, do not say its name.** I am going to take my **hat.** What do you want to take? When you say **"h,"** hold your hand in front of your face so as to feel the breath you are expelling. Encourage the children to do the same when they tell you what they are going to take that starts with **"h."**

Copyright © 2005 by Pan American Montessori Society — Used by permission

Born in Puebla, Mexico, Dr. Feland L. Meadows serves as The Goizueta Endowed Chair of Early Childhood Education in the Bagwell College of Education. This endowed chair enabled Kennesaw State University to become the first institution in Georgia to develop a M.Ed. in Montessori Early Childhood Education, 2.5-6 Year Level and a B.S. in Early Childhood Education, Birth through Five (B-5) which leads to a Teaching Credential from the GA Professional Standards Commission. These programs also lead to International Certification as Montessori Teachers by the Pan American Montessori Society. These programs are accredited by NCATE and are the only Montessori Teacher Education programs nationally accredited by the U.S.D.E. recognized Montessori Accreditation Council for Teacher Education (MACTE) in the state of Georgia. Dr. Meadows has prepared more than 2,500 Montessori Teachers in seven countries.

Expanding Vocabulary Knowledge

Beck, McKeown, and Kuran (2002) stressed the importance of using "robust" vocabulary instruction to help students appreciate the rich meanings of words. Beck recommends that teachers initially determine students' vocabulary knowledge, determine how their vocabulary knowledge is being expanded, and know how to assess word knowledge. Frequent encounters with new vocabulary words help students use new words. Beck suggested that teachers provide students with "friendly explanations" during vocabulary activities. These explanations come from authentic reading passages. The explanation may be stored in vocabulary log books, on vocabulary cards, or exhibited on word walls to be used during reading and writing. Teachers can model how to use descriptive words to determine meanings of words. They can teach students to chunk words into syllables and note the affixes (prefixes and suffixes) and their meanings as well as discover and discuss the origins of the root words to create their descriptors for the vocabulary words. Students can create descriptions of words, as in Table 4.4. This vocabulary activity can be modified for all ages. Teachers may introduce the words and provide a think-aloud with their explanations about the meanings of words and use descriptors, then students can use think-alouds and practice creating descriptors for vocabulary explanations.

TABLE 4.4 Vocabulary Explanations

garland (gar-land) flower wreath
anthology (an-thol-o-gy) collection of pieces of literature
sequence (se-quence) the order that things happen such as the order of letters in the alphabet

Discussing words and relating them to a context helps students retain, note, and use the vocabulary words when reading and writing. For instance, students might describe the activities that an astronaut might do after reading a story about an astronaut. They can also discuss words that an astronaut would use to describe feelings when walking on the moon.

Dale's Four Stages of Vocabulary Knowledge

Beck and McKeown (1991, p. 791) suggested that knowledge of word meanings should be related to Dale's (1965) four stages of vocabulary knowledge:

Stage 1 – Never saw the word before
Stage 2 – Heard it, but don't know what it means
Stage 3 – Recognize it in context as having something to do with . . .
Stage 4 – Knows it well

Students need to discuss the stage they are in and use effective strategies for understanding the meanings of unfamiliar words in order to move from one stage to the next. Dale's four stages of vocabulary knowledge may be used as a framework for many vocabulary activities. An essential aspect of vocabulary knowledge development is *how* teachers and students select vocabulary words to increase comprehension. Students and teachers should both be involved in the process. Before, during, and after reading, students should have time to discuss the meaning of the words they discover. Stating definitions alone does not motivate students to recall the meaning of words. The words need to be significant and meaningful to the students.

Promoting Vocabulary Development

Curtis and Longo (2001) designed a vocabulary intervention as part of the program Reading is FAME. These researchers believe as Beck, McKeown, and Omanson (1987), that students need direct instruction and 10–15 encounters with word meanings.. They stress the importance of expanding students' vocabularies through listening, speaking, reading, and writing. FAME is based on Chall's (1983) stages of reading development. The vocabulary component of FAME features improving reading comprehension and using a word list before presenting the words in context. Students create the contexts for the word meanings. Teachers and students monitor their progress. This is the process for the FAME vocabulary strategy:

1. The teacher first models a discussion of familiar and unfamiliar words in isolation. This may be limited to 10 words per week or less, depending on student needs. Then the teacher discusses each word in context. For example, "The word 'anxious' means that someone is nervous about something. Have you ever been anxious about passing a test? When?" Discussing Dale's stages helps students monitor their vocabulary progress.
2. Next, the teacher presents the words in a variety of contexts:
   a. Prefixes (i.e., *un-* and *re-*) and suffixes (i.e., *-ed* and *-ment*) may be emphasized.
   b. Reader response and read-aloud activities may be included with emphasis on vocabulary.
3. The students practice the strategy. For instance, analogies may be used to expand word meanings (i.e., exuberance is to cheerfulness as melancholy is to _____).
4. The teacher promotes interactive processing. Writing is a way to understand word meaning by using the vocabulary words in stories. For instance, students might write about the word "startled" using this prompt: "If you were startled by a wild animal, what would you do?"

Extending Vocabulary Development through Classification

We have considered the importance of classification for early vocabulary development, and classification is important at all stages of vocabulary development. When students use **semantic clues**, they consider word meaning and learn to develop outlines, effective sentences, and meaningful paragraphs. In order to use effective sentence structure in those paragraphs, students learn to classify words in relation to parts of speech and word usage. Students use **syntactic clues** in this process to synthesize the components of effective sentences. They use **pragmatic clues** as they consider the cultural impact and function of those words. When students conduct morphemic analysis, they learn to classify the parts of words and become familiar with prefixes and suffixes. They use **graphophonic clues** as they look for patterns and consider word structure during morphemic analysis. Students also use graphophonic clues to identify types of words. For effective writing and spelling, they need to be able to recognize types of words, such as **compound words** (two or more words combined) and **contractions** (shortened forms of words).

Emphasizing Affixes during Word Recognition Strategy Instruction

Affixes should be recognized by students to help them pronounce and know the meanings of words. For example, they need to become familiar with frequently used prefixes and suffixes such as the *re-* prefix in the word "repressible." The 20 most common prefixes and suffixes in children's reading materials in grades 3–9 were listed by White, Sowell, and Yanagihara (1989). The common prefixes and suffixes are found in Table 4.5.

Students can look for, discuss, and circle prefixes and suffixes in words they are analyzing to help them recognize and spell subunits in words. It is helpful to underline the spelling patterns/ rimes and always circle prefixes and suffixes.

TABLE 4.5 Common Prefixes and Suffixes

Common Prefixes		
Prefix	**Meaning**	**Examples**
anti	against	anticipate
de	from, away	detach
dis	apart from, not	distract
en, em	in	embedded
fore	in front of, before	foreman
in, im, ir, il	not	invisible
in, im	in or into	inside
inter	between, among	interview
mid	middle	midnight
mis	wrong, bad, not	mistake
non	not	nonprofit
over	too much	oversight
pre	in front of, before	predict
re	back, again	reread
semi	half, partly	semicircle
sub	under, inferior	subzero
super	above, in addition	superman
trans	across, through	transportation
un	not	unhappy
under	too little	undervalue
Common Suffixes		
Suffix	**Meaning**	**Example**
al, ial	relating to	personal
ed	past tense	laughed
er, or	one who	speaker
er	comparative	proper

est	most (comparative)	kindest
ful	quality of	wonderful
ible, able	able to, quality of	possible
ic	like, pertaining to	cubic
ing	ongoing	running
ion, ation, ition, tion	act or state of	addition
ity, ty	state or quality of	activity
ive, ative, itive	tending to, relating to	interactive
less	without	tearless
ly	every, in the manner of	weekly
ment	result, or state of	enjoyment
ness	quality of	neatness
ous, eous, ious	full of, state of	precious
s, es	plural	houses
y	quality, full of	dirty

Decoding Multisyllabic Words

Students decode multisyllabic words strategically when they develop skills in morphemic analysis. This enhances their vocabulary development, comprehension, and fluency. For example, students might use a variety of strategies when reading the word "challenged" in the sentence, "I was <u>challenged</u> during a game of jeopardy." The students could try the following strategies to pronounce the word:

1. **Students use the analogy strategy** and underline the spelling patterns <u>all</u>, <u>en</u>, and <u>ed</u> in the word.
2. **Students identify subunits of the word "challenged."** The students think aloud, "If I know sh<u>all</u>, I can change the sh to ch for ch<u>all</u>. (This shows the ability to interchange phonemes.) If I know t<u>en</u>, I know *eng*. If I know r<u>ed</u>, I know *ed*." The suffix *-ed* should be recognized as a suffix. **Then the students combine the sounds together in syllable subunits to pronounce the word "challenged."**
3. **Students identify** and circle the <u>ch</u> and <u>ed</u> as **chunks that occur frequently in words.**
4. **Students look for small words in the multisyllabic word.** They note that there is only one small word, <u>all</u>, in the word "challenged."

After this analysis, students should discuss the ways they combined strategies to analyze the word "challenged." It would help them to remember that they used the analogy strategy, applied morphological knowledge, and used a decoding strategy of looking for small words in larger words. Teachers need to model and scaffold lessons for student think-alouds during read-alouds of meaningful text. This helps students to overcome fear of decoding multisyllabic words and removes word recognition barriers as they read for meaning independently.

Integrating Literacy Learning Across the Curriculum

As students learn strategies for word analysis and vocabulary development, it is important to use culturally responsive literature in the classroom and provide a literacy-rich environment with multiple opportunities for literacy learning across the curriculum. Here are some ways to promote vocabulary development across the curriculum:

- Have students work together in small, flexible groups to select words from context for word analysis and meaning-making.
- Discuss instructional literacy purposes that are guided by the needs of students. Assessment guides instruction.
- Scaffold literacy learning and make adaptations for students to ensure success.
- Integrate authentic reading and writing experiences to meet and support the needs of diverse students.
- Use multimedia to motivate students and build background knowledge. Model how to use technology for purposes of learning.
- Use tasks that are of interest to students and are open-ended to extend learning (i.e., rubrics, books of interest, etc.).
- Ensure that students are effective literacy strategies during word analysis, spelling, reading, and writing.
- Use centers, or learning stations, that reinforce literacy learning purposes across the curriculum.
- Encourage reflective thinking, multisensory opportunities, and responsible learning. Discuss with students how and why the learning is taking place to promote metacognitive learning (i.e., student think-alouds).
- Include visible word walls and strategy charts to reinforce literacy lessons. Teach students to use the word walls as references during reading and writing.
- Recognize when students understand concepts and effective strategies and provide innovative ideas.
- Personalize literacy learning across the content areas.
- Conference with students and parents about effective literacy strategies for word analysis and making meaning of texts.

Activities to Enhance the Implementation of Word Recognition Strategies and Comprehension in an Integrated Approach

Comprehension is the key to reading, and word recognition activities need to be connected with authentic opportunities to enhance comprehension. The following activities will provide ideas for lesson planning that incorporate word recognition strategies to increase spelling, fluency, and comprehension.

- Develop strategy charts and bookmarks to help students learn to select effective word recognition strategies independently when reading and writing. What would you include on a chart/bookmark for word recognition strategies for your students?
- Prepare lessons for the analogy strategy following the procedures for the analogy strategy outlined in this chapter. What adaptations could you make for ELL students? Go to *http://tesol .org and http://teachers.net/4blocks/article4.5html* for assistance.
- Which IRA language arts standards are addressed by the word recognition strategies discussed in this chapter?
- Create a word search puzzle. Visit *www.funbrain.com.*
- Visit *www.abcteah.com* to use or create word searches/word finds for your students. After searching have them sort words into categories or by spelling patterns/rimes.

- Complete and discuss the KEYS for the chapter. Self-evaluate your assessment, teaching, and learning. Share your learning and suggestions with a partner, small group, or other teachers.
- Create a rubric for word recognition strategy success within a balanced and integrated approach. Visit *www.quia.com*.
- Create an Internet project based on a content-area theme. Include word recognition strategies, authentic literature and writing experiences, software, and games for your students. Table 4.6 presents additional strategies for vocabulary development.

TABLE 4.6   Strategies for Vocabulary Development

Strategy	Strategy Description	Example
Vocabulary Banks and Vocabulary Videos	Students collect words in their vocabulary banks (or file boxes) and choose a certain word to depict in a video.	On video a group of students portray the word "chrysanthemum" by using quotes from the book *Chrysanthemum* by Henkes (2007).
Personal Clue Cards (Carr, 1986)	Students create personal clue cards to enhance vocabulary knowledge and extend background knowledge.	Word: garden Illustration: Image © darios, 2012. Shutterstock, Inc.
Verbal-Visual Vocabulary Squares (Readence, Bean, & Baldwin, 1998)	This strategy helps students remember the meanings of words. The students use a square on a folded piece of paper for each word. The word is written in the middle. In small groups the students find the word in the text. They write the definition, part of speech, create a sentence, and add an image.	Word: sunflower Text: We saw a sunflower in the garden. Definition: A large flower with yellow petals and a cluster of seeds in the middle. Part of speech: noun Image © ultimathule, 2012. Shutterstock, Inc.

Parent Involvement In Vocabulary Development

Children derive tremendous benefits when they listen to bedtime stories and spend quality time reading with their parents. The benefits of those reading sessions are limitless. Parents are the first and most important teachers of their children. It is important for teachers to explore ways to help parents increase their positive impact on children's literacy learning. When parents face challenges with literacy, teachers may need to find innovative ways to include them in their children's literacy learning. Karther (2002) suggests that schools include programs centered around parents' work schedules. Additionally, schools need to provide literacy materials and model how parents can increase their children's literacy learning.

Cullinan (2000) listed seven benefits that result when parents read aloud to their children.

Reading aloud:

- establishes bonds of love
- opens doors
- becomes part of family heritage
- is fun
- builds the desire to read
- gives an educational advantage
- develops the ability to read alone (p. 24)

During reading experiences it is highly beneficial when parents encourage their children's literacy development by drawing attention to features of the print. Explicit attention to both pictures and print enhances the experience, particularly when parents read with their children on a regular basis and make the experience enjoyable. When parents ask specific meaningful questions to draw attention to specific vocabulary words, they help students personalize vocabulary words. This helps students to make text-to-self, text-to-text, and text-to-world connections with the vocabulary words and the stories (Harvey & Goudvis, 2007).

When students need assistance with literacy experiences beyond the school setting, parental involvement may be encouraged with conferences, class newsletters, class web pages, and technology equipment to check out and take home. In some cases, parents may find it challenging to read proficiently in either their native language or English. Mentors, paraprofessionals, and peer buddies can help connect literacy learning to school and home.

It is important to equip parents to support their children's literacy learning through reading, writing, journaling, and Internet literacy experiences. When parents enjoy reading and writing, they help instill a love for reading and writing in the lives of their children. This is particularly true when they engage in intentional vocabulary instruction as they read with their children. Often this is most effective when they ignite their children's natural curiosity and encourage interest in vocabulary in the context of quality literature. Dr. Laura Staal is an enthusiastic professor and conference presenter from the Department of Professional Leadership in the School of Education at the University of North Carolina. She has found meaningful ways to encourage her daughter's vocabulary development through intentional vocabulary instruction.

Intentional Vocabulary Instruction

Dr. Laura Staal

As an educator and parent of five school-aged daughters, I am very interested in my children's experiences at school. I will never forget the incident that focused my attention and professional interest on vocabulary instruction: the day that my second grader received an "F" on a vocabulary quiz. I remember this day clearly. My husband was deployed, and I had a very busy day at work.

Upon coming home, my babysitter explained that my daughter was very upset. She had crumpled up a quiz, had thrown it across the room, and was still crying about it. I picked up the quiz, unraveled it, and investigated its contents. It didn't take long to realize the problem: it was a five-item matching vocabulary quiz, and two of the vocabulary words were synonyms (the words "clustered" and "gathered"). Then I sat down with my daughter and explained about synonyms and how these two words and their definitions can be used interchangeably. Her teacher adjusted her grade and used the experience to teach a class of second graders all about synonyms. This incident motivated me to research effective and creative ideas to foster vocabulary development and instruction in K–12 classrooms. The research revealed that (1) vocabulary is important, (2) there are lots of great vocabulary strategies, (3) there must be a model for consistency, and (4) researching different vocabulary strategies is fun and rewarding.

First, the research was a reminder of the importance of vocabulary development. Duffy (2004) explains that building rich oral and written vocabulary is one of the key characteristics of a literate environment:

> Reading is language and language is made up of words and words reflect experiences, the more experiences you have the more likely it is that you will become a good reader. Because new words come from new experiences, literate classroom environments are characterized by rich experiences with world knowledge and new concepts. These translate into new vocabulary. The richer the vocabulary, the more students are encouraged to become readers. (p. 6)

Too often, children (like my oldest daughter) view vocabulary as a set of weekly drills, practices, quizzes, and tests. But it doesn't have to be this way! One of my favorite authors, Philip Yancy (1997), states "As a writer, I play with words all day long. I toy with them, listen for their overtones, crack them open, and try to stuff my thoughts inside" (p. 12). This is exactly what we want our students to do: We want them to play with words, listen to their overtones, crack them open to experience their richness, and to stuff their own thoughts and experiences inside! So how do we do this? How do we get kids really excited about words?

The second thing that my review of the research identified was the answer to this question! There are a ton of really great vocabulary strategies out there (e.g., Barger, 2006; Beck, McKeown, & Kucan, 2002, 2008; Bromley, 2008; Graves & Watts-Taffe, 2008; Lane & Arriaza-Allen, 2010). For example, one of the most interesting and exciting studies that I came across involved the vocabulary strategy of word walls (Harmon, Wood, Hedrick, Vintinner, & Willeford, 2009). Sixth-grade students were asked to do the following in small groups over the course of several weeks: (1) locate words from the Internet, magazines, TV, etc.; (2) select words according to specific criteria; (3) assign a color to each word; (4) create a symbol to assign to each word; (5) create personal connections to the words through sentences and pictures in meaningful contexts; (6) share their work with the rest of the class; and (7) display their words on the classroom word wall. The researchers of this study found that engaging students in meaningful vocabulary activities gets students excited about words. Just like Yancy (1997), these students experienced the richness of words by stuffing their own ideas, thoughts, and personal experiences into them through media, color, collaboration, connections, and creativity!

There are multitudes of effective strategies to foster vocabulary development out there (preteaching vocabulary words, studying word relationships/word parts, reading out loud, singing, gaming, discussing, thinking out loud, creating word walls and word banks, making connections across the curriculum, acting, and collaborating).

The third thing that the research revealed to me was exciting research by Berne and Blachowicz (2008). Results from their survey study of 72 teachers report that most teachers possess an awareness of research-based strategies and practice them regularly in their classrooms. This is great news! After careful review and analysis, however, they uncovered a larger and more important issue with respect to vocabulary development. They found that teachers have a desire for effective and consistent practice schoolwide. So, Berne and Blachowicz created a simple model to help guide teachers in their growth with respect to vocabulary instruction in the classroom, called "A Model for Consistency." This model involves the following three steps: (1) *Reflect* on current vocabulary practices, (2) *Read* the research for new ideas, and (3) *Research* new vocabulary practices in your classroom. I liked this idea so much that I decided to follow the model myself.

As I began reflecting, I realized that I had already completed the first two steps in Berne and Blachowicz's (2008) model. I *reflected* on my daughter's vocabulary experiences and my own vocabulary practices and started *reading* the research. The part I was missing was the third step, challenging me to *research* the vocabulary practices that I had been reading about. So, I decided to intentionally research vocabulary strategies; some from the research, and some that I created together with my students. Based on observations and the voices of my students, I found the following vocabulary strategies to be the most exciting, effective, and rewarding:

1. **Reading Out Loud.** In my opinion, this is the number one vocabulary strategy. There are cool and interesting words everywhere! When reading out loud, the reader has the opportunity to intentionally pause to clarify and celebrate new vocabulary words. For example, I recently read the book *Dragon Rider* (Funke, 2004) out loud and intentionally stopped to clarify and celebrate the new and interesting word "rapacious." I also chose to pause and celebrate Funke's style of writing a series of words using the literary strategies of synonyms and alliteration: "devour," "destroy," "dismantle," and "despoil." O'Conner (2006) does the same thing in her book *Fancy Nancy: Bonjour Butterfly*: "scowl," "sulk," and "storm." Not only do examples like these get kids excited about words and how they sound, but it also provides them with an effective descriptive writing strategy.

2. **Vocabulary PowerPoint Presentations.** This strategy asks students to create a PowerPoint slide by selecting a font and pictures to describe the new word, definition, and part of speech. For example, for the word "rapacious," one student selected the "chiller" font and pictures of a barracuda, anaconda, and great white shark.

3. **Vocabulary Poetry.** This strategy asks students to create a poem to explain a new vocabulary word. It is helpful to students to share already existing vocabulary poetry such as "Solitude" (Milne, 1996).

4. **Vocabulary Realia.** This strategy asks students to connect an object to a vocabulary word. For example, one student chose a scary-looking dragon from her collection to connect to the word "rapacious" from *Dragon Rider* (Funke, 2004).

5. **Vocabulary Interviews.** This strategy asks students to interview people about their favorite words. This sounded like so much fun to me that one day I decided to interview people, too! My findings: (1) One Army soldier told me his favorite word is "plethora." Why? Because it is from one of his favorite movies and the word conjures up humor. (2) A mother of a preschooler's favorite word is "indubitably." Why? Because it is fun to say! (3) A Walmart greeter's favorite word is "friend." Why? Because he says it all day long, "Welcome to Walmart, my friend."

6. **Word Sightings.** This strategy asks students to be on the lookout for sighting (seeing and hearing) new words. In the book *Becoming Naomi Leon* (Munoz-Ryan, 2004), Naomi keeps a word notebook where she records new and interesting words. She is always on the lookout for word sightings. One night as I was watching the broadcast of the 81st Academy Awards (Condon & Laurence, 2009), I decided to try this out! Some of the first words I sighted were from the announcer's description of Heath Ledger's performance in the movie *The Dark Knight* (Nolan, Roven, & Thomas, 2008): diabolical, menacing, appalling, unleashed.

7. **Vocabulary Timelines.** This strategy asks students to record the page numbers of interesting words that describe a character during reading and to create a vocabulary timeline by describing each word in the order it appeared in the book. See the vocabulary timeline below for the character "Nettlebrand" from *Dragon Rider*.

Photo courtesy of the author.

FIGURE 4.1

8. **Vocabulary Pyramids.** This strategy asks students to create a pyramid by writing the word, part of speech, definition, sentence, and personal connection. A vocabulary pyramid example for the word "rapacious" is displayed in Figure 4.2.

FIGURE 4.2 Word Pyramid

Based on this short vocabulary vignette, what new vocabulary strategy are *you* going to go out and intentionally and indubitably try in your classroom?

BOX 4.1

LITERACY WEBSITES

www.readwritethink.org International Reading Association Lesson Plans and Resources

www.reading.org International Reading Association

www.ncte.org National Council of Teachers of English

www.ldonline.org Learning Disabilities website

www.tesol.org Teachers of English to Speakers of Other Languages

www.nationalreadingpanel.org National Reading Panel report and resources

http://www.ala.org/alsc/awardsgrants/bookmedia/caldecottmedal/caldecotthonors/caldecottmedal Caldecott Awards for Books

http://kids.mymysterynet.com Mystery literature resources for children

www.readingrockets.com Teacher resources for literacy instruction

Effective vocabulary instruction helps students to classify fruit trees and flowering shrubs as they design a garden literally or figuratively. *Starfall.com* and similar websites extend literacy opportunities from emergent literacy to fluent reading. When students have opportunities to experiment with classification, word analysis, and word choice on many levels, they learn to communicate in meaningful ways and develop leadership ability.

© Kendall Hunt Publishing Company; Photograph by Tyler Davis

This picture of spring blossoms in Elaine's garden was photographed by Tyler Davis

Keys for Strategic Instruction to Promote Reading Comprehension

Debra Coffey, Elaine Roberts, and Pam Henry

Chapter 5 focuses on reading comprehension and ways to select and use culturally responsive literature for language development. Consider what you know and want to explore about promoting reading comprehension.

TABLE 5.1

K	E	Y	S
What do you **know** about effective instruction for reading comprehension?	What do you want to **explore** about effective instruction for reading comprehension?	What do you **yearn** to learn after reading and discussing the chapter?	How will you **satisfy** your curiosity? What ideas and concepts will you apply to your teaching?

Enhancing Reading Comprehension

In order to create a lovely garden, Mary was sensitive to the needs of individual plants, considering whether they needed more sunshine, water, or nutrients to become vibrant and healthy. When working with students we check to see what they need individually in order to experience success. Comprehension is the essence of reading. This chapter highlights ways to promote reading comprehension and help each student to become a vibrant, healthy reader.

Literacy learning involves collaboration and respect for individual experiences and ways of learning. Students need opportunities for reading high-interest books and scaffolding for systematic word analysis in the context of meaningful literature. These elements of effective instruction need to be integrated with enjoyable writing, technology, and discussions about purposes and personal interpretations of learning. Chapter 5 emphasizes keys that open doors to understanding and provide opportunities for students to see themselves in the literature they enjoy. This helps them to make meaningful connections and personalize literature. Personal connections motivate them to spend more time exploring literature. The more they read, the more effectively they read. These experiences are catalysts for achievement and success in school. Teachers who are culturally responsive work proactively and assertively to understand, respect, and meet the needs of students from various cultural backgrounds. They use a student-centered approach to remove barriers and open doors for all students to experience success (Pollock & Ford, 2009).

Exchanging ideas in creative ways helps students to understand each other and explore their own thinking processes as they overcome cultural barriers and extend their thinking.

Defining Reading Comprehension

What is **effective comprehension instruction**? How do teachers realize if students use comprehension strategies independently to construct meaning when reading narrative and expository texts? The RAND Reading Study Group (Snow et al., 2002) defined **reading comprehension** as "the process of simultaneously extracting and constructing meaning through interaction and involvement with written language." The RAND Study Group managed a long-term research plan to support students' reading comprehension and integrate reading across the content areas. The study group stressed that comprehension involves three elements: the reader, the text that is comprehended, and the related activity (RAND, *www.rand.org/multi/achievementforall*). The three components are embedded within a cultural context affected by the reader and how the reader interacts with the three components for comprehending text. For example, during reading good readers respond to the purposes for reading and their knowledge, application, and engagement in text in relation to their cultural perspectives.

The article "Reading through a Disciplinary Lens" (Juel et al., 2010) inspires teachers to increase comprehension by helping students focus on the "message in the text and the vocabulary load . . . give students the opportunity to look at texts through the three useful lenses of science, writing, and history" (p. 14). Scientists look for evidence and create questions to learn more about topics as they read. They visualize as they read and search for meaning beyond the text by researching and experimenting in areas of related interest. Writers reflect on other writers' style and purposes for writing and think about how they impact their reading audience. They inspire readers with lively adjectives and vocabulary to enhance settings, themes, characters, and plots. They help readers connect to texts and think about themselves living and learning from passages of interest. Historians are constantly searching for valid facts and proving or disproving information they read. They are like explorers who search the Internet, question the point of view of the author, reread, monitor, and think critically. These are all qualities of readers who comprehend and develop a passion to search, visualize, wonder, and predict in order to learn more. Students who are encouraged to become mini philosophers question and feel free to share opinions. This is particularly true in our age of digital literacies. When teachers give students opportunities to think as scientists, writers, historians, and mini philosophers they become motivated to look closely at texts and comprehend more fully.

The book *Different Just Like Me*, by Lori Mitchell (1999), is about a girl named April who takes a trip to visit her grandmother. April encounters many interesting people before she visits her grandmother. She sees a deaf child, a blind lady, an artist, a handicapped person, and people talking different languages. She noticed that they were in the same places as she was and were doing similar things as she was doing. When she arrives at her grandmother's home she admires her house and flower garden. She decides that people are like flowers, with many different needs, shapes, and colors, just like her. April was a very observant child who wondered, noticed her surroundings, and enjoyed learning about others. This is an excellent book to help students realize the importance of doing the same when reading and writing. They learn that paying attention to the messages of texts is a way to understand, appreciate, share opinions, and expand their views about the uniqueness of people and places they want to know more about.

Villaume and Brabham (2002) discussed text-reader transactions and related strategies used for comprehension to empower readers in their article, "Comprehension Instruction: Beyond Strategies." They shared how good readers immerse themselves in stories to make meaning using **personal connections and interpretation**s to **interact with the author** (i.e., either agreeing or disagreeing with the author). As a result, comprehension strategy instruction includes teaching for **student empowerment and engagement**. When students are comfortable valuing and sharing their beliefs during literature discussions, negative dispositions about reading can be eliminated. Allowing students to select and discuss texts of interest across the content areas and using effective comprehension strategies helps them become active, impassioned readers.

Villaume and Brabham (2002) weave a definition of explicit and systematic comprehension instruction through instruction that proceeds from "the *'outside in'* while other forms proceed from the *'inside out.'* "Teachers teach from the 'outside in' as they try teaching ideas gleaned from professional conversations. They work from the 'inside out' as they reflect on their own reading processes and use these insights to refine their comprehension instruction" (p. 673). Comprehension instruction should embrace both "outside-in" and "inside-out" methods. Students should work from the "outside in" as well as the "inside out" as they learn and talk about their own reading strategies, which they have selected for making meaning during reading.

The article reminded Elaine of her visit to an elementary school in Ireland. She asked students in various grades to describe the strategies they used to make sense of what they read. The responses included, "I reread for clarity," "I use Mary O'Malley's strategy for making meaning by wondering about what I read," and others said, "I ask mystelf questions." How do social interactions within the classroom help students think and talk about strategies used for reading and writing critically? Is there enough time spent reading, writing, thinking, and discussing students' interests to motivate them to read for comprehension?

Villaume and Brabham said that **explicit instruction** is "simply clear instruction; Students 'get' what we are trying to teach" (2002, p. 673). In order to "get" the strategy and become an empowered reader, students discuss what they are thinking while reading. During this process teachers follow up literacy learning goals and clarify misconceptions when students are applying comprehension strategies before, during, and after reading.

Effective comprehension integrates literacy strategies for concept learning with motivating reading and writing activities across all subject areas. Comprehension instruction involves helping students build and activate background knowledge while reflecting about text information that is explicit or inferential.

Naturally, there is more to comprehension than teaching effective strategies. Good instruction takes time. Effective teachers provide and expand **purposes for reading** with an understanding of the variety and complexity of students' responses. It is important for teachers to realize that students' responses to literature are based on students' ethnicity, socioeconomic status, community, home, and schooling experiences (Suarez-Orozco & Paez, 2002). McKnight (2000) stated that "comprehension is a complex and dynamic process in which the reader decodes the writer's words and draws on his own background knowledge to construct an understanding of the text that is similar to the writer's intent yet unique to the reader. The meaning resides in the transaction between the reader and the writer's text" (p. 1). Students' ability to self-monitor their understanding of text, therefore, relates to the unique transaction between the reader and the writer. This is an essential element of the comprehension construction process. Students need time to share their personal reactions to literature to refine their thinking about literacy learning.

What are the Best Comprehension Instructional Practices of Effective Teachers? The Research

Fielding and Pearson (1994) emphasized that comprehension instruction should include four components: (1) time for actual text reading, (2) teacher-directed instruction in comprehension strategies, (3) collaborative learning, and (4) occasions for students to talk to the teacher and one another about their responses to reading. Isabel Beck (1997) agreed that discussions about texts extend comprehension. She noted that teachers should also model strategies for making sense of text.

Nell Duke (2002) summed up five components of effective comprehension instruction:

1. A clear vision of effective comprehension
2. Appropriate attention to underlying skills and dispositions
3. Many opportunities to read and be read to (and for compelling reasons)
4. Lots of talk, writing, and thinking about text
5. Explicit instruction in comprehension strategies

Effective comprehension instruction provides the integration of visual and oral language processes plus complex social and personal interpretations. Oral language involves pitch, stress, and tone for personal emphasis to increase fluency during reading. Thus, reading comprehension is a dynamic process that causes readers to reevaluate the meaning of other texts and reconstruct their meaning (Lemke, 2002).

Transactional Strategy Instruction

Since reading is a transactional process, transactional strategy instruction (TSI) should be practiced in classrooms for students of all ages (Brown, Pressley, Van Meter, & Schuder, 1996; Chi, Glaser, & Farr, 1988; Rosenblatt, 1978). Transactional strategy instruction includes direct explanation, teacher modeling of comprehension strategies, flexible and engaging student discussions, and guided practice of comprehension strategies to help students become more critical and interpretive readers.

Gaskins, Anderson, Pressley, Cunicelli, and Saltlow (1993) found that transactional strategy instruction takes time. These researchers describe ways the transactional strategy movement in comprehension instruction has taken educators away from dwelling solely on teaching individual strategies. Instead, TSI guides teachers toward interactive instruction where the interrelated strategies come to focus and are shared during authentic reading experiences. Guided transactions between readers, authors, and others empower students to believe in themselves as successful readers. Effective teachers build instruction on students' existing knowledge about comprehension strategies of text, scaffold instruction of unfamiliar comprehension strategies, teach students how to use comprehension strategies independently, encourage discussions about purposes for learning, extend student understandings of concepts, and have students discuss personal reasons for reading. The National Reading Research Center studied how teachers model strategies successfully and help students to **self-regulate** the use of effective strategies for reading (Brown et al., 1996). According to the report, effective transactional strategy instruction includes the following:

1. Readers are taught that the meaning of text is not in the text or reader's mind alone but in transactions between them.
2. Students learn to understand texts' meaning through group transactions rather than by individuals.
3. Students' reactions and interpretations during discussions determine the teacher's instructional decisions.

Brown et al. (1996) suggest transactional strategies instruction (TSI) strategies taught for comprehension include:

- **Predicting and verifying predictions** based on the text and/or background knowledge
- **Visualizing** (mental imagery) ideas from text
- **Connecting** information with background knowledge for making meaning of text
- **Summarizing** important main ideas and details in text
- **Retelling** ideas from text in the students' own words

The major focus of literacy instruction, therefore, shifts from individuals to social group transactions where students have the authority and freedom to discuss and think aloud about their learning. They share and explain how they comprehend text (i.e., purposes for making meaning, strategies and personal interpretations elicited during reading). Transactional strategy instruction, indeed, is an empowering process for students.

Research suggests that students benefit from transactional strategy instruction. For example, the Office of Bilingual Education and Minority Language Affairs focuses on the transfer from Spanish reading to English reading. They believe that every teacher is a teacher of reading across all content areas and grade levels. They also stress that all teachers need to be aware of the **cultural and social issues** in students' communities that affect literacy development (i.e., oral language development, availability of materials, varied methods of teaching, etc.).

Teachers need to be aware that in many cases, Latino and African American students are placed in schools with fewer resources, lower-order thinking activities, and lower expectations for learning when they live in lower socioeconomic areas (Paez, 2009). ELL students with limited strategy knowledge are often pushed beyond English texts in third grade to complex texts in fourth grade without understanding text structures. This "fourth-grade slump" can cause frustration for the students as well as the teachers. These students benefit from direct instruction about text structures and ways to use effective comprehension strategies for monitoring their literacy learning. Teachers need to help students learn how to self-monitor their learning through student-centered activities that include:

- Finding purposes for reading
- Differentiating among text structures, differences in narrative, expository (informational books), and e-books online
- Using more informational texts at all grade levels
- Including multisensory activities
- Reinforcing phonemic awareness activities (i.e., rhyming, blending, deleting, segmenting sounds); many ELL students are unfamiliar with English rhyme activities that help with word recognition)
- Featuring effective strategies
- Reading and rereading books aloud to students from a variety of genres (extends fluency skills)
- Encouraging students to share their learning and discover more about their interests

These engaging activities help students overcome gaps in comprehension, especially when they are in the upper grades (Duke, 2000). Low-achieving students in poverty schools also benefit from direct strategy instruction in word recognition, fluency, writing, vocabulary, strategy implementation, and technology support.

Effective Instruction for Reading Comprehension

Scaffolding Strategy Instruction

Teachers' model and scaffold strategy learning by emphasizing the following procedure:

1. Teach students to understand the purpose for the literacy strategy.
2. Model, display, and describe the steps in the strategy using think-alouds.
3. Provide time for student-guided practice and transference of the strategy to independent reading and writing experiences.

Effective teachers scaffold instruction as they teach students how to comprehend texts. A practice guide for comprehension by Shanahan et al. (2010) includes the essential elements for young students' ability to comprehend when reading. They are knowledge and reasoning skills necessary for comprehending texts, thinking skills, and motivation to succeed in school. The authors suggest that students need to be taught and use comprehension strategies, use text organizational structures for comprehension, and take part in higher-level discussions about making meaning of text. It is important for students to read texts that support comprehension development and read engaging texts of interest while learning comprehension strategies.

Scaffolding enhances students' learning of reading comprehension and fluency. As teachers provide guidance, students learn to make meaning, read fluently, and become strategic, skilled readers.

An Integrated Approach

School administrators who provide time for quality teacher collaboration help motivate teachers to plan effective literacy assessment, instruction, and learning. Thus, a shared commitment between teachers and administrators to quality literacy education helps teachers meet the needs of individual students for life-long learning. In order to do so, teachers must enlist the use of various components of literacy, develop models for an integrated approach, and properly assess all their students individually.

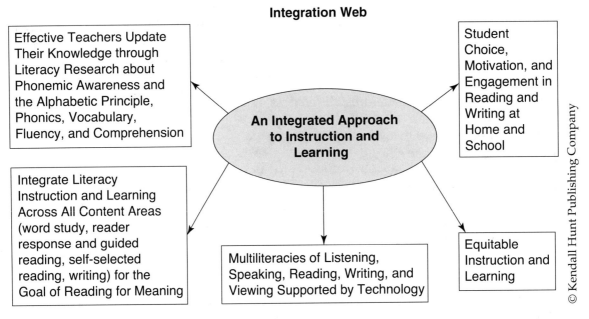

FIGURE 5.1

Folk Tales/Multicultural Literature

Folk tales are short stories based on oral traditions. An example is the book *Lon Po Po* by Ed Young (1996). The teacher can have students discuss what they think will happen in this Chinese version of *Little Red Riding Hood*. After reading the book aloud to the students, they can recreate the atmosphere of the book using artwork found on an Internet virtual trip to China. Word study can involve selecting vocabulary words from the story that can be decoded by using the analogy strategy with key words. For example, select three of the underlined spelling patterns from the following key words: birth/d<u>ay</u>, <u>Sh</u>ang, <u>nut</u>, and <u>gink</u>/o tr<u>ee</u>. Emphasize and circle the "sh" in Shang and find other words with the same consonant digraph "sh" throughout the week. Students can understand the meaning of the words as they compare and contrast information about China and the United States by creating Venn diagrams. The diagrams can help students use new vocabulary words during reader response and writing. They can illustrate stories comparing their lives to the lives of Chinese characters from the book and act out the story. Students also enjoy comparing *Lon Po Po* to other versions of *Little Red Riding Hood*.

Integrated Instruction with Book Clubs

Multiple literacies engage students in authentic reading and writing for comprehension as they focus on digital resources, literacy skills, and strategies. Pearson and Raphael (1999) emphasize a view of balanced literacy assessment, teaching, and learning that integrates the multiple literacies of listening, speaking, reading, writing, and related thinking skills through book clubs. The multiple literacies are extended by children's cultural and social knowledge during book discussions. In addition, they are expanded through media and technology literacy.

The book clubs focus on language as essential to thinking since they include social interactions with peers to increase critical literacy learning. The teacher can model and teach the book club in a teacher-led setting or can act as a facilitator or participant (Au & Raphael, 1998). Some book clubs involve student-led discussion groups. Book clubs are literature-based and include student reading selections from multiple resources. Literature-based curriculums include literacy skills, strategies, and opportunities for cultural reader response and motivation.

Aligning Fluency Skills, Word Recognition, and Comprehension

Fluency involves reading and understanding what is read smoothly and effortlessly. A fluent reader has automatic decoding skills, uses effective word recognition strategies, employs sight word knowledge, and reads smoothly with expression. **Prosody** is using and understanding pausal intrusions, intonation, and stress to read with expression and connect fluency to comprehension (Dowhower, 1991; Hoffman, 1987; Kuhn & Stahl, 2000; Rasinski, & Padak, 2000; Samuels, 1997).

Promoting Fluency

Fluency is developed in first grade through reading and retelling stories, using writing for various purposes, identifying sight words, and representing sounds in spellings (Neuman, Pikulski, & Roskos, 1998; Clay, 1991, 1993; International Reading Association and National Association for the Education of Young Children, 1998). Use of **repeated readings of passages** and related reading rate charts helps students understand their fluency strengths and needs (Samuels, 1997). During repeated readings students reread short passages of interest (50–200 words) until word recognition accuracy and fluency is improved with comprehension. Most children become early readers at the first-grade level. They can learn to use effective reading strategies when teachers model strategies and provide guided practice through reading and writing experiences. Most children at the second grade are transitional readers who can use meaning, grammar, and letter-sound knowledge and recognize a large number of frequent sight words (Clay, 1991; International Reading Association and National Association for the Education of Young Children, 1998). Teachers should foster reflective thinking about reading with fluency and comprehension. Third-grade children are typically fluent readers who enjoy reading. They read for meaning and place less emphasis on decoding. Third graders often use effective literacy strategies for decoding and meaning-making. They make personal connections with texts through reading and writing. They should be encouraged to read and write to expand thinking and discuss literature with others.

To Help Students Develop Fluency

- Continue to develop letter-sound knowledge, sight word knowledge, phonemic awareness, and phonics.
- Encourage students to listen to fluent readers and read to each other with expression.
- Encourage children to read predictable books.
- Have word walls and labels visible to help children with their reading and writing.
- Read aloud to students with expression and have them echo-read what you have read.

- Read to children each day and include authentic literature and purposeful writing experiences in lessons.
- Encourage children to read at their independent level and teach them at their instructional level.
- Model and teach children how to use effective word recognition strategies independently.
- Involve parents in sharing literacy-rich environments and reading aloud with expression with their children.
- Teach children how to use the computer and computer software to increase fluency and explore media in the library.
- Include texts that are influenced by the cultures of the students' homes in both languages for ELL students.
- Assess and monitor students' progress using repeated readings and reading rate charts.
- Readers' Theatre (RT) can be used with groups to increase fluency and comprehension. During RT students read scripts as they act out a story.

Effective Teachers Plan Meaningful Lessons

Meaningful literacy lessons for whole group, small groups, and independent reading include shared and guided reading. **Shared reading** is an instructional approach that emphasizes big books and enlarged texts. Teachers often use a big book with enlarged text to give students opportunities to participate in reading with teacher support. Shared reading usually follows a typical lesson plan format, but it is unique because of the opportunities for students to participate in the reading process. The next two pages describe components of a shared reading lesson.

Planning a Shared Reading Lesson

Topic: Examples, Rhyming Words for Word Study (Phonics and Vocabulary), Fluency, and Comprehension Strategies.
Title of Lesson:
Subject Area: (Language Arts, Science, Social Studies, Math)
Grade Level:
Objectives:
Standards:
Materials: List all of your materials, including culturally responsive literature and technology.

Body of the Shared Reading Lesson Plan Format

Motivation: List your steps for "hooking" your tutee or small group into your lesson and introduce your story creatively using multisensory methods.

1. Introduce new vocabulary: (i.e., List new vocabulary, have students discover new vocabulary in the text, use a graphic organizer such as personal clue cards, technology, and/or add the words to the appropriate word wall)
   a. I will have the students pronounce and discuss what they think each word means.
   b. I will share a definition for each word and use it in a sentence.
   c. I will use the pictures in the book for words so tutee can connect words to objects. I will emphasize the importance of using a phonics strategy to pronounce the words and search for clues in the word and sentences to make meaning (rather than depending solely on picture clues).
2. Begin picture walk
   a. Discuss the cover of the book
   b. Talk about the title, author, and illustrator of the book.
   c. Have tutee look through the book, talking about what tutee sees in the pictures.

Sample questions to ask:
1. What are the characters doing?
2. What do you think is happening in this picture? (comprehension strategy - predicting Write some of your tutee's predictions for later use in the lesson.)

During Reading

1. Today I will be doing a shared reading lesson reading the story _____.
   a. For the first reading, I will read the story to the class modeling how good readers read using automaticity and prosody.
   b. For the second reading, I will read the story again with the class participating by reading _____ (You fill in the blank as to how they are going to participate in the second reading of the story).
2. Minilesson on the following _____(List the focus of your lesson.)
   a. Modeling _____
      1. Explain what you are modeling. Ex. Explain what rhyming words are.
      2. Using page 1 from our story, I will read the sentence _____. I will explain that the words_____ and _____ rhyme because they end with the same sound. I will also read another sentence from the same page _____, modeling the words _____ and _____ explaining that those words don't rhyme because the sounds at the end of the words don't sound the same. (Use the analogy strategy.)
      3. Follow the same procedure as for step 2.
   b. Guided Practice: The class and I will read the rest of the story together, identifying rhyming words as we read each page.
   c. Independent Practice: The class will go through the book and identify all of the rhyming words in the story.

After Reading

1. Discuss the rhyming words they found in the story.
2. I will give the students a word, and they will give me a word that rhymes with my word.
3. I will give the students words pairs. They will identify whether the word pairs rhyme or not.
4. I will have the students use the new vocabulary words when writing a response to their reading in a motivating way.

Centers:

List your center activities dealing with your focus for your lesson, such as rhyming words.
Be sure you describe each center, telling the learning styles/multiple intelligences for which it is designed. (Consider Gardner's Multiple Intelligences and the levels of Bloom's Taxonomy.)
Technology: (This can be one of your center activities.)
Closure: Summarize key concepts and ideas.

Assessment:

- How will you assess your student's understanding on the concept, skill, strategy for today's lesson?
- How will you use your assessment results to determine who will need reinforcement on the skill, concept, or strategy focus for today's lesson? Who will receive enrichment on the skill, strategy, or concept taught in today's lesson in order to use higher order thinking skills?
- Explain in detail the ways you will reinforce concepts and skills during the lesson.
- Explain your enrichment activities.

Accommodations for your diverse students in your classroom:
For this population in your classroom, tell how you will accommodate the needs of hearing impaired, visually impaired, ELL, ADD, ADHD, gifted students during your lesson.

Word Sort

1. Developmental spelling stage
2. Add the appropriate Standard
3. An explanation as to why you chose this word sort
4. Modeling procedures for teaching the word sort
    a.
    b.
    c.
5. Guided Practice: The students and I will do the word sort together.
6. Independent Practice: The students will do the word sort on their own. I will help if needed.
7. Assessment

Word Sort Game

1. Developmental spelling stage
2. Add the appropriate Standard
3. Explanation as to why you chose this word sort game.
4. Modeling procedures for teaching the word sort game.
    a.
    b.
    c.
5. Guided Practice: The students and I will do the word sort game together.
6. Independent Practice: The students will do the word sort game on their own.
7. Assessment

Guided reading gives small groups of students opportunities to read a text on an **instructional level**. During guided reading students have individual copies of texts and they discuss the text as the teacher asks questions and guides them in using strategies to meet their skills needs. Independent reading is designed to match the needs and interests of individual students. Effective teachers concentrate on students' strengths and design instruction to lead them to the next level of development. They use assessments to meet students' needs and enhance their reading and writing expertise. Reading and writing are interwoven throughout this process to build leadership and enhance competence.

Assessments and Motivation

During self-selected reading in the classroom it is important that students have at least 30–40 minutes to read at their independent level. Teachers often provide a supply of small rugs, beanbag chairs, or a reading loft for a reading comfort zone in their classrooms. Age-appropriate e-books on the Internet may also be available for self-selected reading times. It is important for students to understand how to find texts of interest at their independent reading level from multimedia resources. Teachers need to guide students to websites that link them to e-books they can read online or print out and read. For example, *The Tortoise and the Hare*, by Rebeccah J. Kamp, is downloadable from the Internet public literary youth's division at *www.phschool.com/curriculum_support/book_clubs/index.html*. This website links to e-books with a click on Language Arts. It provides the opportunity to select a story to read and print. Older students are motivated to read stories online via *www.pemberley.com/janeinfo/namrgdnc.html*, which includes Jane Austen stories and more.

Effective teachers learn about their students' reading and writing interests and the ways they make book choices after students complete **interest inventories** or **literacy attitude surveys** (Gambrell, Palmer, Codling, & Mazzoni, 1996; McKenna & Kear, 1990; Kear et al., 2000; Graves et al., 2011). An interest inventory estimates reading attitude levels efficiently with reliability (refer to Table 5.2). Students indicate their learning styles as they fill out this chart regarding how (with a partner, small group, alone) and where (in books, in magazines or encyclopedias, on the Internet) they like to search for ideas.

TABLE 5.2 Interest Inventory/Attitude Survey for Reading

Directions: After reading the Garfield Attitude Survey by McKenna and Kear (1990), create an attitude survey based on your grade level and/or content area either using or adapting the following format:
Name _____ Date _____

Books of Interest	Authors of Interest	What I Like to Read	Ways I Like to Search for Ideas

As teachers conference with students about their motivation and attitudes about reading, it may be helpful to administer and analyze a variety of student interest inventories to determine books of interest and hobbies. This helps them to effectively plan instruction to meet individual student needs. Interest inventories also help teachers learn about students' literacy experiences at home. The Motivation to Read Profile by Gambrel et al. (1996) is in Appendix F.

Individualized Instruction to Promote Reading Comprehension

Rather than simply reteaching strategies that students already use effectively and independently, teachers need to help students recognize that a targeted strategy is only one of many strategies that can be activated during reading. Students need to be taught how to select appropriate reading strategies that match their purpose for reading. Keeping enjoyable, interactive reading alive is the main goal. Culturally responsive literature enhances students' enjoyment of the reading process. Assessments at the beginning of a tutorial session help teachers to concentrate on strategies that are most beneficial for individual students.

How Can Teachers Uncover Students' Comprehension Difficulties and Foster Student Problem Solving?

Naturally, effective teachers familiar with research-based reading instruction provide higher-level thinking and learning activities during student literacy experiences. Effective teachers expect students to learn to use strategies independently. Strategies students select to increase comprehension should be shared and praised. In *Comprehension: Crafting Understanding*, by Cathy Collins Block, the author talks about how students enjoy learning as "**meaning makers**" (want to learn how to use effective strategies and make deeper responses to literature), "**transformer titans**" (want to learn how to personally connect to text), "**breadth builders**" (want to learn from a variety of genres), "**word wanters**" (want to use decoding strategies), "**speed mongrels**" (want to increase their fluency), "**memory menders**" (want to maintain information in long-term memory), "**critical analyzers**" (want to learn how to make connections/reflections to the world and other texts when reading), and "**author askers**" (want to ask the author questions to make sense of texts).

Documenting Individualized Instruction

Teachers meet students' needs more readily when they keep student profiles that describe learning experiences and plan reading and writing strategies to enhance development of individual strengths. Throughout this process it is important to provide appropriate scaffolding that highlights students' needs and interests to progressively guide them to the next level of development. Box 5.1 presents a lesson plan format and Table 5.3 presents a lesson plan rubric for scaffolding the learning process.

BOX 5.1

LESSON PLAN FORMAT

Modeling: I do, you watch. You will list the step-by-step procedures you are using to instruct your tutee in the strategy, skill, or concept.

Guided Practice: I do, you help. This is the section in your lesson where you state that you and your tutee will practice the strategy, skill, or concept you just modeled, together.

Independent Practice: You do, I help. This is the section in your lesson where the tutee tries the strategy, skill, concept on his/her own and you are there if he/she needs any assistance.

Application: You do. I watch. This is the section in your lesson where the tutee demonstrates the strategy, skill, or concept without help. **This is where you will do your assessment.**

Modeling Writing — Suggestions for modeling writing:
Refer to your Blackburn-Cramp writing assessment. Look at the level of writing where your tutee demonstrated needs in his/her writing. Do the following:

1. Model effective sentences (where your tutee demonstrated a need) by writing a sentence and giving an explanation as to why those sentence components are written that way. List your modeling procedures.
2. Guided practice: Give your tutee some sentences that you prepared before class that contain miscues relating to the conventions on which you are working. Ask your tutee to **verbalize** where the miscues are, how to fix the miscues, and why miscues are evident. (Example: The first word of a sentence or a proper nouns should begin with a capital letter, etc.)
3. Independent practice/Application: Have your tutee write his/her summary of the story, read his/her favorite part of the story, or read about a favorite character in the story, demonstrating the correct use of conventions of writing. **It will be helpful to combine your independent practice with application and assessment.**

Reflection — Suggestions for your reflection:
After you have taught your lesson, remember to reflect on those things that went well. Include reflections on changes you would make, such as improving your instruction (modeling procedures) for the area your tutee found challenging. Consider your approach or method that you will use to more effectively meeting the needs of your tutee.

Future Plans — Suggestions for future plans for your next lesson:
For each component in your lesson plan, include an assessment to determine whether or not your tutee needs reinforcement with that skill/strategy. Go back to your objectives and determine whether or not your tutee met the expectation for accuracy for each of these skills/strategies. Use that information to tell what your next step will be in your next lesson for each of those skills/strategies. **Example:** For the assessment of the word sort on long e, my tutee was to achieve 100% accuracy according to my objective. However, based on the assessment of the word sort on long e, my tutee demonstrated only 85% accuracy. Based on these results, I will continue working on long e using different long e words for our sort and change my modeling procedures for the word sort. **Follow the same procedure for your other assessments.**

TABLE 5.3   Lesson Plan Rubric

Student Name: _____ Lesson #_____ Date_____	

Quality of Lesson
Elements:
 	
1. Objectives well written
   ___objectives are specific
   ___outcome based
   ___measurable
   ___relates to what the student should be able to do after the instruction
2. Performance Standard
   ___relates to lesson
   ___compatible with objectives
3. Essential Questions
   ___promotes understanding, inquiry, and transfer of learning
4. Writing Proficiencies
   ___Ideas
   ___Organization
   ___Style
   ___Sentence Fluency
   ___Word Choice
   ___Conventions (grammar and spelling)
	_____/_ points

Appropriate Books Elements: ___appropriate for the lesson ___appropriate for the student's instructional level ___appropriate for the student's interest	_____/_ points
Effective Literacy Strategies Elements: ___strategies for reading ___strategies for writing	_____/_ points

(continued)

All Components Show Attention to Detail	_____/_ points
Elements: ___motivation ___modeling procedures ___guided practice ___independent practice ___closure ___assessment(s)	
Reflection	_____/_ points
Elements: ___analysis of how well each component in the lesson worked ___analysis of what didn't go well in the lesson ___analysis of how it can be changed ___assessment results are used to determine if objectives were met and to guide instruction for the next lesson	
Total	_____/__ points

Grading Code: A √ Denotes an Element in Lesson Plan; an X Denotes Element Missing in Lesson Plan

Literacy Development for Strategic Reading and Writing

Literacy activities in the classroom and the tutorial process are designed to help students become strategic, skilled readers. Table 5.4 may be used to identify the characteristics of strategic skilled and unskilled readers in order to identify students' specific needs.

TABLE 5.4 Recognizing Differences between Strategic, Skilled Readers and Unskilled Readers

Strategic, Skilled Readers	Unskilled Readers
Select effective strategies for word recognition and comprehension	Lack effective strategies for word recognition and comprehension
Make automatic spelling-to-speech correspondences	Skip unfamiliar words
Read unfamiliar words in effective chunks, not letter by letter	Try to pronounce words solely by individual letters
Often spend a great deal of time reading	Read as little as possible
Read for meaning: Interpret the author's message through vocabulary Use syntactic and semantic clues and background knowledge Reflect and make personal connections Select effective strategies	Read to decode words Lack understanding of effective strategies
Reread for clarity	Seldom reread for meaning
Uses visualization to increase meaning	Lack visualization strategies to enhance meaning

Motivated to read	Lack interest in reading due to frustration
Self-questions while reading	Does not self-question while reading
Self-monitors during reading	Does not self-monitor during reading
Read fluently	Does not read fluently (choppy reading, repeats phrases, etc.)

Table 5.5 presents a variety of strategies for the reading and writing process. These literacy strategies provide students with tools for success.

TABLE 5.5   Strategies for Reading Comprehension

Strategy	Strategy Description	Example
Pre-P (Pre-Reading Plan; Langer, 1981)	Before reading, the teacher guides students to make word associations with concepts. Students brainstorm their thoughts and compare their knowledge. Next, they self-assess their prior knowledge. Pre-P helps the teacher to plan support for individual students.	Word associations are brainstormed on a thematic chart for the word "streams." Lists include running water, creeks, banks, fish, swift water. After brainstorming the words, students share their experiences with streams and self-assess their increased knowledge.
Graphic Organizers (Webs, Character Maps, etc.; Ausubel, 1968)	Organizers help students categorize information in a visual representation. Teachers and students can build background knowledge through the use of graphic organizers.	The Carrot Seed by Ruth Krauss Perseverance Success
Thinking Maps (Hyerle, 1995)	**Thinking Maps** are visual maps for learning. There are eight maps that correspond with different thinking processes. They provide a visual image for information and are often used for taking notes across the content areas. The eight types are the radial tree (defining information), concept map (adjectives and information), flow chart (sequencing), brace map (part/whole relationships), tree map (classifying information), double bubble map (compare/contrasting), flow map (cause/effect) and bridge map (analogies).	Flow chart: What are the phases of matter? Solids- Holds Shape Liquids -Fixed Shape Gas- Container shape

(continued)

VFTP (Virtual Field Trip Partners; Roberts, 2012)	Student partners build background knowledge through Internet field trips.	Visit Butchart Gardens on the Internet with a partner to build knowledge about growing plants. Write your reflections about your experiences during the trip in a dual journal as if you were on a real trip together. Include illustrations and ideas about the plants you will grow in your own gardens.
Rereading to Clarify	Teachers model and students learn how to find where they need to look in a passage to reread and clarify meaning.	Teachers model and students learn where to look for information in the beginning, middle, and end of a story or informational book.
DRTA (Direct Reading, Thinking Activity; Davidson & Wilkerson, 1988)	Students make predictions by using clues from the author prior to reading, stop during reading to reconstruct predictions, and repeat the process throughout reading. Using a prediction chart helps visual learners.	First, the teacher models the strategy and have students notice how to predict, reread, and share probing questions ("Why do you think the author said that?"). Then the students discuss predictions during appropriate parts of the text. They refer back to the text to substantiate predictions for clarity.
KWL Plus, KWLA (Ogle & Carr, 1987; Mandeville, 1994)	Before reading students chart and brainstorm what they **know** about a topic and what they **want** to learn. After reading, they write what they **learned** and how it **affected** them personally.	<table><tr><td>**K**</td><td>**W**</td><td>**L**</td><td>**A**</td></tr><tr><td></td><td></td><td></td><td></td></tr><tr><td></td><td></td><td></td><td></td></tr></table>
Cinema (Wenzel & Roberts, 2012)	Dramatize a story on storyboards using background knowledge.	Students create storyboards as visual representations of learning.
Personally Connecting to Text	Students learn to think and personally connect to the text from their experiences, and they compare the author's interpretations to their own. These connections can be used for creative writing.	The teacher uses a think-aloud to talk about how to personally connect to a story ("This is an exciting part . . . . Something happened to me like this . . . ."). Next, the students share a think-aloud while they read to make personal interpretations and connect their own experiences to the story before, during, and after reading. Finally, students learn to use connections to the text as a strategy for comprehension while the teacher asks guiding questions to help them consider what good readers do and relate the story to their lives.

Bookmark OWL Strategy (Keene, 2007)	Students use the OWL bookmark when reading to enhance comprehension.	O – What do you **observe** or notice? W – What do you **wonder**? L – **Link** it to your life.
Story Maps and Literature Webbing	Prediction and Use of Prior Knowledge - Before reading, events from the literature are written on cards. The cards are mixed up out of sequence. The students try placing the cards in order of what they believe will happen in the story in a web.	The teacher reads the story. Then the students place the cards in the correct sequence of events. Information is added to a web or thinking map during student discussions, rereadings, and writings about the text.
QAR (Question–Answer Relationship Strategy; Raphael, 1986)	This strategy involves four types of questions for analyzing a book and answering questions: - **Right There** (within the text, explicit) - **Think and Search** (search for clues in the text – explicit and implicit) - **Author and You** (add your own background knowledge to the author's information) - **On My Own** (answer the question based on personal knowledge without going back to the text)	Find **right there** questions in the text ("Where were . . .?"). **Think and search** questions are answered by searching for clues that are explicit and implicit within the text ("Why do you think . . .? Provide evidence for your answer"). **Author and you** questions involve adding your background knowledge to the author's information to synthesize, analyze, and evaluate information ("Maybe . . ."). **On my own** questions require answers based on personal knowledge without using the text ("What personal experiences does this story make you consider?").

More Literacy Comprehension Strategies to Enhance Individual Instructional Plans for Literacy Case Studies and Classroom Literacy Experiences

Summarization Strategies

Summarization strategies increase comprehension of texts, and teachers use a variety of them for modeling and scaffolding instruction across the content areas (Dole, Duffy, Roehler, & Pearson, 1991; Pressley, Johnson, Symons, McGoldrich, & Kurita, 1989; Wiesendanger, 2000). Students experiencing reading difficulties may have problems summarizing and discussing information due to problems with narrative and expository text structures, story grammar, vocabulary, fluency, limited background knowledge, concept knowledge, and lack of task persistence (Bos & Anders, 1990; Gersten et al., 2001).

Slow processing of information due to long-term memory difficulties can also interfere with summarization skills. These problems can seem overwhelming to students when they are required to read whole chapters and summarize information without using effective comprehension strategies. Helping students use graphic organizers, thinking maps, study guides, questioning and predicting strategies, mnemonic devices to enhance memory, multisensory activities, and self-correcting strategies can provide students with problem-solving tools. These tools help them summarize what they understand before, during, and after reading.

Summarization strategies combined with self-monitoring of meaning-making and peer interactions enhance comprehension (Graves, 1986; Jitendra, Cole, Hopes, & Wilson, 1998; Klinger, Vaughn, & Schumm, 1998). Effective teachers use scaffolding (Vygotsky, 1976) to model summarization by instructing students on how to search for important ideas/themes within texts and represent the ideas within an interesting summary. Summaries can be based on **story grammars** (i.e., students pay attention/record information about characters, setting, problems, events, and resolution of problems during reading to increase comprehension). **Graphic organizers** can be used to outline the structure of a story for narrative texts to help students retain information. After teachers model ways to use story grammars, scaffolding of learning involves social activities to help students learn from each other. For example, peers/buddy readers may collaborate to create story grammar graphic organizers in the format of webs/maps before, during, and after reading to focus on main ideas and important details. Finally, individual students can use the graphic organizers independently to increase comprehension after they have learned from the teacher's modeling and scaffolding as well as interactions with peers.

Cunningham (1982) created the Generating Interaction between Schemata and Text, or **GIST**, procedure for scaffolding summarization instruction. During GIST students create 15 or fewer words for summaries of increasingly large amounts of texts. Initially, they use single sentences and eventually build to an entire paragraph. The GIST summary process includes scaffolding instruction to be (1) modeled to a whole class, (2) used in small groups, and (3) implemented by students as they read independently.

The International Reading Association website (*www.readwritethink.org*) has excellent resources for summarizing and using GIST. For example, there is a lesson titled "Get the Gist: A Summary Strategy for all Content Areas" that includes the following:

Discuss and read the text.
Complete a 5W's plus H graphic organizer about the passage (5 W's Plus H: Who, What, Where, When, Why plus How).
Write a summary using the information from the 5W's plus H graphic organizer.

Reciprocal Teaching

Reciprocal teaching (Palincsar & Brown, 1984) includes summarization to increase comprehension. When using the reciprocal teaching strategy students learn multiple strategies: (1) to ask higher-level questions, (2) to predict, (3) to clarify, and (4) to summarize information. The teacher initially models reciprocal teaching and then has students practice the four parts of the strategy in small groups or with partners. For example, the teacher models higher level "why" questions after reading a part of the text ("Why do you think ___happened?"). Then the student asks the teacher a "why" question after reading the next part of the text. Thus, the student plays the role of the teacher (reciprocal teaching). The strategy takes time to learn and can be repeated during paired reading. Finally, students learn to transfer the four reciprocal teaching strategies by using higher-level questions, making predictions, clarifying, and summarizing information when reading independently. Literacy journals help students transfer the strategies across the content areas. During independent or paired reading students stop and note in their journals how they use the four strategies learned during reciprocal teaching.

Klinger et al.1998 found that **peer-mediated small groups** using **multiple strategies** benefited when the groups were informed of specific tasks/**purposes for reading**. The tasks were building background knowledge by previewing material, predicting, monitoring learning, finding main ideas, and summarizing.

Instruction for Students Experiencing Gaps in Reading Comprehension

Addressing the gaps that occur in knowledge about how to teach reading comprehension can be especially complex when teaching students with reading comprehension difficulties. Some studies suggest that students with **learning disabilities**, especially dyslexia, have serious reading problems comprehending text and need more explicit comprehension instruction (McIntyre & Pickering, 1995; Moats & Farrell, 1999; Smith, 1999; Pressley, Brown, El-Dinary, & Afflerbach, 1995; Pressley, 2000). **Dyslexia** can be inherited by both genders and is associated with language disorders and phonological processing problems that can create difficulties with phonemic awareness and word recognition. These problems can decrease fluency, cause frustration, create a lack of background knowledge due to attention problems, and cause organizational difficulties that affect comprehension negatively.

Smith (1999) clarified comprehension instruction for students with dyslexia when she stated, "The difference in teaching students with dyslexia and readers without dyslexia is not *what* is taught but *how* it is taught. Students with dyslexia require explicit instruction and need more practice than do readers without dyslexia" (p. 185). Students with dyslexia need explicit/direct instruction and guided practice in phonemic awareness, word recognition, spelling, writing, vocabulary, fluency, and comprehension strategies with individual adaptations. Comprehension strategies and related activities should be reinforced regularly across the content areas for all students. English language learners, while not learning disabled, are affected by instructional methods. Too often they are placed in special education classrooms rather than in general education classrooms.

Based on research, Pressley (2000) encourages teachers to overcome students' comprehension difficulties by teaching phonics and vocabulary strategies, build word knowledge through self-questioning, and teach comprehension strategies. He stresses the importance of teaching students to self-monitor their comprehension by checking pronunciations and meanings of words to determine whether what they are reading makes sense. If students discover problems, they need to use effective strategies (fix-up strategies) to resolve the problem. Teachers need to continue mini-lessons for comprehension and have students practice until they learn the strategies.

Reading Logs

Students should keep dated reading logs with comments and new vocabulary to share their reading interests during self-selected reading. Reading logs are charts of books read by students. Frequently, there is a contract with the teacher, parents, or mentor describing a reward for reading books (i.e., after reading so many books the student can read their favorite book to a younger student). Students should also record their comments about the books listed in their reading log and whether the book is fiction or nonfiction. They can include whether they would recommend a book to a friend. Furthermore, reading logs are a great addition to students' literacy portfolios to help them realize the number of books they are reading, practice new vocabulary during writing, and analyze their book preferences. During discovery discussion lessons, small groups of students may meet and share strategies they use to improve reading. According to Block (2004), students need to teach each other about how they "craft meaning" while reading.

Multisensory Instructional Activities

Best comprehension instructional practices include **multisensory** activities, especially for students experiencing reading difficulty. Multisensory activities involve two or more senses to teach and learn a concept. Multisensory programs include both synthetic and analytic instruction (McIntyre Pickering, 1995). Researchers define **synthetic instruction** as teaching the parts of the language and then how the parts work together to form a whole. **Analytic instruction** presents the whole and how it can be broken down into component parts. Examples of multisensory programs include Montessori (1912) and Ferma and Keller (1921). These programs initially addressed the needs of nonreaders who had normal intelligence and came from low socio-economic environments. The programs include hands-on activities such as tracing words (tactile and kinesthetic sense), visual and auditory discrimination, repetition, and guided practice. Smith and Hogan (1991) suggested the following procedure for multisensory instruction:

1. Summarize previously taught information before introducing new information.
2. "Set the stage" for guided discovery. Use pictures, for example, for demonstrations (include hands-on learning).
3. Ask questions to motivate learning.
4. Engage the students in enjoyable activities during the presentation.
5. Use brief mini-lessons that include strategies and last 3–10 minutes.

Visually Display Comprehension Strategies on Charts/ Bookmarks

Teachers can provide parents with information about effective comprehension strategies to help students use strategies independently by sending home bookmarks describing how to use reading strategies. These bookmarks should include the students' home language and English. Since expository texts can be more complex than narrative texts, teachers need to model and help students and parents discover strategies for understanding the different structures of narrative, expository, and electronic texts. Students, parents, and teachers should discuss which strategies work best for each type of text structure and content during conferences and email. These discovery conversations help students feel more comfortable reading a variety of texts. The discussions about strategies should be summarized on charts as visible clues in classrooms and as strategy bookmarks at home to be used before, during, and after reading. These chart summarizing strategies and how they are implemented are essential visual references to help students transfer their knowledge about strategic learning to content areas.

Effective teachers use a variety of organizational and management structures in their classrooms to promote independent use of effective comprehension strategies. They teach children how to comprehend different genres of texts. They provide opportunities for students to feel comfortable taking risks when asking questions and searching for new and interesting information. This comfort zone extends their strategic literacy learning.

Instruction to Motivate Readers to Develop Task Persistence

Techniques to motivate students include task persistence (student use of effective comprehension strategies consistently). Students who have curiosity and are motivated usually have good comprehension, according to research by Guthrie et al. (2007). The researchers interviewed students about interest, student choices, self-efficacy (person's belief about their abilities to learn), student involvement (large amount of time spent reading), and student interactions about texts. They found that motivated students had high interest and good comprehension while unmotivated students lacked interest in reading and had less comprehension. The unmotivated students need to be motivated by teachers and peers to become engaged readers, build self-efficacy, and share preferences for reading. Students who face challenges with comprehension particularly need positive reinforcement through extrinsic motivators, intrinsic motivation, teacher modeling, feedback, teacher and student self-monitoring, and peer interactions when transferring comprehension tasks/strategies across the content areas (Dewitz et al. 2009; Gersten et al., 2001).

All students need to be motivated to share comprehension strategies and undertake more difficult tasks with teacher and peer support across the content areas. Shared discussions and social transactions during learning activities can enhance task persistence and lead readers and nonreaders to develop an eagerness to read. The resulting shared interpretations about authentic literature of interest motivate students to enjoy reading and writing. They become more successful readers who can self-monitor their comprehension and apply effective strategies (Baumann, Jones, & Seifert-Kessel, 1993; Bradshaw, 2001; Brown, Armbruster, & Baker, 1986; Paris, Lipson, & Wixson, 1983; Turner & Paris, 1995).

Comprehension instruction involves making time for collaborative reader responses to literature, understanding purposes for reading, motivating students to read, enhancing metacognition, and encouraging the use of effective reading strategies. Effective strategies include summarization, visualization, personally relating to text, text-to-text connections, think-alouds for discussing information at higher levels of thinking/reflecting, rich vocabularies and skills for decoding words, transferring, integrating, and making connections between reading and writing experiences.

When students collaborate successfully they learn to view themselves as successful "comprehenders" who can balance word/world knowledge, reader responses, and writing and self-monitor use of effective strategies before, during, and after reading. The goal is transference (task persistence) of automatic, effective comprehension strategies for comprehending and interpreting information during fluent reading and writing in all content areas.

Unfortunately, best practices for comprehension assessment and instruction are not evident in all classrooms. Durkin (1978) observed upper-grade comprehension instruction and Pressley et al. (1998) observed fourth-and fifth-grade comprehension instruction. The researchers found little scaffolded strategy instruction and independent student use of comprehension strategies was happening in the classrooms. Instead, they found that comprehension testing was the main instructional tool used by teachers (simply asking comprehension questions after reading a text). Instead, what authentic comprehension assessment, instruction, and learning would be more appropriate?

When identifying the strategies that will be most beneficial to students, a strategy development chart may be highly beneficial for determining the impact of a variety of strategies. After teachers identify the characteristics and needs of learners, they are ready to identify the strategies they need to use. Table 5.6 is a tool for documenting the impact of those strategies to determine the most effective strategies for each child.

TABLE 5.6 Strategy Development Chart

Date	Text/ Technology	Strategies for Word Recognition	Strategies for Fluency and Comprehension	Why Did I Choose this Strategy?	What is Next?

Enhancing Metacognition: Encouraging Effective Thinking for Successful Learning

Teacher scaffolding of think-aloud instruction and learning provides an avenue for sharing and extending existing knowledge to enhance comprehension. Teachers need to allow time for students to talk about what they are reading, writing, and thinking. Thinking about their thinking is metacognitive ability and refers to "the ability to manage and control one's cognitive activities and evaluate whether or not they are performing successfully . . . improving their strategic processing of material and making them more active readers" (Gersten et al., 2001, p. 281).

Gersten et al. (2001) examined comprehension research for instructional effects on learning-disabled students and found three instructional components that impacted student learning: (1) controlling task difficulty, (2) using interactive groups, and (3) directing response questioning.

While using direct response questioning, it is important to teach students how to question during reading using a specific format of strategies. Students experiencing processing problems may lack skills for using comprehension strategies and think-alouds during reading. Think-alouds require metacognitive skills for self-monitoring to think/check/self-monitor/talk about whether or not they comprehend text. To help students understand the importance of think-alouds, teachers can orally model how they think aloud during reading. For example, "What does this mean to me? What strategy(s) do I need to use? What have I learned?"

Teachers can encourage use of strategies by asking students, "What strategy would you try?" If students are unsure, teachers can suggest a strategy and model how and why a particular strategy would be effective. Students need to talk about strategies when they use them and explain why they use them. Teachers can provide mini-lessons for teaching new strategies and for revisiting strategies that students need additional help with during reading. When this social process for learning strategies and thinking about strategies during reading is extended over a period of time, students become more interested in reading, offer personal suggestions/interpretations, and share strategies with others.

During think-alouds readers build personal ideas about meaning of text. Thus, a social constructivist framework is used when thinking aloud (Kucan & Beck, 1997; McCarthey & Raphael, 1992; Palinscar, Ogle, Jones, & Carr, 1986; Pressley & Afflerback, 1995; Resnick, 1991). Think-alouds draw attention across the text, reader, and the context during peer collaborative interactions to build meaningful discussions about text. As a result, students talk about their understanding of text content and learn to reframe meaning-making during conversations about texts. Pontecorvo (1993) coined the term "think-alouds" to indicate "forms of discourse (that) become forms of thinking" (p. 191). The think-alouds build strategic readers who become constructive, reflective readers (Pressley et al., 1992). Teachers need to remind students that this type of think-aloud participation empowers them when they highlight their thinking processes to make meaning, increase reading fluency, and extend their personal inferences when reading independently.

High correlations exist between oral reading fluency measures and some standardized measures for reading comprehension. Repeated readings of texts increase reading fluency and motivation (Armstrong, 1983; Dowhower, 1994; Gersten et al., 2001; Fuchs, Fuchs, & Maxwell, 1988; Samuels, 1997).

TABLE 5.7 Self-Monitoring Checklist for Comprehension Progress

Name_____ Date _____	
Directions: Fill in the checklist while reading a passage to identify what you need to learn, what you learned, the new vocabulary you discover, and strategies you use during reading.	
Comprehension Check – Prior Knowledge What do I already know about this topic?	
Book or Resource – Fiction or Nonfiction? What is my purpose for reading the passage?	
The Author's Message What is the author saying? Does it make sense? What are my (how and why) questions about what I have read?	
My Opinions How do I feel about what I have read? Does it remind me of an experience?	

New Vocabulary Words What new vocabulary words did I find? I will write the word and the sentence. Then I will list the words I need to learn.	
Reading and Writing Strategies What strategies did I use?	
Sharing Strategies What strategies will I suggest to a friend?	

Literacy Development for Strategic Reading and Writing

As students use strategies with appropriate scaffolding, these tools help them to experience more success in school. This success often results from the ability to think clearly and effectively. Table 5.8 presents ways that teachers can use effective questions to guide students toward higher levels of thinking.

TABLE 5.8 Effective Questioning for Higher Levels of Critical Literacy Learning

Literal Questions – Bloom's Taxonomy Knowledge Level (Recalling Literal Information):   **Model and ask** students to generate higher-level questioning skills during independent reading and use reciprocal teaching strategies for questioning others. Examples of lower-level literal/ explicit questions found in texts should be charted or available in students' portfolios: Where did the story take place? (literal)   Who were the main characters? How were they represented? (literal)   Find in the story . . . (literal)
Beyond Literal Questions: **Model and ask** students to find criteria that relate to the following levels of thinking for higher comprehension: **Application** – Extending learning   **Comprehension** – Meaning-making   **Analysis** – Determining relationships   **Synthesis** – Determining and extending information   **Evaluation** – Assessing information
Examples of Higher-Level Questions for Critical Literacy: -What cultural understandings did the author stress?   -What do you wonder about the story?   -What is the purpose of the story?   -Do you agree or disagree with the point of view of the author? Why or why not? Tell me in your own words . . .   -Where could you find out more information about the topic?   -What do you think the main character felt about . . .?   How would you talk someone else into reading the story?

Literacy Development for Strategic Reading and Writing

It is important for teachers to use quality literature to increase students' engagement and enjoyment of reading as they integrate literacy skills and strategies at every grade level to promote life-long learning. They need to assess and integrate literacy skills to verify that all students can learn to use reading and writing strategies independently. When students notice that their teachers are enthusiastic about reading, they are motivated to enjoy reading. They actively participate in cooperative learning experiences, whole and small group activities, and individual reading. When students are taught to be strategic learners who take ownership for their learning through authentic, natural assessments, they learn to value themselves as readers and set purposes for learning. These experiences help them to use higher-order thinking skills. When teachers collaborate to design effective instruction together, their discussions typically revolve around the development of literacy skills and strategies that connect to individual student needs. Since they realize that students in their classrooms will not be reading at the same level or have acquired the same literacy skills, their successful collaboration, when grounded in research, will lead to a creative vision of literacy learning (National Council of Teachers of English, 2002).

In this chapter we have explored ways to help each individual in a learning community learn to become a skillful, strategic reader who interacts successfully with peers. When each individual experiences success, this helps the entire community to become more vibrant and opens doors for meaningful interaction.

© Kendall Hunt Publishing Company; Photograph by Tyler Davis

This picture of a flower in Elaine's garden was photographed by Tyler Davis

Keys for Promoting Creative Exploration in a Literacy-Rich Environment

Chapter 6 explores assessment and emphasizes the importance of synthesizing the components of literacy for a balanced program. Chapter 6 features The Four Blocks Method and the Literacy ROOTS Progress Monitoring Tool. Consider what you know about promoting reading and writing success in the classroom.

TABLE 6.1

K	E	Y	S
What do you **know** about promoting reading and writing success in the classroom?	What do you want to **explore** about promoting reading and writing success in the classroom?	What do you **yearn** to learn after reading and discussing the chapter?	How will you satisfy your curiosity? What ideas and concepts will you apply to your teaching?

Balanced, Integrated Classroom Instruction

While Mary nurtured individual plants in her garden, she was aware of the overall plan to create a lovely garden of plants with strong roots. She knew that strong roots would help them to withstand environmental challenges. Chapter 6 focuses on the components of reading for individual and classroom instruction. The components of the Four Blocks Literacy Model form the basis for our framework of instruction that builds strong literacy roots to help students overcome challenges during the reading process. We will consider ways to use writing experiences to strengthen reading ability as we design lessons to promote enthusiasm for reading and document growth. Throughout this chapter we explore creative ways to provide quality, culturally responsive literature to nurture the development of literacy roots and enrich the reading and writing process.

Patricia Cunningham and fellow literacy researchers (Cunningham & Cunningham, 1992; Cunningham & Hall, 2007; Cunningham et al., 2008) emphasized that a balanced, integrated approach to literacy leads to life-long learning. Their research indicates that literacy learning increases when students participate in the Four Blocks Literacy Model, which includes **working with words, guided reading, self-selected reading,** and **writing**. Within each of the Four Blocks teachers provide mini-lessons that include skills and reading strategies that are reinforced throughout the content areas.

This integrated, four-block instructional method emphasizes student choice and provides opportunities for reading a wide range of books from different genres to keep students motivated and interested in literacy learning. Expository texts, such as science trade books, and narrative texts, are used for both guided and independent reading experiences. Cunningham stresses the need for teachers to utilize organization and management skills to make successful use of the components of The Four Blocks.

Components of the Four Blocks Literacy Model

Working with Words Block

During **word study** (Cunningham & Allington, 1999, 2003; Cunningham & Hall, 2007; Cunningham et al, 2008), students review high frequency words, participate in phonics-based activities, increase vocabulary knowledge, and learn strategies for decoding words and spelling. Sessions focus on decoding words, vocabulary exploration, and spelling activities in which children learn how changing letters changes words. They explore ways to categorize words by similar spelling patterns and learn how to decode, using familiar words to pronounce unfamiliar words with the same spelling patterns. Through these activities students learn to recognize spelling patterns that can help them spell and decode other words. For instance, they realize that the "at" in "cat" can help them decode "bat" and the initial spelling pattern "at" in the word "attachment." Words that do not follow traditional phonics generalizations are also discovered. Each day students review high frequency words on a classroom word wall, verbalizing them and participating in reading and writing activities that focus on the letters, sounds, and spelling patterns as well as stressing the importance of comprehension. These words may be accompanied by pictures on the word wall for a visual connection that creates a visual image in the mind. The goal is for the words to become familiar without the use of picture clues.

During the word study block and the writing block, spelling is highlighted because word recognition is highly correlated to developmental spelling. Bear, Invernezzi, Templeton, and Johnston (2007) emphasize the correlation in the book, *Words Their Way: Word Study for Phonics, Vocabulary, and Spelling.* This book provides activities to help students with spelling strategies from emergent to mature stages. It includes personalized classroom lessons and numerous instructional ideas to help students develop a mental framework for understanding words and reading for meaning.

Guided Reading Block

Guided reading and reader response activities help students to use reading strategies effectively and move them toward independent silent reading with comprehension and fluency (Burns & Johns, 2001; Cunningham, 1999; Fountas & Pinnell, 1996, 2001; Pressley et al., 2006; Johns & Lenski, 2009). Guided Reading exposes children to various types of literature. Instruction includes mini-lessons with reading strategies to increase background knowledge and comprehension before, during, and after reading. Students learn how to read books at increasing levels of difficulty as they develop reading strategies and skills. Strategies, skills, interests, and instructional levels are considered for grouping students. During these sessions students can read from a basal, multiple copies of trade books (narrative and informational), big books, and digital resources. Written responses to literature enhance guided reading sessions and help students connect more fully with literature.

During guided reading sessions teachers and students begin by selecting books of interest at appropriate reading levels. Leveled books help teachers and students to select books that match students' instructional levels. Teachers support student reading in numerous formats. For example, students can *whisper read* in groups *or partner read* by using choral reading (students share reading together) and echo reading. During echo reading the teacher or a student reads. Then other students read the same passage. Mini-lessons are carried out as literacy needs dictate. Teachers use progress monitoring such as anecdotal notes that are recorded by teachers during reading sessions. They note observations of each student's performance and help plan future grouping and instruction.

Before, during, and after reading, teachers challenge readers to us phonics, fluency, and vocabulary strategies while reading for meaning. They ask meaningful questions and clarify information for readers when it is important to do so. After guided reading sessions, a teacher often conferences and administers a running record to a student from the group in order to determine the student's progress and use of effective reading strategies. A **running record** is an assessment tool for collecting reading behaviors tied to oral reading that can be analyzed for students' reading strengths and weaknesses. Ongoing assessment can help teachers decide whether a student should be included in a specific small group mini-lesson where students with similar reading skill needs receive specific strategy instruction. Hence, guided reading groups are flexible and purposeful.

Guided reading in upper grades helps students respond more fully and personally to texts. Reader-response is consistent with a student-centered approach to reading where emphasis is placed on student reactions to literary selections. Louise Rosenblatt (1938, 2005) defined **reader-response theory** as a text and reader transaction that spurs a stimulus for the reader's interpretation during authentic reading experiences. Wilfred Guerin (1992) explains Rosenblatt's impressions of reader-response as a balancing act between the text and the reader. Students bring their personal experiences to the reading transaction.

During reader-response, teachers use small group reading to establish discourse about the selected texts (Encisco, 1992; Hancock, 2004). The group often meets after the students have finished reading a selection of a text. Group time for discussing, reading, and writing about a text may extend for 3–4 weeks. According to McAlpine and Warren (1997), students should have enough latitude to enjoy a free-flowing discussion with little teacher intervention. Once the teacher helps the reader response groups organize according to their interests, students have an opportunity to take over the teacher's role as they interact. They are encouraged to learn how to conduct conversations about individual interpretations and view themselves as thinkers. Through a gradual release of responsibility, students eventually determine which titles they want to read and how they want to proceed. They also share and use reading strategies to extend comprehension.

Researchers agree that an integrated, balanced approach to literacy learning helps students transfer reading strategies to other content areas. When students view themselves as successful readers and writers they transfer reading strategies to other subjects. Visit the MCPS Early Literacy Guide at the following Web address for suggestions for guided reading and reader response: *www.mcps.k12.md.us/curriculum/littlekids*.

Self-Selected Reading/Independent Reading Block

Students need to read a variety of genres at their independent level for **self-selected reading**. Opportunities for self-selected, independent reading should occur daily. To motivate students to read, teachers can share the beginning of a narrative or an informational text and engage students' interest. Age appropriate digital books on the Internet should be available during self-selected reading. It is important for students to understand how to find books of interest at their independent reading level from Internet resources. For example, teachers can guide students to websites that link them to books they can read online or print out and read. For example, *The Tortoise and the*

Hare, by Rebeccah J. Kamp, is downloadable from the Internet public literary youth's division at *www.phschool.com/curriculum_support/book_clubs/index.html*.

This website links you to E books by clicking on Language Arts and selecting a story to read and print. The website *www.pemberley.com/janeinfo/namrgdnc.html* is appropriate for older students. It features stories by Jane Austen and more selections to spark student motivation.

Writing Block

Writing strategies learned during guided reading, self-selected reading and word study are reinforced and implemented independently, encouraging critical thinking and meaning-making of the process. This is accomplished through mini-lessons and individual progress monitoring. As with the other blocks in Cunningham's method, the writing block begins with a mini-lesson as in a writer's workshop. In the writing mini-lesson, the teacher models the behavior of a writer in front of the class using an overhead projector, computer, dry-erase board, or other device. For example, a teacher might model the thinking process of choosing a subject to write about and planning how to write it. Depending on the mini-lesson, the teacher may also model how to revise and edit one's writing as well as the publishing and illustrating aspects of writing.

Each day's mini-lesson may focus on a different type of writing, some days will highlight shorter pieces, whereas other sessions may focus repeatedly on longer work. Once the mini-lesson is finished and students begin to write drafts on their own, the teacher then has a chance to hold individual conferences with students. Peer conferences are also constructive discussions about writing for positive revision, suggestions, and editing. The writing block is often the one in which teachers will see the greatest variation of literacy levels among their students, since it is not limited by the availability or acceptability of appropriate books. To ensure the success of all the student writers in one's class, a student's choice of a writing subject is important, as is time to work on their writing during writer's workshop. The final aspect of the block is often the *Author's Chair*, in which a few students share their writing work with the class daily.

Lesson Planning in a Balanced Literacy Program

Lesson planning ties all of the components of a balanced literacy program together. Lesson plans form the framework for effective teaching, and they synthesize all of the components of instruction into a meaningful experience. A Shared Reading Lesson is particularly beneficial for young children because they have the opportunity to read with the teacher. This may be in the form of echo reading or choral reading as they enjoy the rhythm and rhyme of the text while looking at the words in a big book. A shared reading lesson may form the basis for an author study. A shared reading lesson designed as an author study helps students to personalize books and make connections with authors. During a shared reading lesson, word study and phonics activities may be designed to coordinate with a specific text. Similar components form the basis for whole group, small group, and individualized instruction. As teachers develop plans for students' active involvement in shared reading lessons, our text Appendices A-C provide frameworks, stories, and vault graphic organizers for motivating lessons. During all types of instruction we want students to develop strong literacy roots so they will be competent readers and writers.

Literacy ROOTS Progress Monitoring Tool for Integrating Literacy Across the Content Areas

The Literacy ROOTS Progress Monitoring Tool is a visual tool for assessment, lesson planning and monitoring individual students' literacy progress. It helps teachers analyze multiple literacy assessment results and plan lessons related to the National Reading Panel dimensions of phonemic awareness, phonics, spelling, vocabulary, writing, fluency and comprehension. Students note their progress and become motivated to obtain their academic and social goals. Literacy ROOTS helps teachers' document strategic instruction to increase literacy learning across the content areas. It assists students and their caretakers in understanding the literacy strengths, needs, and goals of students. It provides a thinking framework based on the Four Blocks Literacy Model for a balanced approach to teaching and learning. The Literacy ROOTS Progress Monitoring Tool also focuses on student interest, guided by cultural responsiveness, and student centered instruction and learning (Au, 2001; Gillet et al., 2012). The Literacy ROOTS Progress Monitoring Tool may be adapted to a favorite electronic format (Figure 6.1–6.3).

Assessments are the central roots for instruction. Reading strategies and goals derive from the assessments for meaningful instruction. This visual tool can be used to capture the essential components of individualized instruction or tutoring. It may be used for a specific summary and analysis of the overall impact of instruction on student learning, or it may be used for lesson planning during tutorial sessions.

The Components of the Literacy ROOTS Progress Monitoring Tool include:

- **R** — Reflection (reflecting upon insights from the home and school culture that indicate the student's literacy knowledge and experiences)
- **O** — Ongoing Assessments (analyzing pre assessments and ongoing assessments to guide the student's literacy instruction)
- **O** — Organizing A Balanced Approach to Literacy Instruction with Multimedia (organizing the student's reading and content area Four Blocks lessons by selecting appropriate reading strategies, texts, and digital resources based on test results)
- **T** — Talents and Interests (identifying the student's diverse needs to plan student-centered instruction)
- **S** — Student's Post Assessments and New Academic and Social Goals (planning student academic and social goals that are based on the results of post assessments and previous instruction)

FIGURE 6.1 Literacy ROOTS Progress Monitoring Tool for Monitoring Student Progress

Figure 6.1 (Roberts, E. 2012) **Page 1 of 3**	Student Name: Student age:_____ Student grade level:___
R Section — Reflections	
R Section — **Reflections about Culture of Home:** Reflect upon family literacy interactions and culture.	**R—Reflections about Culture of School** Reflect upon school literacy experiences and student preferences for learning: grouping and peer interactions.

(continued)

O Section — Ongoing Assessments	

O Section — **Ongoing Assessments:**
 	
Pre Assessments *(name of tests)*:
 	
Date:
 	
    1. **Phonemic Awareness and Alphabetic Knowledge results:**
	Ongoing Assessments:
	
	Pre Assessments:
	
	Date:
	
	    2. **Phonics and Spelling results:**
	
	Word list reading levels:
	
	Independent grade level ___
	
	Instructional grade level ___
	
	Frustration grade level ____

Ongoing Assessments:
 	
Pre Assessments:
 	
Date:
 	
    3. **Writing results:**
	Ongoing Assessments:
	
	Pre Assessments:
	
	Date:
	
	    4. **Vocabulary results:**

Ongoing Assessments: Pre Assessments: Date: 5. **Fluency and Comprehension results:**	**Ongoing Assessments: Fluency and Comprehension** Reading grade levels of oral and silent reading passages: **Independent grade level** ___ **Instructional grade level**___ **Frustration grade level** ___ **List Reading Strategies Needed:**

<u>O Section — Organizing</u>

Page 2 of 3 <u>A Balanced Approach to Literacy Instruction with Multimedia</u>

<u>O</u>: Organizing A Balanced Approach to Literacy Instruction with Multimedia (Organizing the student's reading and content area **Four Blocks lessons**: Include appropriate reading strategies, texts, and digital resources based on pre-test results)	(Note: Remember to reinforce reading strategies across all Four Blocks. The strategies should also be included in content area reading) **Reading Strategies to be reinforced in all Four Blocks:**
Word Study	**Writing**
Guided Reading Use texts at the instructional level. Reading Strategies and Lessons Focus:	**Self-Selected Reading**

Page 3 of 3	<u>T Section: Talents and Interests</u>

Name and date of Interest/Attitude Survey:

Results:

Favorite Books:

Interests:

<u>S Section: Student's Post-Test Results and New Academic and Social Goals</u>

a. Post Assessment result and date (Informal Reading Inventory, etc.):

New Academic Goal:

New Social Goal:

b. Post Assessment result and date:

New Academic Goal:

New Social Goal:
Post Test Reading Levels:
Independent word list reading grade level ___

Instructional word list reading grade level ___

Frustration word list reading grade level ___

Independent oral reading grade level ___

Instructional oral reading grade level ___

Frustration oral reading grade level ___

Explanation of Literacy ROOTS Page 1

R: Reflection on the cultural influences on the student.

This part of the progress monitoring tool helps teachers understand the student's literacy experiences and cultures at home and school. To complete this section, reflect on the student's home and schooling literacy experiences. Does the student prefer working in small groups or alone? How does the student interact with others? Does the student have opportunities to visit the library? Is the student an English language learner? Was the student proficient in the mother tongue and related literacy learning? Note any pertinent information.

O Section — Ongoing Literacy Assessments.

This part of the progress monitoring tool is related to the National Reading Panel (NRP) dimensions. It includes areas for literacy pre-assessments, dates, and results in the progress monitoring tool.

Assessment Examples for the NRP Related Dimensions of Section O:

1. Phonemic Awareness and Alphabet Knowledge
Yopp-Singer Test of Phoneme Segmentation
  Administer the test to determine the student's ability to segment sounds in words. Include assessments for phonemic awareness as needed. Also test for alphabet knowledge of letters and sounds.

2. Spelling and Phonics
Use appropriate assessments to determine students' ability to recognize words, apply their understanding of phonics and spelling, and determine their word recognition grade levels for words in isolation. An Informal Reading Inventory (IRI) can be used to assess word recognition and comprehension skills and determine reading levels. Examples of informal reading inventories include John's (2011) *Basic Reading Inventory* and Leslie and Caldwell's (2010) *Qualitative Reading Inventory-5.*

Spelling Assessments
Bear et al. Spelling Inventory (2008)
Richard Gentry Monster Spelling Test, (2004)
Administer the spelling test to determine the student's ability to pronounce and spell words. Notice if the student correctly recognizes and spells affixes (prefixes and suffixes), spelling patterns, and other patterns in words.

3. Writing
Ask the student to write a paragraph. Use this paragraph to determine the student's organization, ideas, style, voice, word choice, sentence fluency, and conventions of writing. Use a related rubric or developmental writing scale to assess writing strengths and needs. Analysis of writing samples may be based on the Blackburn Cramp Developmental Writing Scale levels for writing or other writing assessments.

4. Vocabulary
Administer vocabulary assessments to determine the student's ability to understand the meaning of words with affixes, multiple meaning words, and problems with limited prior knowledge.

5. Fluency and Comprehension
The goal of reading is reading fluently with comprehension. This section is featured at the bottom of page 1 to denote that it provides the roots for successful reading. Administer assessments to determine the student's ability to read with accuracy, automatic word recognition, prosody (read with inflection and phrasing) and comprehension.
  Administer an Informal Reading Inventory to determine word recognition, fluency and comprehension strengths and needs. The National Assessment of Education Progress (NAEP) Oral Reading Fluency Scale Rubric is available for analysis of fluency results. Fluency assessments include the

Repeated Reading Procedure. There are also reading rate charts to record and monitor student progress for words read per minute (wpm) with comprehension. (For examples, see Rasinski, 1985, 2003; Samuels, 2002).

During the assessments determine the student's use of effective reading strategies by discussing the following questions:

How do you pronounce unfamiliar words?

Does the student have effective word recognition strategies? Remember to find out specifically how the student sounds out a word (i.e., Chunking words into syllables, chunking by onset and rime/spelling patterns, looking for small words in multisyllabic words, understanding patterns, understanding prefixes and suffixes, and origins of root words).

What do you do if you are reading and it doesn't make sense?

Does the student use effective comprehension strategies (i.e., rereading, asking questions, making connections, etc.)? Does the student understand the importance of making meaning during reading?

Literacy ROOTS Focuses on Comprehension, Increasing Reading Levels and Student Strategy Use for Successful Reading and Writing

Note that the student's knowledge of phonemic awareness, phonics, spelling, vocabulary, and fluency impact reading comprehension. An informal reading inventory is suggested as one assessment of these literacy skills. **Informal reading inventories** can be used to determine students' reading levels. **Reading levels** are assessed as independent, instructional, or frustration levels. At the independent level, a student has word recognition accuracy of 99% and reading comprehension of 90%. Reading materials at this level are to be read by the student with little or no assistance. Texts at this level are known as "independent" reading material that students can read on their own with minimal errors and understanding. The Instructional Level indicates accuracy in word recognition at 95% and reading comprehension at 75%. At this level, students need assistance in reading by the teacher or caregiver. Words are more difficult to pronounce and the story is more difficult to comprehend by the reader. The Frustration Level is when word recognition accuracy is below 90% and reading comprehension is below 50%. This level should be avoided when selecting reading materials for the student and can cause frustration due to errors and lack of fluency.

Explanation of Page 2 of the Literacy ROOTS Progress Monitoring Tool

O — Organizing A Balanced Approach to Literacy Instruction with Multimedia.

This section of the progress monitoring tool includes an integrated approach to teaching based on multiple pre-test results using the Four Blocks Method for instruction. (Refer to Figure 6.1 for a blank copy of the Literacy ROOTS Progress Monitoring Tool.)

Use Cunningham et al. Four Blocks for an integrated and balanced approach to teaching literacy across the content areas. The four blocks are: Word Study, Writing, Self-Selected Reading, and Guided Reading/Reader Response across the content areas. Create and list the main components in instructional lessons based on academic and social goals with texts at the student's appropriate reading levels, multimedia resources, and focus on specific reading strategies. Reinforce the reading strategies across each of the four blocks.

Examples of Reading Strategies:
Word Recognition-Phonics, Spelling and Vocabulary

- Letter-sound matching with segmenting and blending sounds
- Analogy strategy with key words, onsets and spelling patterns, and think alouds ("If I know b<u>oat</u> (keyword), then I know c<u>oat</u>, etc.")
- Look for patterns-vowel sounds and patterns
- Look for special features in words such as prefixes and suffixes (fly, flying; cycle, recycle), small words in big words
- Use context, questioning and graphic organizers for vocabulary

Fluency and Comprehension

- Retelling and Rereading
- Summarizing
- Predicting
- Asking Questions (students become the teacher and ask high level questions to themselves or others) and other comprehension strategies

Students need to ask themselves: Does what I am reading make sense?

Page 3 of the Literacy ROOTS Progress Monitoring Tool: Talents and Interests, and Student's Post Tests with New Academic and Social Goals. [Refer to Figure 6.1]

T-Talents and Interests

Assess student's motivation, talents and interests. Administer an attitude survey and/or interest inventory to determine the student's attitude about reading and writing to plan motivating instruction.

Assessment Examples:

Motivation to read can be assessed with the *Elementary Reading Attitude Survey* based on the Garfield character by McKenna and Kear, 1990.

Administer and analyze the results of *The Motivation to Read Profile and Conversational Interview* by Gambrell et al. (1996). *Available in Appendix C of this textbook.*

Discover the student's values and attitudes about reading by sharing questions, discussing the student's favorite Internet websites, other multimedia resources, and personal talents.

Include the assessment titles and results in the Literacy ROOTS progress monitoring tool to help guide instruction based on students' interests and inquiry learning.

S-Student's Post Assessments and New Academic and Social Goals: Administer and analyze post tests based on page 1 pre tests of Literacy ROOTS. Develop new student academic and social goals related to student progress and conferencing among the student, caretakers and teacher. If the student needs to continue to work on reading strategies note the need to continue specific strategy instruction on page 3 of Literacy Roots. Attach or keep notebooks with copies of completed assessments, lessons, and learned strategies to motivate students to view and value their literacy progress across the content areas.

Reflection on an Example of a Completed Literacy ROOTS Progress Monitoring Tool and Lesson

Reflect on the example of a tutoring lesson and completed Literacy ROOTS Progress Monitoring Tool for 2nd grade student Brianna written by her teacher Rachel Royal. How do you think the use of the Literacy ROOTS Progress Monitoring Tool will be beneficial to the student, teacher, and caretakers? Why?

An Example of the Literacy ROOTS Progress Monitoring Tool with Tutorial Plan

Tutoring Lesson Date 6/21 & 6/22

Tutor: Rachel Royal   **Student First Name:** Brianna   **Grade Level:** 2

Instructional Reading Level Narrative: First
Instructional Reading Level Expository: Primer
Instructional Focus for Tutoring:

1. Phonics and Spelling: Review short and long vowel sounds in words to improve phonics and comprehension.
   Word Sort Activity: Sort short vowel words and long vowel words that end with *e, CVCe*; add new key words to her word wall dictionary.
   Teach the analogy strategy key word " b<u>eat</u>" with the /eat/ spelling pattern. Add the keyword to the word wall dictionary. Create word family words with the spelling pattern "eat."
   > Use the Talk to Yourself Chart by Gaskins et al., (1996/97)
   > to reinforce the analogy strategy. (An example of the chart
   > can be found in Chapter 3 of this textbook).

2. Comprehension: Use an expository text for summarizing and synthesizing information.

Text: *We Need Farmers* by Lola M. Schaefer   **Reading Level of the Text:** First

READ ALOUD: *The Milk Makers* by Gail Gibbons

- Discuss facts, questioning, and retelling for comprehension.

Learning Objective:

- The student will retell *We Need Farmers* by Lola M. Schaefer. The teacher and student will write a retelling/summary.
- The student will differentiate between the "long *e*" and the "short *e*" in words in the text.

Before Reading:

- Hook: View pictures of farm animals
- Insure Successful Reading: We will activate Background Knowledge about farms.
- Comprehension Strategy: Retelling, Summarizing, and Synthesizing Information
- Begin Chart:
  - The teacher and Brianna will begin a chart for facts, questions, and the retelling/summary.

During Reading:

- The student is thinking about the important facts from the story and recording them on Post-its.
- We will stop at several places to record our thinking about the text on the chart.

After Reading:

- The student will retell the information.
- The teacher and the student will work together to record the facts, any questions, and the retelling/summary.
- The student will add any new words to the word wall dictionary.

Assessment of Objective:

- Brianna reread the book, *We Need Farmers.*
- While she read the book, she wrote down facts and questions about the book to create a chart for summarizing information to increase comprehension. Throughout the book, I continued

to ask her several comprehension questions, which she answered well. We created a progress monitoring tool of the types of farmers that were in the book. We also wrote a retelling of the book together based on our chart information and discussions.

- She completed a word sort by sorting words according to the "long *e*" and the "short *e*." She used phonics cards to compare the spelling patterns.

Reflection:

Brianna and I finished this tutoring session in two days. We had some interruptions on day 1. On the first day, Brianna began by reviewing the sounds and spellings for the short and long vowels. Then she did a word sort for "short and long *e*" words. One of those words happened to be "eat," and we used "beat" as our key word to create a word family with the spelling pattern "eat." She is becoming very good at this and came up with words with the spelling pattern.

As she read the book, she stopped to write down different facts and questions from the text. We also discussed the different types of farmers from the book. We worked together to write a retelling of the story. I really want to work with her on retelling. During the informal reading inventory, she really struggled with the retellings.

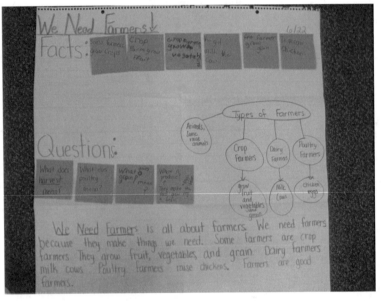

FIGURE 6.2   Brianna's Facts, Questions, and Retelling for summarizing developed during a tutoring lesson

Example of Literacy ROOTS Progress Monitoring Tool for Monitoring Student Progress

Figure 6.1 (Roberts, E. 2010) **Page 1 of 3**	Student Name: Brianna
	Teacher Rachel Royal
	Student age:____ Student grade level:___
R Section — Reflections	
R Section — **Reflections about Culture of Home:** Reflect upon family literacy interactions and culture.	**R—Reflections about Culture of School** Reflect upon school literacy experiences and student preferences for learning: grouping and peer interactions.

R: Reflection: Culture at Home Brianna's family is very supportive. She lives with her mom and twin sister. She also spends a lot of time with her grandmother, cousins, and other family. Brianna's mother is very interested in Brianna's success. Brianna often does homework and plays "school" with her twin sister. Both are about to be in second grade.	**R: Reflection:** Culture at School She attends a very small public school (150 students) that is scheduled to combine with another for the upcoming school year. Brianna is extremely social and loves to talk with her classmates. She's very outgoing and likes to be successful. She needs to be encouraged to feel comfortable taking risks.

O Section — Ongoing Assessments	

O Section — **Ongoing Assessments:**
   1. Phonemic Awareness and Alphabetic Knowledge Pre Test Results:
Yopp-Singer (date-6/18): Segments most words either by each sound or by onset and rime/ spelling patterns. She knows the letters and sounds of the alphabet.
 	
:
	O:Ongoing Assessments
	   2. Phonics and Spelling: Pre Test Results:
	Qualitative Reading Inventory (Informal Reading Inventory)
	(date-6/14)
	Word List Reading Grade Levels:
	Pre-primer **Independent level**
	Primer and 1st grade **Instructional level**
	2nd grade **Frustration level**
	She needs phonics strategies.
	Results Spelling:
	Bear Spelling Pre Test: She spelled 4 out of 10 words correctly. She has problems with spelling patterns and vowel sounds.

Ongoing Assessments:
   3. Writing Pre Test Results:
Writing sample results: (6/22) Needs help with writing complete sentences, organization and punctuation
	Ongoing Assessments:
	Pre Assessments:
	Date: (6/22)
	   4. Vocabulary Pre Test Results:
	Pre Test and During Tutoring We worked on vocabulary throughout our readings. She took a quiz on 6/22 and scored 100%. She's very skilled at using context clues and clues from the pictures to determine meaning of unfamiliar words.

Ongoing Assessments: **5. Fluency and Comprehension Pre Test Results:** *Qualitative Reading Inventory* (Informal Reading Inventory) (6/14) and *Repeated Reading Procedure* test (6/21) Date: (6/14) Informal Reading Inventory Oral Reading Passages Results (date-6/14)	**Strategy Instruction Needed** *Word Recognition-Phonics, Spelling and Vocabulary:* letter-sound matching analogy strategy with key words look for patterns-vowel sounds and patterns look for special features in words use context, questioning and graphic organizers for vocabulary *Fluency and Comprehension:* Retelling

(continued)

Oral Reading Grade Levels: Narrative passages: Primer **Independent level** First **Instructional level** Second **Frustration level** Expository passages: Preprimer **Independent level** Primer **Instructional level** First **Frustration level** She needs comprehension and fluency strategies. *Fluency and Comprehension:* (date-6/21) Read passage Fluency Pre Test-Repeated Reading Procedure; Word recognition accuracy: 98%; 48 words per minute (WPM) with comprehension	Think Alouds Read Write Think Predicting Ask Question at higher levels Ask herself - Does it make sense? *Essential: Authentic Reading and Writing Experiences*

O Section — Organizing
Page 2 of 3 <u>A Balanced Approach to Literacy Instruction with Multimedia</u>

<u>O</u>: Organizing A Balanced Approach to Literacy Instruction with Multimedia (Organizing the student's reading and content area **Four Blocks lessons:** Include appropriate reading strategies, texts, and digital resources based on pre-test results)	(Note; Remember to reinforce reading strategies across all Four Blocks. The strategies should also be included in content area reading) **Reading Strategies to be reinforced in ALL Four Blocks during tutoring:** *Phonics and Spelling Strategies* The analogy strategy with key words, blending and segmenting sounds (sound letter matching), special features of words and context *Comprehension Strategies* Retelling, summarizing, Read Write Tell, graphic organizers, rereading
Word Study Create a word wall dictionary: • Add the **analogy strategy** keywords *ride* and *beat* to the word wall. Discuss the CVCe pattern in the keyword *ride*. The spelling pattern is /ide./Use words with the same spelling pattern in sentences and activities. Use the analogy strategy for the vowel digraph /ea/ with the CVVC pattern – The keyword is *beat* . The spelling pattern is /eat/. Find words during reading and writing with the new spelling patterns.	**Writing** 1. Write a response to literature using selected word wall words. 2. Note punctuation and capitalization. 3. Use complete sentences and different types of sentences for reader interest. 4. Focus on story stages: beginning, middle, and end. *Reinforce the **analogy strategy**. Include use of words with the spelling patterns practiced during word study. Discover and correct spelling of words with new spelling patterns. Ask: Does my writing make sense?

- Use the "Talk to Yourself Chart" for letter sound matching and the analogy strategy (Gaskins et al., 1996/97). Find words with the same spelling patterns in texts and discuss their special features and meaning.

Guided Reading	Self-Selected Reading
Read texts at her instructional level from the pre tests. Reading Strategies and lessons focus: 1. Monitoring Comprehension-Does it make sense when I am reading? Think Aloud Read, Write, Talk 2. Activating Background Knowledge 3. Summarizing and Synthesizing- Work on retelling with chart *Include review of **analogy strategy** to decode unfamiliar words when reading and spelling.	1. Practice rereading expository texts (informational texts) of interest. 2. Read daily to continue to build confidence and fluency. 3. Choose informational books at appropriate levels. (Interests include families, animals, and farms). 5. Include review of **analogy strategy**. Use a bookmark with the strategy when reading independently to help pronounce and discover unfamiliar words. 6. Create a reading log.

Page 3 of 3	T Section: Talents and Interests

Name and date of Interest/Attitude Survey:

Results: Attitude Survey - Motivation to Read Profile by Gambrell (6/14)

Brianna likes to sing, write, and cheer. She wants to be a cheerleader. She also likes to play hand-clapping games.

Favorite Book: Brianna's favorite book is *No, David!* by David Shannon.

Interests: Brianna likes to watch her favorite TV shows on the Internet.

S Section: Student's Post-Test Results and New Academic and Social Goals

Post Assessment result: 7/14; *Bear Spelling Inventory*: She struggles with long vowel spellings. Ex: The word "sight" with long vowel /i/ and the /ight/ spelling pattern.
New Academic Goal: Continue to use the analogy strategy to create keywords and families to focus on chunking by onset-spelling patterns and reinforce during spelling, reading and writing.
New Social Goal:
 a. Raise hand and share learning in class.

Post Assessment result: 7/22; Fluency Test-*Repeated Reading Procedure*; Word recognition accuracy: 98%; 48 WPM
New Goal: Read and reread without as many pauses, focus on reading smoothly with an even pace. Keep a reading rate chart to see progress.
New Social Goal:
Read with a partner quietly.

(continued)

Post Assessment result: 7/26; *Informal Reading Inventory:* read with a 91% accuracy rate for 2nd-grade narrative oral passage with comprehension. She needs to continue reading expository texts of interest.

New Academic Goal: She reads with a few miscues and needs to work on fewer pauses. Reread familiar texts to practice fluency and use a reading rate chart for progress.

New Social Goal: Reread and retell favorite books to friends and family.

Post Test Reading Grade Levels: (She increased her independent reading level from Primer to 1–2 grade level)

Independent oral reading grade level __1–2_

Instructional oral reading grade level __2_

Frustration oral reading grade level __3_

Post Test Results: *Yopp-Singer* test (7/22): Segments all but one word either by each sound or by onset and rime/spelling pattern

New Academic Goal: Continue to focus on segmenting and blending sounds and letter sound matching.

New Social Goal:

Use think alouds about reading, spelling and writing strategies with friends. Use website phonics games and discover familiar and unfamiliar words to add to word wall dictionary for writing.

FIGURE 6.3   This picture shows plants with strong roots in Elaine's garden

Keys for Encouraging Creativity and Evaluating Writing Performance

Stephanie L. McAndrews

TABLE 7.1

K	E	Y	S
What do you **know** about evaluating writing performance and encouraging creativity?	What do you want to **explore** about evaluating writing performance and encouraging creativity?	What do you **yearn** to learn after reading and discussing the chapter?	How will you **satisfy** your curiosity? What ideas and concepts will you apply to your teaching?

Writing composition is the "process or result of arranging ideas to form a clear and unified impression in order to create an effective message" (Harris and Hodges, 1995, p. 38). Writing is essential to life; it is needed to communicate for functional purposes as well as for sharing our thoughts. As Routman (2005) states, "I want students to write with passion and ease. I want them to be motivated, confident writers who see writing as an everyday, useful, even enjoyable tool" (p. 1). Writing instruction is sometimes neglected in the teaching curriculum and is often a neglected topic in national and state legislation because it is not one of the National Reading Panel Report's identified five important areas. The International Reading Association has embraced the need for effective reading as well as writing instruction in the Standards for Reading Professionals–2010. Composing and comprehending are interrelated and parallel processes, readers and writers both compose meaning (Kucer, 2005; Tierney & Pearson, 1984). The more students use reading and writing together, the more they learn from both of them. Learning to comprehend in a given genre supports the written composition in that same genre and vice versa.

The 6+1 Writing Model helps teachers instruct and assess students' writing skills. The 6+1 Traits are ideas, organization, voice, word choice, sentence fluency, conventions, and presentation. The six-trait writing model integrates the writing process with essential components that make up quality writing. The traits are frequently used as a basis for state writing rubrics. The 6+1 Traits were developed in the mid-1980s to address the needs for an assessment tool for effective writing. The Northwest Regional Educational Laboratory worked with educators to develop the traits and related scoring resources for training teachers to improve writing skills of students. In 2002 the National Assessment of Educational Progress shared results of writing studies that raised concerns about student writing. They found that the number of students achieving at the proficient level or below was only 28% in grade 4, 31 % in grade 8, and 24% in grade 12 (Persky et al., 2003). A research study was completed by Kuzlow and Bellamy (2004), titled, *Experimental Study on the Impact of the 6+1 Writing Model on Student Achievement in Writing*. The study focused on the importance of effective training in the 6 +1 Traits. Teachers in the study attended a two-day 6+1 Traits writing workshop. The results suggest that the teachers did not fully implement the traits and, therefore, should have longer periods of training to improve student writing achievement.

The progression for teaching the 6+1 Traits is:

1. The teacher introduces one trait at a time as well as related scoring criteria.
2. Students write pieces in a variety of forms and revise with peers, focusing on the selected traits.
3. The teacher uses whole-group scoring and discusses good writing using sample papers. They follow with discussions about strategies for using the selected trait effectively.
4. The teacher conferences with individual students and provides feedback.
5. Students create writing folders for writing goals and works in progress. They track their progress related to the traits and the standards.

Providing ongoing assessment, instruction, and regular opportunities for writing are essential for a child's literacy development. One effective assessment and instructional tool is the Composition Assessment for the Writer (Figure 7.1), which was adapted from both the Primary and Advanced Narrative Revising and Editing Checklists (McAndrews, 2008).

Figure 7.1 presents an assessment for evaluating the use of each of the 6+1 Traits of Writing: ideas, organization, voice, word choice, sentence fluency, conventions, and presentation (Spandel, 2007) during the writing process. The goal for this assessment is to plan instruction and to identify the writer's growth in the content and conventions of narrative and expository writing composition.

FIGURE 7.1 Composition Assessment for the Writer

Author: Date:

Title: Evaluator: Self or Teacher

Genre: Narrative, expository, persuasive, descriptive, letter/journal, poetry (Circle one)

Directions and Scoring: Circle either student or teacher in the score column. After reading the entire composition, read each of the descriptors in the rubric and evaluate each element with a plus sign (+) for excellent, a checkmark (✓) for satisfactory, or a minus sign (−) for needs improvement. Underline any descriptive words that seem appropriate. Then analyze with specific examples from the composition.

Composition Assessment for the Writer

Prewriting
__ I brainstormed a topic I was interested in or I knew about.
__ I collected resources about my topic.
__ I made a concept map of the important ideas or events.
__ I interviewed people about my topic.
__ I wrote at least one draft.

Title
__ I wrote a catchy or informative title and capitalized the appropriate words.

Organization
__ My lead gets the reader's attention and lets the reader know what my composition will be about.
__ My ideas are sequenced in a way that makes sense.
__ The format goes with the purpose or style of writing: narrative, expository, persuasive, or descriptive.
For narratives:
__ I had a clear beginning describing the characters and setting (place and time).
__ I had a clear middle where I described the plot or events in detail.
__ I had a clear ending where I described the resolution and made an interesting closing statement.
For expository:
__ I used titles and subtitles if appropriate to identify ideas.
__ I used bullets or numbers if appropriate to help make the information easy to find.
__ My conclusion reinforces, supports, and/or restates my main point.

Sentence Fluency
__ My sentences flow from one idea to the next.
__ My sentences begin in a variety of ways.
__ My sentences are different lengths.
__ My sentences are clear, not too wordy or too short.
__ I use linking words such as *also* and *in addition*.
__ I used transitions to connect ideas such as *first, second, then, next, finally*.

Word Choice
__ I included vocabulary words specific to the topic.
__ I used specific nouns or proper nouns, avoiding vague words such as *stuff* and *things*.
__ I used a variety of strong verbs, limiting my use of words such as *went* and *put*.
__ I used descriptive adjectives (describing nouns) and/or adverbs (describing verbs).
__ The words I chose are right for my audience.
__ The meaning of every word is clear. Any confusing words are defined or examples are given for them.
__ I used words to make strong images, including using the senses.

Voice
__ I included my honest feelings, emotions, and opinions.
__ I included ideas to show emotions such as humor, sadness, happiness, suspense, excitement, etc.
__ I used words to show I care about my topic.
__ I included details from my five senses so that the reader can visualize my writing.
__ I used words that show my personality.
__ I used a variety of sentence structures for declarative (for telling), interrogative (for asking), exclamatory (for showing excitement), and dialogue (for stating what people say).
__ I used literary elements (similes and metaphors) to make comparisons.

Conventions
__ Every sentence in my paper is a complete sentence.
__ Every sentence is grammatically correct.
__ The verb tense is consistent throughout each paragraph.
__ I edited my paper for capitalization.
__ I edited my paper for punctuation.
__ I edited my paper for spelling. (I used strategies and resources as needed.)

Publishing
__ I wrote in my best handwriting, checking for correct letter formation, spacing, and margins.
__ I included pictures, diagrams, charts, and/or other graphics that are related to the ideas in order to help the reader better understand my writing.
__ I eagerly shared my writing with other people.

Teacher Analysis: Describe the composition strengths and needs, including specific examples from the writing composition.

Writing Assessment

To plan for instruction, the teacher must first decide the genre: descriptive, expository, journals and letters, narrative, persuasive, or poetry. To improve writing, teachers need to scaffold students' thinking and writing throughout the writing process. There are a variety of steps of the writing process, including prewriting, cyclical steps of drafting, revising, editing, and conferencing, and finally publishing and sharing. While there are many strategies for writing depending on the genre or purpose, most importantly students need to write for a purpose and reread what they write to be sure that it is accurate and clearly conveys their message. To improve in their writing development, students need to write on a daily basis and for different purposes. They should also analyze models of good writing and choose the writing pieces they want to prepare for publication.

Mrs. Gomez, a second-grade teacher, is starting a unit on narrative writing and she wants to activate background knowledge for this experience. She initially assesses her students' current understanding of composing personal narratives.

1. She tells her students that they are going to be doing a unit on personal narratives. A personal narrative is a composition that retells a personal experience based on something that really happened. All details come together to create a complete story with a beginning, middle, and end.
2. She says, "Today you are going to write a personal narrative. I want you to think about an event or topic you know well. Tell a partner about it."
3. Draw a picture or make a web of the important ideas you want to include.
4. Now, explain it in writing with as much detail as possible. Please write on every other line for revision purposes.
5. When students are finished writing, she tells them, "Please reread what you wrote and make any changes to help the reader understand what you wrote."
6. The Composition Assessment for writers is used to identify the strengths and needs of each student and score the writing piece. Then she writes specific feedback or comments on the Writing Composition Summary Sheet.
7. Scoring: For each writing element, examine the indicators and put a plus sign (+) if it is excellent, a checkmark (✓) if it is satisfactory, or minus sign (−) if it needs work in the left column as well as provide feedback about the traits/elements. Provide specific examples of strengths and needs in the analysis section.
8. An analysis of this information is used to plan lessons and share information with students to further develop the student's writing.
9. Mrs. Gomez wanted to support all of her students in writing, but she particularly noticed that Maurice (pseudonym) finished early and did not write much for his personal narrative. The following is Maurice's writing and assessment summary.

Initial Writing Composition Assessment Composition and Summary: Maurice, Grade 2

Me and my bab go fishing. I cach a bluingel my bab cach a cat fr,fishing (changed the *r* to *i*)

Student's reading: Me and my dad go fishing. I catch a bluegill and my dad catch a catfish.

Evidence of prewriting: He talked about it, but didn't write or draw anything.

Evidence of revision and editing: He did not do any revision, but edited the spelling of *fishing*.

Number of sentences: 2 (only one period)   Number of paragraphs: 1 (incomplete)

Average number of words per sentence: 6 words in the only complete sentence

Appropriate length for topic: No, too brief with limited details

Instructional Implications and Extended Lesson Plan

The following is an extended lesson plan based on the composition assessment summary. When introducing the lessons for each day, Mrs. Gomez orally explained the objectives, strategies, and procedures for the students. The essential elements of the traits were shared and written down for the students to follow. Mrs. Gomez composed her own narrative of when she went on a dog-sledding trip last spring. She used her prewriting and drafts to model and explain each of the steps of the writing process. (Connections with the 6+1 Traits are in bold type.)

Day 1:

Objectives: Identify elements of effective narrative writing.

Strategy: Use a teacher text modeling good writing rather than *mentor text*? Mentor text and writing composition rubric.

Procedure:

1. Teacher reads a mentor text with examples that exemplify the trait and/or elements that you want to teach.
2. Students identify traits/elements in the writing that the author used that they thought made the writing interesting.
3. Introduces or reviews the writing composition rubric.
4. Finds elements in the mentor text.

Homework Objectives: Find out more details, with specific words related to the topic, events, senses, and setting.

Strategy: Gather resources for content through interviews and multimedia.

Procedure: Draft plus **ideas trait**: The teacher selects a topic for writing her personal narrative on a dog-sledding trip in Minnesota. She shares her journal, photos, brochure, maps, books, and Internet articles about dog-sledding equipment and training.

Homework - Have Maurice talk to his dad about the fishing trip. Write down words or phrases about ideas and equipment names that were shared. Bring in any of the following: pictures from the trip, brochures or maps, fishing books, or Internet articles.

Day 2:

Objectives: Revision plus **ideas, organization, style, and word choice traits:** Include more details, with specific words related to the topic, events, senses, and setting.

Strategy: Concept mapping (Figure 7-2)

Procedure: Use resources from home, Internet, and memory to complete the concept map. The headings in the bubbles were provided.

Note: The descriptions of the fish and the location of the lake were found online.

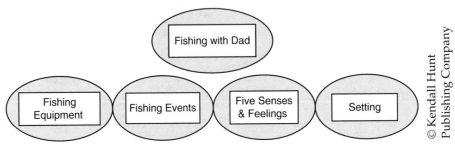

FIGURE 7.2 Concept Mapping Example

Fishing Equipment	Fishing Events	Five Senses & Feelings	Setting
Cabela's All Pro Spincast fishing rod and reel	Tying on hook Putting on bobber 2 feet from end	Water clear, cold Little bit windy on the water	Stockton Lake near Springfield Missouri
Tackle box	Cutting worms and baiting hook	Hear the fish splashing exciting	June after school got out
Long hooks Bobber	Go to the shallow water, where wind is blowing on us. By brush waited	Bluegills- big bodies & small mouths, backs and sides are brown with stripes, gills and mouths are blue, orange belly.	in our fishing boat
Bait—worms and night crawlers	Felt a pull on my line No worm Put on new worms, catch a bluegill, take off the hook Dad catch catfish	Catfish—long bodies with forked tails, spots, brown on top and light green on belly, whiskers.	Slept in a tent with my dad
Tracker Jon boat	Cooked it and ate it	Tastes good	

Day 3:

Objectives: Write a second draft of the story in sequence with more details.

Strategies: Partner sharing and draft using the concept map for **ideas and organization traits**

Procedure:

1. Author: Tell the story to a partner and include as many details from your concept map as possible.
2. Partner: Listen to the story and make at least two comments about what is interesting and at least two statements with ideas about who, what, where, when, how, why.
3. Author: Write notes of new ideas shared.
4. Both: Read the content section of the writing composition rubric.
5. Author: Compose a second draft on every other line using ideas from the concept map and notes.
6. Author: Use a phonics strategy to help write an unfamiliar word. For example, the student might *sound it out phonetically and write letters for each of the sounds they hear* initially. They can circle the word as a reminder to go back and edit it after finishing the story. When editing the story, he can be taught to use an effective phonics strategy such as the analogy strategy to chunk and spell words accurately. For example, "fish" can be spelled correctly by teaching the student the spelling pattern /ish/ and reminding him to think "If I know d<u>ish</u>, I know f<u>ish</u>." The key word /fish/ can be added to his word wall dictionary for future use when reading and writing words with the same spelling pattern. Remember it is better to write interesting words than only words you can spell when drafting a story.
7. Author: Reread your composition.
8. Author and Partner: Review the content section of the writing composition rubric and evaluate the composition.
9. Author: Revise your composition for content **ideas and word choice traits**. You can insert words/ideas by making a caret and writing it above or writing it on a Post-it note, delete words/ideas by marking one line through them so they can still be read, move ideas by circling them and making an arrow to where they should be moved.

Day 4:

Objectives: Revise composition for content and then edit for conventions

Strategies: Use Composition Writing Rubric to self-assess composition and partner sharing

Procedures:

1. Review the content section with the six traits of the writing composition rubric.
2. Reread and evaluate your own composition for content.
3. Revise your composition for content as you did on day 3.
4. To check for sentence fluency, make sure there is no missing information from one sentence to the next. Read the first word in each sentence to make sure you are using a variety of words for flow and interest of the reader.
5. Reread your composition and make any additional revisions to content and the six traits.
6. Review the conventions section of the composition rubric.
7. Edit for grammar, punctuation, capitalization, and spelling.
8. For spelling, work on writing the word by chunking the sounds into onset-rime. For example, for the word b/ed, b is the onset (initial consonant) and ed it the rime or spelling pattern. For the b/d reversal, have him use the bed strategy of making bed with your thumbs and fists to select the correct letter.
9. Have author and reader conversations to revise and edit the paper.
   Author: Read your composition to a different partner.
10. Partner: Listen to the story and make at least two comments about what is interesting and two statements about who, what, where, when, how, why.
11. Author: Write notes about new ideas to add.
12. Author: Revise and edit draft.
13. Partner: Read your third draft.
14. Author: Sign up for conference with the teacher.

Day 5:

Objective: Student conferences with the teacher.

Strategies: Student-led writing conference

Procedure:

1. During the conference the student reads the draft to the teacher and then explains how each element of the rubric was addressed.
2. Teacher evaluates the composition based on the rubric focusing on the writing process and the six traits.
3. Teacher provides oral and written feedback to the student. The teacher should not write on the student's paper. Revision notes should be made on the writing composition summary form and/or on Post-it notes. For incorrect spelling the teacher should support the student in writing letters for each of the sounds by chunking by syllables, finding affixes, and finding the onset-rime/spelling patterns in the root word. Then decide which words the student should look up and add to a word wall or be provided by the teacher.
4. Teacher states that either the student needs to write another draft or the student is ready to write the final copy with a few minor changes.

Day 6:

Objective: Students publish their writing

Strategies: Write final copy of composition, Author's Chair, publish composition in newspaper.

Procedure:

1. Once the teacher has met with the students and has determined they are ready, students write their final copy of their composition in their best handwriting or use a computer attending to letter formation, spacing, and margins. They could include optional illustrations or graphics.
2. Students read their compositions to the class while sitting in the Author's Chair.
3. The audience listens for what effective elements of writing the author used and what they learned from the composition. They can also use the writing composition rubric for ideas or all of the 6+1 Traits.
4. The audience and then the teacher orally share these specific positive comments.
5. Teacher, aides, or volunteers type their compositions into a newspaper format. Graphics are then added. The newspaper is then printed and distributed to families, peers, faculty, staff, and/or administrators.

The following is Maurice's third draft and final copy.

Catching my First Fish

Maurice, Author and Illustrator

My dad and I went on a fishing trip in June after school got out. We (-went, ^drove) all the way to Stockton Lake near Springfield (^,) Missouri. We put up (-are,^our) (^ little green) tent in the campground. We (-went , ^walked) right to the loading ramp. The water was really clear and still kind of cold. I helped dad carry the fishing rods and (-takl/^tackle) our Tracker Jon boat. Dad got me (-a/^an) All Pro Spin Cast rod and reel from Cabela's for my birthday. First dad showed me how to put the bobber about 2 feet from the end and tie on the long hook. I dug the worms and night (-crolers, ^crawlers) out of the dirt and cut them with my knife. Then I (-put, ^ squished) it on the hook. We (-went, ^trolled) to the (^shallow) water

Image © Deklofenak, 2012. Shutterstock, Inc.

near the brush. The wind was blowing a bit. My dad and I (–put, ^dropped) in our lines and waited. We had to be quiet and not rock the boat. My bobber went under a bit and I felt a pull on my line. I checked it and there was no fish and no bait. Then, I put on a night (-croler,^crawler). Dad got a bite and he reeled it in slowly. He (-cacht, ^caught) got a big catfish! It was long and had spots. The top and sides (-was, ^ were) brown and the belly was light green. It had (-wiskers, ^whiskers) (^ like a cat). Then I got another bite. I reeled it in really slowly. The fish was still on the hook! I held the fish while my dad pulled the hook out. It was wiggling all around. I(–put, ^ dropped) it in the bucket. My dad said it was a bluegill. It had a big body and a small mouth. It (–has, ^ had) a brown back and sides and had stripes. Its belly was orange. It got the name (becuse, ^because) it is blue around the gills and mouth. I was so (-exited, ^excited) (-becuse, ^because) it was the first fish I ever (cacht, ^caught)! That night we cut the fish open and pulled out the guts. Then we (put, ^ laid) it on the hot grill. Dad (-put, squeezed) lemon juice on them. They were so (-delishus, ^delicious)! We climbed (went) into the tent to go to bed. My dad said I am a great angler!

Evidence of Prewriting: He made a concept map, shared it with peers, and wrote three drafts before his final copy.

Evidence of Revision and Editing: He made numerous and substantial revisions and editing changes between each of his drafts. For the final copy he substituted active verbs for most of the passive verbs. He also corrected all of the spelling errors.

Number of sentences: 40   Number of Paragraphs: 1 (complete)

Appropriate length for topic: Yes

Maurice was able to significantly add to the content through this scaffolded instructional process. He sat in the author's chair and eagerly read his story to the whole class with expression and appropriate intonation. His writing, along with the writing of his peers, was published in the class newspaper that went home to the families. His father exclaimed that he shared his newspaper with all the family members. Now Maurice has started taking notes and asking more questions on our family trips. When we came back from our last trip he wrote the captions for the photographs. He also wants to read my fishing magazines. Maurice has developed as a confident writer. On a subsequent writing composition assessment, Maurice was able to transfer many of the writing skills he learned to a new piece of writing. He wrote on his pinewood derby experience in Cub Scouts. On his own, using the rubric to revise and edit, he wrote 15 sentences with significant detail. It had a clear beginning, middle, and end. His voice was clearly evident in his disappointment he didn't win, but he had fun making the car and racing it. Sentences generally flowed from one to another, except for two run-on sentences. He used specific words related to the building and racing of the car. He would benefit from revising some of the passive verbs to more active ones. He was able to spell most of the high-frequency words correctly and phonically spelled and chunked the others to the point that they were all decodable. He did check for and revise words that had the potential for a b/d reversal. Maurice was able to successfully meet all of the objectives for the writing instruction that were determined based on his initial writing and transfer this knowledge to his new writing. More importantly, Maurice is more engaged in the processes of language, reading, and writing for his own purposes.

This chapter provided an example of a writing composition assessment that includes the 6+1 Traits that can be used to inform instruction and promote student understanding of the writing process for quality writing. Students need opportunities to see themselves as writers and authors. Maurice and his classmates have seen writing as a meaningful endeavor and hopefully these experiences will encourage them to continue to develop as readers, writers, and thinkers.

Keys for an Effective Balanced Literacy Program

Debra Coffey, Elaine Roberts, and Stacy Delacruz

Chapter 8 highlights designs for planning and implementing a balanced literacy program that encourages young readers to blossom into life-long readers. Consider what you know about a balanced literacy program.

TABLE 8.1

K	E	Y	S
What do you **know** about a balanced literacy instruction program?	What do you want to **explore** about a balanced literacy instruction program?	What do you **yearn** to learn after reading and discussing the chapter?	How will you **satisfy** your curiosity? What ideas and concepts will you apply to your teaching?

Balanced Literacy Programs

A balanced literacy program helps students to explore literature in context as they develop a thorough understanding of skills and strategies for effective reading. As a framework designed to help all students learn to read and write effectively, balanced literacy builds connections in the classroom, school, and community. This makes the classroom like a vibrant garden. Pearson and Raphael (1999) emphasized the ways a balanced approach integrates the **multiple literacies** of listening, speaking, reading, writing, and related thinking skills. The multiple literacies of listening, speaking, reading, writing, and thinking are extended by children's cultural and social knowledge. Additionally, they are expanded through media literacy. Pearson and Raphael described the components of literacy as (1) student-centered instruction, (2) reader response/text-driven understandings, and (3) use of narrative and expository texts to integrate literacy skills across the content areas. When these components are supported by media, literacy students are provided with a myriad of choices to extend reading and writing skills (Reinking & McKenna, 1997; Puckett, Shea, & Hansen, 2011) described an inclusive classroom setting in which students with physical disabilities participate and interact with other students using computers and other forms of assistive technology to enhance collaboration during reading and writing activities.

Balanced Literacy Instruction Nourishes Young Readers with Beneficial Curriculum Components

In this chapter we consider the key features of literacy instruction designed to nourish young readers and match their needs and interests with beneficial curriculum components. A balanced literacy program focuses on the literacy components of listening, speaking, reading, writing, and thinking across the content areas with comprehension as the foundation for learning. It includes student implementation of reading strategies to help with phonemic awareness, phonics, vocabulary, fluency, and comprehension. A balanced literacy program includes:

- Strategies for phonemic awareness, phonics, spelling, vocabulary, comprehension, and fluency are (1) modeled, (2) practiced, (3) used independently, and (4) applied to reading and writing in context. Teachers strategically integrate the five major components of reading with curriculum components that match the developmental levels of students to inspire growth.
- Guided and/or content area reading includes teacher modeling and scaffolding. This modeling process includes the teaching of reading strategies and opportunities for students to use these strategies in the context of quality literature as a group. Read-alouds and think-alouds are used to stimulate active engagement in learning. Students apply what they learn during class sessions and guided practice. During this time the teacher moves around the room, providing appropriate scaffolding and conferencing with groups and individuals. Conferencing sessions provide opportunities to reinforce strategies learned during word study and discuss creative writing to reinforce learning. Tables in the classroom display books that relate to concepts and themes emphasized during class sessions. Students have opportunities to select high-quality literature at appropriate levels. Throughout this process reading comprehension is the foundation for reader response and interaction as students explore concepts and themes.
- Independent reading provides opportunities for students to practice using reading skills automatically as they become enthralled with good books. During these sessions they keep logs of favorite books and record their responses to literature.
- Writing workshop connects personal writing experiences to strategies learned during word study, the writing process, and use of new vocabulary. Students explore lively adjectives for narrative and informational writing. Mini-lessons help students develop ideas, organize their thoughts, select engaging words, study authors' styles, and use conventions such as punctuation accurately.
- Hands-on activities for curriculum integration are used throughout this process to make the curriculum tangible and provide connections with life beyond the classroom walls. Displays and bulletin boards throughout the classroom are used to reinforce those connections and extend learning.

Balanced Literacy Programs Feature Motivating and Imaginative Writing

Balanced literacy programs feature integrated opportunities for motivating and imaginative writing experiences that often derive from narrative and expository stories. Students write to learn and inform, and writing brings enjoyment. Imaginative writing motivates them to use descriptive words and entertain their audience. They can use the structure of story elements to write scripts for plays, write to pen pals, and engage in various forms of digital writing. Students enjoy chalk writing and opportunities to write about artwork. They benefit from opportunities to take notes as detectives, write mystery stories, and interview others for quotes and suggestions for topics and themes of interest. Students enjoy dual journal writing where each student has a side of the notebook to write on to respond to the other student's writing or adds illustrations for persuasive or narrative writing.

Switch writing is another way to motivate students to write. Each student writes the first sentence of a story that is fun and appropriate. They then pass their paper to the person on their right side, and that person adds the next sentence to the paper. The process continues until each story is completed and shared. During the switch-writing process, the teacher also writes and adds descriptive sentences to the stories to keep the story interesting. The teacher reminds the students of story elements as they write. For example, initially they focus on the beginning of the story with the setting and characters. Then they consider problems and events leading to the climax. Finally, they discuss the resolution of the story. Certain sentences from the stories may be selected by students to be modified and used as a mini-lesson that sparks a future story.

A Balanced Classroom with Hands-on Activities for Literacy Development

If you walked into Debra Coffey's classroom, you would have seen a balanced literacy program in action. Students in her third-grade class enjoyed collaboration through switch writing, and they were enthralled and amused by the outcome of a group story. Through the seasons of the year, her students engaged in purposeful activities to connect the curriculum with the world beyond the class-room. These meaningful experiences integrated literacy with the content areas and connected the classroom with activities students enjoyed after school. When she read the book *How a Seed Grows*, by Helene Jordan (1992), students planted lima bean seeds in egg shells. Then the egg shells were removed during the sequential stages of growth to reveal the roots, leaves, and stems of the lima bean plants as they grew in the egg shells. Students drew their own diagrams and recorded the plant growth in their journals as they observed real examples of the stages of plant growth, which were depicted in the book. Students saw plant growth from another angle when they planted seeds in zip-lock bags with paper toweling and hung the bags in the windows to view the stages of growth. When they planted marigolds in cups after these experiences, they could easily visualize the roots beneath the soil. Throughout these experiences students explored narrative and expository texts featuring plants, recorded their experiences in journals, and shared insights with their friends.

During a tasting party Debra Coffey's third-grade class read about plants we eat. Then they identified the parts of plants they were eating with ranch dressing. For instance, they noted that carrots are roots, and broccoli is a flower. During this unit on plants, students read about the growth of pumpkins, viewed sequencing posters for the stages of pumpkin growth, and drew faces on real pumpkins using magic markers. Later, groups of third-grade students planted pumpkins near the school parking lot where they could observe the growth process. After watching the stages of growth and recording observations, they were excited to eventually see pumpkins growing among the vines.

In January her students brought their baby pictures and wrote about the growth they had experienced. Then they considered the specific ways they wanted to grow during the new year. During certain weeks of the year students had special opportunities to share their own cultural backgrounds, their interests, and timelines showing their accomplishments. The opportunity to be Student of the Week enhanced their leadership ability, while writing workshop activities made them more metacognitively aware of their own progress and built a strong sense of community.

Each student in this third-grade class adopted a tree and described changes throughout the seasons. On Arbor Day students in Debra Coffey's class planted a tree as a culminating activity. During writing workshop sessions, students created their own books about events from the year or other topics they found significant. They used cardboard and fabric to create special covers for the books, and they stitched the pages together in collaboration with parents. When they were all official authors, they shared their books with parents and classmates during a school-wide Author Tea.

When Debra Coffey taught various grade levels, interactive read-alouds and hands-on activities in learning centers were often catalysts for writing activities. After her first-grade students read books about apple trees and Johnny Appleseed's adventures, they enjoyed an apple celebration. As they rotated among centers, they had an apple-tasting party, graphed their favorite apples, and made applesauce. In one learning center apples were cut in half, and students made apple prints with green and red paint. In the afternoon they drank juice that was squeezed from apples, using a juice press that was brought to school. Then they prepared journal entries with pictures and descriptions of what they learned during the day. Later, they shared their journal entries and discussed the sequence of events using their pictures of the celebration.

Students in Debra Coffey's classes had many opportunities for listening, speaking, reading, writing, and thinking creatively. When she was teaching fifth grade, her students designed many plays and presentations during the year. Near the end of the year they created a play about *The Giving Tree*, by Shel Silverstein (1964). That play gave them the opportunity to review the stages in the growth of an apple tree and the joys of giving to others.

Debra Coffey planned thematic class activities with a team of teachers during afternoon sessions. These collaborative sessions enhanced the teachers' ability to provide balanced, integrated instruction and create literate environments as they transformed their classrooms, using pictures, displays, and bulletin boards with monthly themes. For certain activities students moved among rooms and worked together. A shared commitment to quality literacy education helped the team of teachers to capture imaginations, make memories, and meet the needs of individual students for life-long learning.

In the next sections of this chapter we explore a variety of strategies and activities to encourage enthusiasm for reading and writing in the classroom. We consider ways to incorporate technology to enhance these experiences through a balanced literacy program that integrates all of these components across the curriculum.

Research on Interactive Read-Alouds

*The single most important activity for building the knowledge required
for eventual success in reading is reading aloud to children.*
—Jim Trelease

Reading aloud is one instructional part of a balanced literacy program. A traditional read-aloud is often associated with a straight-through read-aloud, with the teacher as a facilitator and students as listeners. "In an interactive read-aloud, the teacher pauses at significant points, asks the students for comments, shares their own thinking, and invites brief discussion" (Fountas & Pinnell, 2006, p. 16). An interactive read-aloud makes the student a more active learner throughout this instructional time.

Interactive read-alouds involve many literacy aspects. Students participate in active listening, comprehension strategies, and talking activities. Teachers can scaffold student thinking while using techniques such as think-alouds and text talks.

A study completed by Conrad, Gong, Sipp, and Wright (2004) found that "using the strategy known as text talk with K–2 students improved their oral language and comprehension abilities through a more focused approach with read-alouds" (p. 187). Text talk involves the teacher selecting key vocabulary and planning activities during the interactive read-aloud to help scaffold student learning. For example, when conducting a unit involving plants, the teacher may read *How a Seed Grows*, by Helene Jordan, and preview the text before reading it to select key vocabulary words to focus on throughout the reading. This book also has a science experiment where children can plant a bean seed, tree seed, and flower seed to see which seed grows and what any seed needs to be able to grow.

The teacher may create labels using sentence strips with a plant part on each. A plant diagram may also be drawn out on chart paper. As a new plant part is introduced in the book, the teacher may place the label on the chart paper. As the book continues, the teacher may have higher-level thinking questions planned using Bloom's Taxonomy (1956) as a guide. A vocabulary sort may be completed after reading to determine the vocabulary the students became familiar with during the story.

Another study related to the planning and implementation of interactive read-alouds was completed in grades 3–8. "Teachers were observed by two researchers as they conducted a read-aloud, and the components of it were noted and then compared to read-alouds exhibited by the 'expert' teachers" (Fisher, Flood, Lapp, & Frey, 2004, p. 10). Expert interactive read-aloud teachers were recommended to the researchers by teacher leaders and the principals (Fisher et al., 2004). The results indicated seven components of an effective, interactive read-aloud that teachers implemented. These components include:

1. Text selection: Including high-quality children's literature that met the children's interests and needs.
2. Previewed and practiced: Teachers previewed the text before reading it, and practiced phrased, fluent reading.
3. Clear purpose established: Reminded students the purpose of the lesson.
4. Fluent reading modeled: Teachers modeled clear pronunciation and the sequence of the text.
5. Animation and expression: Participants were engrossed in the books due to the teacher provoking animation and expression.
6. Discussing the text: Book discussions were used before, during, and after the read-aloud. Sticky notes placed in the books ahead of time helped with questioning.
7. Independent reading and writing: Teachers connected their read-aloud to independent reading and writing that occurred throughout the day. (Fisher et al., 2004, p. 13)

These steps can be followed with practically any text selected by the teacher. For example, students in older elementary grades who had experience in the past with plants but need instruction in measurement could listen to the text, *Beanstalk the Measure of a Giant: A Math Adventure*, by Ann McCallum. This is the tale of Jack, who climbs the beanstalk only to meet a giant named Ray. Ray and Jack become friends and want to play games such as checkers and hoopball, but they find it difficult to play fairly because Ray is giant size and Jack is average size. The text contains real-life math problems to help the two friends play their games fairly.

A fourth-grade teacher may find that the book fits her student's needs. Initially, she would preview and practice reading the book so she is familiar with it, and to select any vocabulary or story elements she would like to highlight. The teacher would set the purpose by stating the performance standard that the lesson would highlight for the goals and strategies that she would expect the students to learn. The teacher would then model phrased, fluent reading and stop at particular points throughout the book for discussion related to the standards or students' needs. The read-aloud would be followed by additional, supportive reading or writing or content-area work. In this case, the teacher may pause at points in the book where Ray and Jack encounter a math problem, and have her students solve the problem using the book to check their answers when finished. Interactive read-alouds allow the students to become active participants. *The Seasons of Arnold's Apple Tree*, by Gail Gibbons (1988), gives young learners the opportunity to engage in meaningful discussions. Students may benefit from opportunities to turn and talk to a partner during key moments of an interactive read-aloud to share interpretations, make connections, and increase comprehension.

Writing Genres

As students engage in the writing process during writing workshop or other activities, they need to think about the purpose of their writing. The purpose influences the form that the writer will take. Is the student writing to inform, persuade, or entertain? Teaching the writing genres and scaffolding the genres with students leads to better comprehension and deeper levels of understanding. Students will organize the writing differently and vary the elaboration and details depending on the genre.

The most common writing genres are commonly found in state standards and state and district writing assessments. They are narrative writing, persuasive writing, expository writing, descriptive writing, and response to literature. This chapter explains the different types of writing genres and gives practical teaching ideas for instruction in each genre.

Narrative Writing in Grades K–5

"Miss Delacruz, I have to tell you about my weekend and what happened to my arm," Cody excitedly stated. As Stacy Delacruz turned to acknowledge Cody as he entered her classroom, she saw his little, second-grade arm in a huge cast. She was curious about what happened, so she stated, "Hold that story for writer's workshop today, and I can't wait to hear all about it!"

Each child has a story. It may be a small moment story, like the accident story Cody was about to tell, or a larger story that entails adventures from a summer vacation. Narrative writing involves telling a story while engaging the audience so that they learn from the experience. Creating a mini flip book of writing ideas or a class chart of everyday topics are ways to encourage students to think about their true-life stories.

While the events in a narrative are grounded in a student's life, they also need to incorporate aspects of characters and the plot. Examining picture book narratives and dissecting them by doing a deconstruction of text (Stead, 2005) will help students understand these important story elements. For example, students listen to the story *The Carrot Seed*, by Ruth Krauss (1945), in an interactive read-aloud. As the teacher reads, the students can deconstruct the text by placing the story elements in a story map. In this minimal tale, everyone tells a little boy that his seed will never sprout. The little boy perseveres by watering and tending the seed each day until the seed grows into a large carrot.

Figure 8.1 presents a sample deconstruction of *The Carrot Seed*:

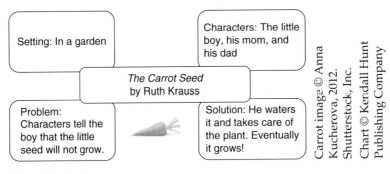

FIGURE 8.1

Children transfer their learning into their own narratives when a teacher gives them a story map and gives them the opportunity to construct and prewrite a story. Perhaps it is a personal narrative about their own seed given to them in science class.

Persuasive Writing

Persuasive writing is another writing genre taught in K–5. This type of writing convinces the audience to take a particular side to an issue. A creative way to begin a lesson on persuasive writing is to hand each student an Oreo cookie (pending they don't have any allergies to the cookie). Then ask the students to state what they think an Oreo has to do with persuasive writing. They may give reasons such as, "I have to persuade you why you should let me eat this cookie!" and "The Oreo has layers like in persuasive writing." Both of these statements are closely related, and the Oreo stands for the following acronym:

O – Opinion (Your opinion on the topic)
R – Reasons (Give at least three reasons why you feel the way you do)
E – Explain (After each reason, explain with supporting details why the audience should feel the same way)
O – Opinion Restated (Close your persuasive essay with your opinion restated to keep it fresh in the mind of the reader)

Mentor texts that try to persuade the reader are keys for modeling this trait. *Time For Kids: Plants!* by Brenda Iasevoli (2006), discusses various types of plants. After reading this book during an interactive read-aloud, teachers could use the sites listed below during workstations or computer lab time. Students would research their favorite plants and discuss their opinions (why certain ones are their favorites), their reasons (color, size, location, helpfulness), and explanations.

BOX 8.1

PLANT RESOURCES ON THE WEB

Chomp! Meat-Eating Plants
http://kids.nationalgeographic.com/kids/stories/animalsnature/meat-eating-plants/

Desert Plants
www.mbgnet.net/sets/desert/

Flowers in Bloom
http://kids.nationalgeographic.com/kids/photos/flowers-in-bloom/

Plant Videos
www.neok12.com/Plants.htm

Expository Writing

Nonfiction writing designed to explain and describe understanding of a subject is called **expository writing**. Technology skills can be easily integrated into expository writing. In the fall when pumpkins were readily available, Stacy Delacruz read *The Pumpkin Book*, by Gail Gibbons (2004), to her second-grade students. This book describes how a pumpkin grows from a seed planted in the ground. Near the end of the text there is a page titled, "How to Carve a Jack-O-Lantern." Stacy Delacruz asked her students what they noticed on this page. Some students noted the safety precautions and tools that were mentioned at the beginning of the page. Some students noticed the author's use of transitional phrases to describe each step in numerical order. Others noted that each step had a clear picture that matched.

Stacy Delacruz used this page from the mentor text to model the procedure for writing how to do a particular activity. The students brainstormed three possible topics they could write about. Stacy Delacruz explained that they should be an expert in the area they were to write about in order to teach their peers something new. The prewriting stage consisted of a think–pair–share with a partner to discuss their three possible ideas.

Then on a template adapted from Lucy Calkin's *The Art of Teaching Writing* (1994), the students started drawing the steps of how to do something. Her students were creative and thought of various subjects, such as how to throw a surprise party for your mother, how to make origami, and how to give your dog a bath. The prewriting continued as students sketched out pictures that showed their "how-to" topics.

Students started drafting their pieces as they looked at each picture and wrote succinct directions to go with each step. They referred to a transitional words list they had made during interactive writing to help them transition to each step. Once the drafting was done on the second day of the writing workshop, students traded with a peer editor.

Before peer editing began Stacy Delacruz brought in bread, peanut butter, and jelly. She showed students a draft that she had created, titled "How to Make a Peanut Butter and Jelly Sandwich." She explained that she would use her draft to act out how to make the sandwich. She asked her students to peer-edit her draft to see if they found anything confusing or any parts left out. Her students quickly noticed that she left out important details, including opening the lids to the jars.

After her main mini-lesson, students wrote directions for an activity. After reading the directions, each editor read and acted out (if at all possible) the steps of a student's direction. Part of the editing was to write down questions they had for a peer. Some found the directions difficult to follow because steps were missing. Once the editing and revisions were complete, students used their drafts to form final published versions. Students typed the steps in Microsoft Word. Then they copied and pasted the text into a book they made. Some students brought in photographs to include in their books, while others drew and colored pictures. Many websites provide materials and graphic organizers related to expository texts. For instance, highly beneficial resources can be accessed through *Scholastic.com*: *www.scholastic.com/teachers/lesson-plan/how-books*

Descriptive Writing

Descriptive writing gives students opportunities to use all of their senses to paint pictures with words. They may use imagery, similes, and metaphors to describe an experience or object. One of Stacy Delacruz's most memorable experiences with descriptive writing came during her student teaching experience in a first-grade classroom. The students were studying fall fruits and vegetables for the harvest season. In order to prepare students for a field trip to an apple orchard, the teacher and Stacy Delacruz read various apple-themed books and conducted experiments with apples.

For descriptive writing, they used the passage *The Little Red House with No Doors and No Windows and a Star Inside* adapted from a story by Carolina Sherwin Bailey. The story is meant to be read aloud to a class with an apple in hand for demonstration. The teacher began by telling the story, and when she read about the mother cutting the apple, she cut an apple, revealing the star (that the seeds make) inside the apple.

It was quite a surprise for the first graders to see the star inside the apple. The teacher left the halves with the apple star on a table for the students to use as they wrote a descriptive piece. The students were allowed to taste, touch, and smell the apple. A sense chart graphic organizer from *www.eduplace.com* was used for students to record their data. After the prewriting took place, the students drew the apple star in their science journals and wrote a descriptive piece about apples.

Response to Literature

Making connections to a piece of literature being read is at the heart of the response to literature genre. This form of writing occurs when the author examines the elements of a text (characters, theme, plot, rising action, climax, falling action) and reacts to the main points. It is important to note that a response to literature is not a retelling or plot summary of an entire story.

A prime example of a response to literature occurred after a first-grade class read *The Seasons of Arnold's Apple Tree*, by Gail Gibbons (1988). Throughout the interactive read-aloud, the teacher stopped to prompt discussion. This book highlights the different seasons and the activities Arnold does by his tree during each season. For example, during Halloween night, Arnold picks apples and carves faces on them. The book can be a mentor text for modeling how to write recipes, since the book includes an apple pie recipe. Students can keep a science journal to draw and predict what their seeds may grow into and what the plants may look like in each season.

After the text was read, students dispersed into learning stations. At one learning station, the students folded a 12 × 18-inch sheet of construction paper into four sections, one fold horizontally and one vertically, as indicated in Figure 8.2.

© Kendall Hunt Publishing Company

FIGURE 8.2 Response to Literature: Art Learning Station

At the art learning station, students responded to the text by labeling and drawing what each tree would look like during each season of the year. The summer tree would be covered with apples, the fall tree with colored leaves, the winter tree with snow, and the spring tree with flower buds. Students would use cotton swabs and finger paints to dab the right amount of paint onto each tree.

At the writing learning station, students completed a written response to literature by explaining which season they felt Arnold liked best, supporting their responses with details from the text. Then the students described their favorite season and explained their choices. Students could use text-to-text, text-to-self, or text-to-world connections to describe their response to the text. Dr. Stacy Delacruz, who is now an Assistant Professor at Kennesaw State University in Kennesaw, Georgia, shares these ideas and many more with her university students.

These ideas are just a few of the ways writing genres can be taught using mentor texts, and there are many other resources available to teach the genres. Classroom resources are readily available with ideas for sharing anchor and exemplary papers written in each of the genres. RubiStar is a free website that allows teachers to create or use premade rubrics (*www.rubistar.4teachers.org*). After creating a genre rubric or finding one that identifies the key traits of each genre, teachers may want to introduce the rubric to the students by sharing anchor papers with them. An anchor paper is a paper that demonstrates a specific score from the rubric. These anchor papers may include exemplars that demonstrate the highest rating as well as papers with below-average or average ratings. Before sharing any anchor or exemplar paper with students, it is important to ask the student for permission and white-out any identifying factors. It is also a good idea to use papers from past students so that the students in your class do not try to guess whose paper it may be. Anchor papers and exemplars with writing rubrics are assessment pieces that help guide students' writing. They also help students identify the traits and key qualities of each genre of writing.

Writing experiences are engaging and creative when teachers implement the various writing genres in the classroom. These websites provide appropriate mentor texts or mini-lessons for each genre:

http://writingfix.com/genres/informative.htm — Expository Writing Lessons and Mentor Texts
http://teacher.scholastic.com/activities/writing/index.asp?topic=Persuasive — Persuasive Writing
http://teacher.scholastic.com/writewit/diary/ — Descriptive Writing with Virginia Hamilton
http://writingfix.com/genres/narrative.htm — Narrative Writing

Designing an Effective Writing Workshop Experience

We have emphasized the importance of helping elementary students to develop literacy skills and become **strategic learners** who transfer these skills and strategies during real reading and writing experiences. Effective writing workshop opportunities help students to develop the ability to use word recognition and comprehension strategies independently and collaboratively. Steps of the writing process are (1) brainstorming, (2) drafting, (3) revising and conferencing, (4) editing, and (5) publishing. It is important to appreciate that students are often at different stages in the writing process. It is important for students to feel a sense of flexibility and freedom as they are writing.

Lucy Calkins (1994, 2002) has written numerous books about writer's workshop to help teachers motivate and guide students as they write. Writing workshop is a time when students write individually or collaboratively about topics of interest. The teacher facilitates the writing sessions with modeling and develops a community of motivated writers. The key components of the writing workshop, suggested by Calkins (1994), include:

1. **Starting Components** — The teacher shares a read-aloud and mini writing lesson with shared reading (5–10 minutes).
2. **Writing and Conferencing** — The teacher shares additional strategy mini-lessonwhile conferencing with students (20 minutes).
3. **Small-Group Peer Conferences** — Students provide feedback and plan mini-conferences for each other to discuss their writing (20 minutes).
4. **Sharing Sessions** — Students sit in the Author's Chair to share their work and discuss suggestions for editing and revision with their peers (10 minutes).
5. **Writing Celebrations** — Students celebrate their success during weekly publication celebrations that may be audiotaped or videotaped at the end of a grading period.

Calkins suggests guiding questions for mini-lessons, such as:

- What did we learn in our last mini-lesson?
- How is your writing like a favorite author's writing?
- What do you do when you are unsure of how to end your writing?
- How can we share and help others when we are conferencing without distracting them from their writing?

As Lucy Calkins stated, "Our job in a writing conference is to put ourselves out of a job . . . they learn how to interact with their own developing drafts" (1994, p. 229). Mini-lessons and conferencing sessions motivate students to become confident, independent writers.

Media Literacy Knowledge

Technology often enhances the writing experience and provides new opportunities to extend students' understanding of curriculum content. Technology can empower a teacher to take students on a field trip well beyond the scope of an ordinary classroom. The technology of YouTube and similar resources gives students a shared experience that builds a sense of community.

Multimedia is an excellent resource to extend background knowledge across the curriculum. Technology implemented in a diverse social constructivist classroom promotes critical thinking, increased knowledge of content, and opportunities for student self-assessment of literacy learning (Palinscar, 1998; Wilson, 1995). Media and various forms of technology support language and content learning as learners gather, discuss, and disseminate information through the Internet (Egbert, Paulus, & Nakamichi, 2002; Reinking, 1997) Encourage use of who, what, where, when and why questions for higher-level thinking. The questions below may be included on a bookmark during self-selected reading and writing online to help students transfer the questioning strategy. Students may find it beneficial to ask themselves or a partner these questions in order to help comprehend what they read in an online text:

1. What was your favorite part of the story?
2. Could the main character have made other choices?
3. How would the story be different in another setting, such as another country?
4. What do you think will happen next?
5. Who would like this story?
6. What was the purpose of this story?
7. Would the impact of the story change if there were no illustrations?
8. What are your feelings about . . .?

Technology Enhances a Balanced Literacy Program

Thematic connections to Internet content can be used to help students enjoy learning and develop literacy skills through themed lessons (i.e., multilayered activities that relate to literature and topics related to the curriculum as units of learning). Students are motivated to read by experiencing talking books (i.e., digital versions of stories that use multimedia for animation, music, and highlighted text and model fluent reading, etc.). Software such as Kid Pix Studio or Wikis can also be used to illustrate stories and encourage inventive and accurate spellings of words during writing experiences. Students learn a great deal from guided Internet inquiry projects.

Effective teachers help students use appropriate literacy strategies to gain meaning from multimedia resources during inquiry learning. According to Coiro and Dobler (2007), strategies for reading and writing involving multimedia include: planning, predicting, monitoring, and evaluating the content area information. The information learned can be added to a graphic organizer to help students discuss, write, and discover diverse cultural understandings about what they learned from the Internet sources.

In order to enhance the discussion of videos during content area learning, teachers can teach students the strategy of Stop, Think, and React (Harvey & Goudvis, 2007) to increase comprehension and cultural awareness. For example, during a video the students take notes using a graphic organizer for main ideas, important details, predictions, and/or personal connections. The teacher stops the video when appropriate and asks students to share their notes and discuss the information learned with a partner. The interactions help students develop critical literacy by extending and reconstructing their thinking as they react to each others' responses.

Internet Inquiry Projects

Internet inquiry projects can increase letter-sound knowledge, phonemic awareness, and concepts of print. For example, teach children how to surf the Internet to find pictures of objects that demonstrate the targeted beginning sounds of words, as in the following example:

- **First, model and bookmark a selected website, such as** *www.learningplanet.com.*
- **Second, select online alphabet books.** Find a selection that demonstrates how the children can choose a letter of the alphabet to make the letter and an animal appear that begins with the letter-sound (i.e., select *m* and a monkey appears on the computer screen).
- **Third,** have the children **practice** how to select letter-sounds for the pictures on the Internet website.
- **Fourth, model** how to select three letters and three animals from the website to **draw and write a story** on the computer, Smart board, or chart paper.
- **Fifth,** have the **children select** three animals of their choice from the website. Tell the children to select three letters and their related animals and draw a story about the animals. They should also feel comfortable using invented spelling to write a story in a book format about the three animals and underline the beginning letters.
- **Finally, display** the books plus animal trade books in the classroom for students to learn more about the animals. The students should find their animals and share what they learn with classmates. In addition, **bookmark** animal **websites** for a center activity to help students increase their knowledge and discuss animals of interest. The children and teacher can create an animal **word wall** and a **KWL chart** to share information. Children should dramatize the actions of the animals and wear their animal's letter on their backs. Then other students will have the opportunity to guess their animal.

Image © Aaron Amat, 2012.
Shutterstock, Inc.

One important key to success is
self-confidence. An important key to
self-confidence is preparation.
—Arthur Ashe

Graphic Organizers

During the lesson-planning process graphic organizers help students to communicate ideas effectively, and they provide frameworks for capturing significant ideas. Effective communication is highly valuable and it is closely linked with the level of student achievement. Many of the activities for effective reading and writing in this textbook can be used with various ages. The Key and Vault graphic organizers in Appendix B provide a framework for capturing those treasured moments and writing persuasively. These Key and Vault graphic organizers were created by David W. Anderson as he collaborated with his team to enhance the quality of students' persuasive writing. As the English Department Chair at Canton McKinley Senior High School, he discovered that these graphic organizers helped students to organize their thoughts and present ideas effectively.

Inspiring Reading and Writing through Culturally Responsive Literature

Culturally responsive classrooms are like flourishing gardens with different varieties of flowers. Culturally and linguistically responsive teaching links content to the cultural backgrounds of students. Instruction is designed to overcome biases and stereotypes that students and teachers might bring from home to the classroom. The use of accurate cultural literature promotes cultural integrity, reduces prejudices, and provides a rich classroom environment with equal opportunities and literacy goals for all students (Au & Kawakami, 1994). As students become aware of their peers' cultural backgrounds, they build on their combined experiences and appreciate each other. Culturally responsive literature depicts the accurate representation of cultures and builds awareness, acceptance, caring, and responsive teaching and learning. It provides a framework for social justice and equality for all students and teachers. Yokota (2009, p. 67) provides guidelines for selecting culturally responsive literature:

- Do the author and illustrator present authentic perspectives?
- Is the culture portrayed multidimensionally?
- Are cultural details naturally integrated?
- Are details accurate and is the interpretation current?
- Is language used authentically?
- Is the collection balanced (with representation from a wide variety of cultures)?

A Balanced Literacy Program

A balanced literacy program synthesizes all of the components of literacy instruction. This makes the classroom like a lovely garden with many types of students who appreciate many perspectives as they satisfy their curiosity and explore multiple literacies. Figure 8.3 presents the components of a balanced classroom with culturally responsive instruction. A balanced literacy program acts like a trellis as teachers provide scaffolding, using culturally and linguistically responsive instruction. This helps students to thrive as they explore their connections with literature through an integrated curriculum.

Balanced Literacy in the Classroom

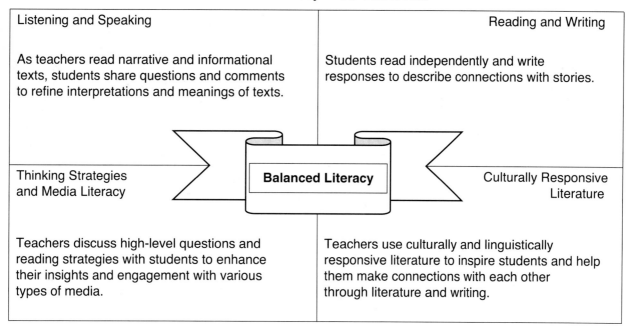

FIGURE 8.3 Balanced Literacy in the Classroom

APPENDICES

Appendices of this book provide additional resources for scaffolding and creative literacy instruction for individuals, small groups, and the whole class.

APPENDIX A

The Underwater Adventures of James and Natalie

by Elaine Roberts and Gary Wenzel

Create stories in a book format using this text describing James and Natalie's adventures. Children may enjoy opportunities to illustrate the stories and chant the repetitive patterns.

Predictable and Repetitive Patterns in Stories

Page 1 — A baby goldfish was born on September fifth. His mother called him James. He had gold and black scales.

Page 2 — James learned how to glide and hide under the ocean waves. He was happy swimming with his mother.

Page 3 — As James grew older, he knew he wanted to find a friend. He looked and looked.

Page 4 — He saw starfish, perch, sailfish, and sea horses.

Page 5 — He knew he wanted to find another goldfish to be his friend. He looked and looked as he glided through the water.

Page 6 — Suddenly, he saw a goldfish hiding and gliding behind the coral reef. James glided over to the goldfish. The goldfish smiled and said, "My name is Natalie." Then she swam away.

Page 7 — James was very sad because he wanted Natalie to stay and play.

Page 8 — That night James had a dream that Natalie became his friend.

Key Words

hide (glide)
play (stay)
fish (goldfish, starfish, sailfish)

James Searches for Natalie

Page 1 — James, the goldfish, glided to the place where he had seen Natalie, another goldfish, hiding in the coral reef.

Page 2 — When he looked behind the coral reef, a scary Mo<u>ray</u> Eel sn<u>app</u>ed and wr<u>app</u>ed its body around James!

Page 3 — James tried to swim away. The eel said, "Don't go aw<u>ay</u>. St<u>ay</u> and pl<u>ay</u>." My name is Mo<u>ray</u>.

Page 4 — James and Moray became friends and played hide and seek all d<u>ay</u>.

Page 5 — James told Moray that he was looking for a goldfish to be his friend, not an eel. Mo<u>ray</u> said, "I want to be your friend, too."

Page 6 — James said, "I will be you friend, but I also want to find Natalie again. We can all be friends. Please help me find her." Mo<u>ray</u> and James looked for Natalie.

Page 7 — During their search they saw a big, flat Manta R<u>ay</u> gliding in the water above them. The Manta R<u>ay</u> dived down after them. They were afraid of the Manta R<u>ay</u>!

Page 8 — When they tried to swim aw<u>ay</u>, the Manta R<u>ay</u> said, "My name is R<u>ay</u>. Stay and pl<u>ay</u>."

Page 9 — They played and played all day.

Page 10 — James said to Ray and Moray, "Let's find Natalie." They all glided back to the coral reef.

Page 11 — A large, gray fish started swimming after them. They tried to hide behind the coral reef, but the big gray, shark saw them!

Page 12 — The shark swam quickly after them.

Page 13 — Suddenly, a small goldfish swam out and said, "Get aw<u>ay</u>, unless you want to pl<u>ay</u>."

Page 14 — The shark stopped and said, "My name is G<u>ray</u>. Can I st<u>ay</u> and pl<u>ay</u>?" The little goldfish smiled and said, "My name is Natalie." Then she smiled and swam aw<u>ay</u>.

Key Words

play (day, away, Ray, Moray, Gray)

sn<u>ap</u> (snapped, wrapped)

The Fish and the Magic Dish

Page 1 — James, the goldf<u>ish</u>, found a magic d<u>ish</u>.

Page 2 — He made a w<u>ish</u> and rubbed the magic dish.

Page 3 — Sw<u>ish</u>, Sw<u>ish</u>!

Page 4 — James, the goldf<u>ish</u>, said, "I w<u>ish</u> I could find my friend Natalie."

Page 5 — Sw<u>ish</u>, Sw<u>ish</u>!

Page 6 — The f<u>ish</u> got his w<u>ish</u>.

Page 7 — The magic d<u>ish</u> turned into another goldf<u>ish</u>!

Key Words in the story (The spelling patterns are initially underlined)
d<u>ish</u> (f<u>ish</u>, sw<u>ish</u>, w<u>ish</u>)

The Gold Fish and His New Friend

Page 1 — James, the goldfish, had a new friend because of his wish.

Page 2 — "What's your name?" asked the goldfish.

Page 3 — "C<u>all</u> me Natalie," said the new friend.

Page 4 — "What's your <u>name</u>?" asked Natalie.

Page 5 — "C<u>all</u> me <u>James</u>," he said as he moved swish, swish!

Page 6 — "Our <u>names</u> are not the <u>same</u>," said Natalie as she moved swish, swish!

Page 7 — They played water <u>games</u> with a b<u>all</u> and were happy. James had his wish!

Key Words

Review of "dish" for 'ish' spelling patterns

New Key Words: <u>name</u> (same, game(s)), <u>James</u>; b<u>all</u> (c<u>all</u>)

The Adventures of James and Natalie

Page 1 — James and Natalie became good friends.

Page 2 — Each day they played and played in the ocean.

Page 3 — One day they decided to play with a <u>jell</u>yfish that had come to the top of the water to find food.

Page 4 — James and Natalie looked at the <u>jell</u>yfish.

Page 5 — Natalie asked the <u>jell</u>yfish, "Are you <u>jell</u>y or a fish?"

Page 6 — The <u>jell</u>yfish laughed and said, "I am not <u>jell</u>y or a fish!"

Page 7 — "I am in the family of sea anemones and coral."

Page 8 — "I do not have a heart, blood, brain, or gills."

Page 9 — Natalie said to James, "<u>Jell</u>yfish like to eat small animals and other <u>jell</u>yfish!"

Page 10 — James said, "Don't get too close to the b<u>elly</u> of the <u>jell</u>yfish because it will sting you!"

Page 11 — James and Natalie laughed when they saw two tiny crabs hiding under the <u>jell</u>yfish. The crabs were not worried about getting stung!

Page 12 — James and Natalie saw a large turtle coming down the beach. They were worried that the turtle was going to eat the <u>jell</u>yfish!

Page 13 — James and Natalie made loud swish, swish sounds, and the turtle went away.

Page 14 — James and Natalie were happy. They saved the <u>jell</u>yfish that day!

Key Words

Review of <u>fish</u> (sw<u>ish</u>)

d<u>ay</u> (pl<u>ay</u>, pl<u>ay</u>(ed), aw<u>ay</u>); <u>jell</u> (b<u>ell</u>); <u>beach</u> (<u>each</u>)

Visit *http://nationalgeographic.com* **for a virtual fish bowl. You can add fish and create stories.**

APPENDIX B

Key and Vault Graphic Organizers Saving Treasured Ideas for Effective Persuasive Writing

David W. Anderson

The Key and Vault is a graphic organizer that will help students of various ages to capture what is most important as they engage in persuasive writing. Noting that the students were demonstrating difficulty in successfully responding to two-point and four-point persuasive writing response items, particularly by providing supporting statements but no clear answer, our team developed the Key and Vault graphic organizer as a visual metaphor to help the students recognize and develop the two interdependent components of a satisfactory answer that included the most significant components for persuasion.

The steps to the Key and Vault graphic organizer begin with the most significant ideas. The answer is the first step in the process of responding. It is the key without which there is no access to the reasoning that is the true value of the response. As students repeatedly responded to questions and prompts in this format, they demonstrated improved ability to completely structure satisfactory responses to two-point and four-point comprehension assessments for persuasive writing. Once students learn to use this format for effective persuasive writing, it can be replaced with a foldable to eliminate copying costs.

We subsequently modified the format to allow for recognizing gradations of quality in both response and supporting statements, focusing primarily upon eliminating equivocal responses and redundant supporting statements. The Key and Vault has proven so accessible to our students that we often see them sketch in the "key" around their responses when pre-writing before composing their actual response on standardized tests. Appendix B includes Key and Vault graphic organizers for various age levels:

- A Two-Point Key and Vault Graphic Organizer — This is more appropriate for young children.
- A Key and Vault Graphic Organizer for the Best Season — This four-point graphic organizer may be used for a variety of topics in the intermediate grades and beyond.

- Key and Vault Graphic Organizer for the Story "Marigolds" — This graphic organizer focuses on key points for a persuasive paper about the story "Marigolds."

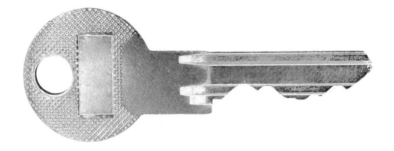

Name: _____

Group: _____ Date: _____

Question/Prompt:

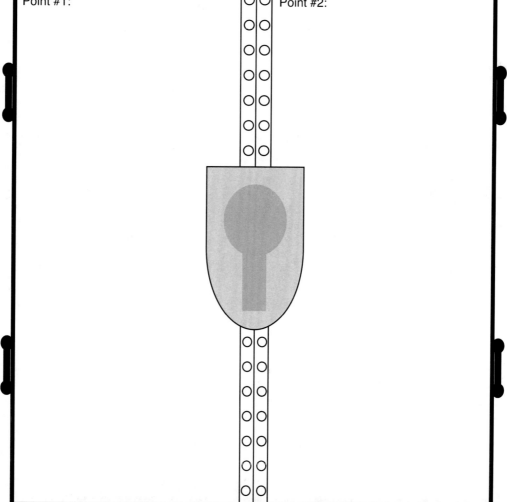

Answer the question/
respond to the prompt
to unlock your score.
Make sure to include
all the *key* words from
the question/prompt
in your answer.

Supporting Arguments

Point #1:

Point #2:

Name: _____

Group: _____ Date: _____

Question: What is the best season: summer, autumn, winter, or spring?

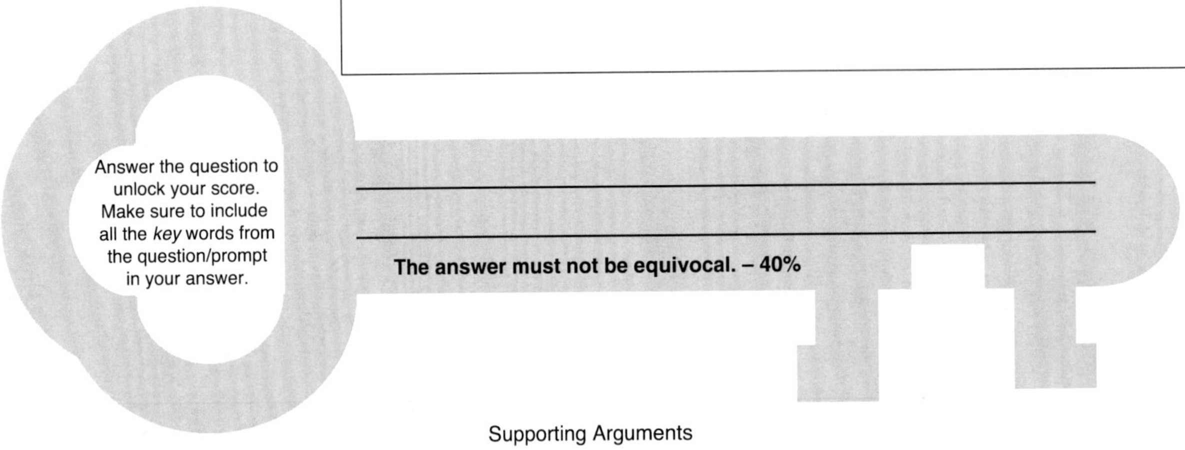

Answer the question to unlock your score. Make sure to include all the *key* words from the question/prompt in your answer.

The answer must not be equivocal. – 40%

Supporting Arguments

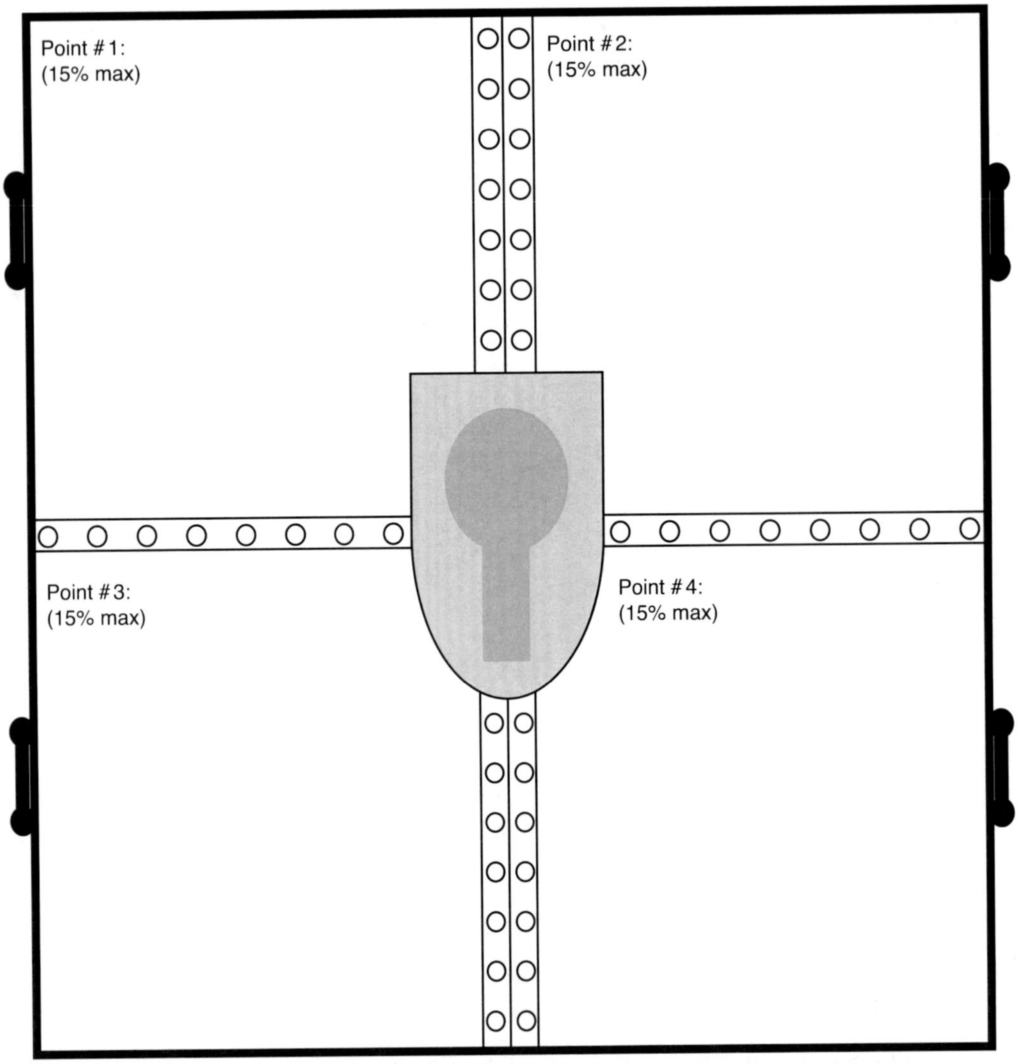

Point #1:
(15% max)

Point #2:
(15% max)

Point #3:
(15% max)

Point #4:
(15% max)

Name: _____

Group: _____ Date: _____

Prompt: Identify the major issue that influences life in the story "Marigolds," and cite four examples of behavior that result from it.

Respond to the prompt to unlock your score.

The major issue that influences life in the story "Marigolds" is poverty.

Supporting Arguments

Point #1:

If it weren't for poverty, the girl's father wouldn't cry in the middle of the night.

Point #2:

If the girl's father hadn't been crying about their poverty in the middle of the night, she wouldn't have left the house.

Point #3:

If the girl hadn't left the house because her father was crying over their poverty, she wouldn't have ruined her neighbor's garden.

Point #4:

If it weren't for poverty, all the children wouldn't be bored, with nothing to do, and causing a ruckus.

REFERENCES

Adams, M.J. (1990). *Beginning to read: thinking and learning about print.* Cambridge. MA: MIT Press.

Afflerbach, P., Pearson, D., & Paris, S. G. (2008). Clarifying the differences between reading skills and reading strategies. *The Reading Teacher, 61*(5), 364–373.

Allington, R. (2003). The schools we have, the schools we need. Retrieved September 11, 2003, from http://cela.albany.edu/schools/rtinvite.html.

Allington, R.L. & McGill-Frazen, A. (1994). Reading and the mildly handicapped. *International Encyclopedia of Education*, Oxford, U.K.: Pergamon.

Allington, R., & Johnston, P. H. (2001). What do we know about effective fourth-grade teachers and their classrooms? In C.M. Roller (Ed.), *Learning to teach reading: Setting the research agenda* (pp. 150–165). Newark, DE: International Reading Association.

Allington, R. L., & Johnston, P. H. (Eds.). (2002). *Reading to learn: Lessons from exemplary 4th grade classrooms.* New York, NY: Guilford.

Alvermann, D. E. (2002). Effective literacy instruction for adolescents. *Journal of Literacy Research, 34*(2), 189–208. Retrieved from http://www.coe.uga.edu/reading/faculty/alvermann/effective2.pdf

Armstrong, Steven W. (1983). "The effects of material difficulty upon learning disabled children's oral reading and reading comprehension." *Learning Disability Quarterly* 6, 339–348.

Aronoff, M. (1994). Morphology. In Purves, C.A., Papa, L., Jordan, S. (Eds.). *Encyclopedia of English Studies in Language Arts, 2,* 820–821. New York, NY: Scholastic.

Au, K.H, & Kawakami, A.J. (1991). Culture and ownership: Schooling of minority students. *Childhood Education, 67,* 280–284.

Au, K. & Kawakami, A. (1994). Cultural congruence in instruction. In E. Hollins, J. King & W. Hayman (Eds.). *Teaching diverse populations: Formulating knowledge base* (pp.5–23). Albany, NY: State University of New York Press.

Au, K. & Raphael, T. (1998). Curriculum and teaching in literature-based programs. In T.E. Raphael & K. H. Au (Eds.), Literature-based instruction: reshaping the curriculum (pp. 123–0148). Norwood, MA: Christopher-Gordon Publishers.

Au, K.H. (2001). Culturally responsive instruction as a dimension of new literacies. Reading Online, 5(1).

Ausabel, D.P. (1968). Educational psychology: a cognitive view. New York:Holt, Reinhart & Winston.

Barger, J. (2006). Building word consciousness. *The Reading Teacher.* 60(3), 279–281.

Baumann, J.F., Jones, L.A., & Seifert-Kessell, N. (1993). Using think alouds to enhance children's comprehension monitoring abilities. *The Reading Teacher, 47,* 184–193.

Bear, D., Invernizzi, M., Templeton, S., & Johnston, F. (2000). *Words their way: Word study for phonics, vocabulary, and spelling instruction.* Columbus, OH: Merrill Prentice Hall.

Beck, I.L. & McKeown, M.G. (1991). Conditions of Vocabulary Acquisition. In P.D. Pearson (Ed.), *The Handbook of Reading Research*: Vol. 2 (pp. 789–814). New York: Longman Press.

Beck, I., McKeown, M., & Kucan L. (2002, 2011). *Bringing words to life: Robust vocabulary instruction.* New York, NY: The Guildford Press.

Beck, I., McKeown, M., & Kucan L. (2008). *Creating robust vocabulary: Frequently asked questions & extended examples.* New York, NY: The Guildford Press.

Berne, J., & Blachowicz, C. (2008). What reading teachers say about vocabulary instruction: Voices from the classroom. *The Reading Teacher.* 62(4), 314–323.

Bender, W., & Larkin, M. (2004). *Reading strategies for elementary students with learning difficulties.* Thousand Oaks: CA. Corwin Press.

Biemiller, A., & Slonim, N. (2001). Estimating root word vocabulary growth in normative and advantaged populations: Evidence for a common sequence of vocabulary acquisition. *Journal of Educational Psychology, 93,* 498–520.

Blachman, B., Tangel, D., Ball, E., Black, R., & McGraw, D. (1999). Developing phonological awareness and word recognition skills: A two year intervention with low-income, inner-city children. *Reading and Writing: An Interdisciplinary Journal, 11,* 230–273.

Blachowicz, C., & Fisher, P. (2010). *Teaching vocabulary in all classrooms,* (4th ed.). New York, NY: Allyn & Bacon.

Block, C.C. (2004). *Teaching comprehension: The comprehension process approach.* Boston, MA: Allyn & Bacon.

Bornstein, H., & Saulnier, K. (1987). *Sign/Word Flash Cards,* Gallaudet University Press.

Brabham, E. G. & Villaume, S. K. (2002). Vocabulary instruction: Concerns and visions. *The Reading Teacher, 56,* 264.

Buckingam, B.R., Edward W Dolch, E.W., (1936). *A Combined Word List.* Boston, New York: Ginn and Co.

Block, C. (2004). *Teaching comprehension: The comprehension process approach.* Boston, MA: Allyn & Bacon.

Bloom B. S. (1956). *Taxonomy of Educational Objectives, Handbook I: The Cognitive Domain.* New York, NY: David McKay Co.

Bodrova, E., Leon, M. (2007) *Tools of the Mind: The Vygotskian Approach to Early Childhood Education,* 2/E. Boston, MA: Allyn & Bacon.

Bos, D.S., & Anders, P.L. (1990). Effects of interactive vocabulary instruction on the vocabulary learning and reading comprehension of junior high learning disabled students. *Learning Disability Quarterly, 13,* 31–42.

Bromley, K. (2007). Nine things every teacher should know about words and vocabulary instruction. *Journal of Adolescent & Adult Literacy.* 50(7), 528–537.

Brown, R., Pressley, M., Van Meter, P., & Schuder, T. (1996). A quasi-experimental validation of transactional strategies instruction with low-achieving second grade readers. *Journal of Educational Psychology, 88,* 18–37. doi:10.1037/0022-0663.88.1.18

Brown, A.L., Ambruster, B.B., & Baker, L. (1986). The role of metacognition in reading and studying. In J. Orasanu (Ed.), *Reading comprehension: From research to practice.* Hillsdale, NJ: Erlbaum.

Brozo, W.G., & Puckett, K. (2008). *Supporting content area literacy with technology: Meeting the needs of diverse learners.* Boston, MA: Allyn & Bacon.

Bruck, M. (1993). Components of spelling skills of college students with childhood diagnosis of dyslexia. *Learning Disability Quarterly, 16,* 171–184.

Bromley, K. (2007). Nine things every teacher should know about words and vocabulary instruction. *Journal of Adolescent & Adult Literacy, 50*(7), 528–537.

Calkins, L. (1994). *The art of teaching writing.* Portsmouth, NH: Heinemann.

Calkins, L. (2002). *A field guide to the classroom library: Level C grades 1–2.* Portsmouth, NH: Heinemann.

Carr, E., & Wixson, K. (1986). Guidelines for evaluating vocabulary instruction. *Journal of Reading, 29,* 588–595.

Celce-Murcia, M. (Ed.). (2001). *Teaching English as a second or foreign language* (3rd ed.). Boston, MA: Heinle & Heinle. (TESFL).

Chall, J.S. (1983). *Stages of reading development.* New York: McGraw-Hill.

Chi, M. T., Glaser, H.R., & Farr, M.J. (1988) *The nature of expertise.* Hillsdale, NJ: Erlbaum.

Clark, L.W., & Whitney, E. (2009). Walking in their shoes: Using multiple perspective texts as a bridge to critical literacy. *The Reading Teacher, 62,* 530–534.

Clay, M. (1979). *The early detection of reading difficulties.* Portsmouth, NH: Heinemann.

Clay, M. (1991). *Becoming literate: The construction of inner control.* Portsmouth, NH: Heinemann.

Clay. M. (1993). *Reading Recovery: A guidebook for teachers in training.* Portsmouth, NH: Heinemann.

Coady, J. (1994). Lexicon/vocabulary. In Purves, A. C., Papa, L., & Jordan, S. (Eds.), *Encyclopedia of English Studies and Language Arts, 2* (pp. 736–737). New York, NY: Scholastic.

Coiro, J., & Dobler, E. (2007). Exploring the online reading comprehension strategies used by sixth-grade skilled readers to search for and locate information on the Internet. *Reading Research Quarterly,* 214-257.

Condon, B., Laurence, M. (Executive Producers). (2009, February 22). The 81st Academy Awards. New York: American Broadcasting Company.

Conrad, N.K., Gong, Y., Sipp, L., & Wright, L. (2004). Using text talk as a gateway to culturally responsive teaching. *Early Childhood Education Journal, 31*(3), 187–192.

Cullinan, B. E. (2000). *Read to me: Raising kids who love to read.* New York, NY: Scholastic.

Cunningham, P.M., & Cunningham, J.W. (1992). Making words: Enhancing the invented spelling-decoding connection. *The Reading Teacher, 46,* 106.

Cunningham, P. M., & Allington, R. L. (1994, 1999, 2003). *Classrooms that work: They can all read and write* (3rd ed.). Boston, MA: Allyn & Bacon.

Cunningham, P., & Allington, R. (2010). *Classrooms that work: they can all read and write* (5th ed.). Boston, MA: Allyn & Bacon.

Cunningham, P., & Hall, D. (2007). *Making words.* Greensboro, NC: Carson-Dellosa.

Cunningham, P., Hall, D., & Segmon, C. (2008). *The teachers guide to the four blocks literacy model.* Four Blocks Publishers.

Cunningham, P. (2000). *Systematic Sequential Phonics They Use: Grades* 1–5. Greensboro, NC: Carson-Dellosa.

Cunningham, J. W. (1982). Generating interactions between schema and text. In J. A. Niles & and L. A. Harris (Eds.), *New inquiries in reading research and instruction* (pp. 42–47). Rochester, NY: National Reading Conference. Cunningham, A.E. 1990. Explicit versus implicit instruction in phonemic awareness. *Journal of Experimental Child Psychology* 50:429–444.

Curtis, M.E. 1980 Development of components of reading skill. *Journal of Educational Psychology* 72: 656–669.

Curtis, M. E., & Longo, A. M. (2001, November). Teaching vocabulary to adolescents to improve comprehension. *Reading Online.* Retrieved from http://www.readingonline.org/articles/curtis/

Cunningham, P. (1991). *Phonics they use: Words for reading and writing.* Boston, MA: Allyn & Bacon.

Dale, E. (1965). Vocabulary measurement: Techniques and major findings. *Elementary English, 42,* 895–901, 948.

Davidson, J. L., & Wilkerson, B. C. (1988). *Directed reading-thinking activities.* Monroe, NY: Trillium Press.

Deneger, S. C. (2009). Using literature to build home and school connections. In D. A. Wooten & B. E. Cullinan, *Children's literature in the reading program: An invitation to read* (pp. 156–165). Newark, DE: International Reading Association.

Dewitz, P., & Dewitz, K (2003). They can read the words, but they can't understand. Refining students' comprehension or reading. *The Reading Teacher, 56,* 422–435.

Dewitz, P., Jones, J., and Leahy, S. (2009). Comprehension strategy instruction in core reading programs. *Reading Research Quarterly, 44(* 2), 102–126

Duffelmeyer, F. A., Baum, D. D., & Merkley, D. J. (1987). Maximizing reader-text confrontation with an Extended Anticipation Guide. *Journal of Reading, 31,* 146–150.

Duffelmeyer, F. (2002). Alphabet activities on the Internet. *The Reading Teacher, 55(7),* 631–635.

Dole, J.A., Duffy, G.G., Roehler, L.R., & Pearson, P.D. (1991). *Moving from the Old to the New: Research on Reading Comprehension Instruction.* Review of Educational Research, 61, 239–264.

Dowhower, S.L. (1991). Speaking of prosody: Fluency's unattended bedfellow. *Theory to Practice, 30,* 158–164.

Duke, N. K. (2000). 3.6 minutes per day: The scarcity of informational texts in first grade. *Reading Research Quarterly, 35,* 202–224.

Duke, N., & Pearson, D. (2002). In *What Research has to say about reading,* (3rded.). Newark, DE: International Reading Association.

Duke, N. K., & Carlisle, J. F. (2011). The development of comprehension. In M. L. Kamil, P. D. Pearson, E. B. Moje, & P. Afflerbach (Eds.), *Handbook of Reading Research, Volume IV* (pp. 199–228). London, England: Routledge.

Duke, N. K., & Pearson, P. D. (2002). Effective practices for developing reading comprehension. In A. E. Farstrup & S. J. Samuels (Eds.), *What research has to say about reading instruction* (3rd ed., pp. 205–242). Newark, DE: International Reading Association.

Egbert, J., Paulus, T., & Nakamichi, Y. (2002). The impact of call instruction on classroom computer use: A foundation for rethinking teacher education. *Language Learning, & Teaching, 6(3),* 108–126.

Ehri, L. C. (1991)Learning to read and spell words. In L. Rieben & C. Perfetti (Eds.), *Learning to Read: Basic Research and its Implications* (pp. 57–73).

Ehri, L. (1992). Reconceptualizing the development of sight word reading and its relationship to recoding. In Gough, P., Ehri, L., and Treiman, R. (Eds.) *Reading Acquisition.* (pp.107–143), Hillsdale, NJ:Lawrence Erlbaum.

Ehri, L.C. (1995). Phases of development in learning to read by sight. *Journal of Research in Reading, 18,* 116–125.

Ehri, L.C. (1997). Learning to read and learning to spell are one and the same, almost. In C.A. Perfetti, L. Rieben, & M. Fayol (Eds.), *Learning to spell: Research, theory, and practice across languages* (pp. 237–269). Mawah, NJ: Erlbaum.

Ehri, L.C. (2002). Phases of acquisition in learning to read words and implications for teaching. *British Journal of Educational Psychology: Monograph Series, 1,* 7–28.

Ehri, L. (2004). Teaching phonemic awareness and phonics: An explanation of the national reading panel meta-analyses. In P. McCardle & V. Chhabra (Eds.), *The voice of evidence in reading research.* Baltimore, MD: Brookes Publishing Company.

Ehri, L., Nunes, S., Stahl, S., & Willows, D. (2001). Systematic phonics instruction helps students learn to read: Evidence from the National Reading Panel's meta-analysis. *Review of Educational Research, 71*, 393–447.

Ehri, L.C. and Robbins, C. (1992). Beginners need some decoding skill to read by Analogy. *Reading Research Quarterly, 27*, 13–26.

Ehri, L.C., Satlow, E., & Gaskins, I.W. (2009). Grapho-phonemic enrichment strengthens keyword analogy instruction for struggling young readers, *Reading and Writing Quarterly, 25*, 162–191.

Enciso, P. (1992). Creating the story world: A case study of a young reader's engagement strategies and stances. In J. Many & C. Cox (Eds.), *Reader Stance and Literary Understanding* (pp. 75–102). Norwood, NJ: Ablex.

Fielding, L., & Pearson, P.D. (1994). Reading comprehension: What works. *Educational Leadership, 51*(5), 62–68.

Fisher, D., Flood, J., Lapp, D., & Frey, N. (2004). Interactive read-alouds: Is there a common set of implementation practices? *Reading Teacher, 58*(1), 8–17.

Ford, M., & Opitz, M. (2011). Looking back to move forward with guided reading. *Reading Horizons, 50*(4), 225–240.

Fountas, I., & Pinnell, G.S. (1996). *Guided reading.* Portsmouth, NH: Heinemann.

Fountas, I., & Pinnell, G.S. (2001). *Guided reading videotapes.* Portsmouth, NH: Heinemann.

Fountas, I., & Pinnell, G.S. (2006). *Teaching for comprehension and fluency: Thinking, talking, and writing about reading, K-8.* Portsmouth, NH: Heinemann.

Fox, B. (2003). *Word identification strategies: Phonics from a new perspective* (3rd ed.). Upper Saddle River, NJ: Prentice Hall.

Fry, E.B., Kress, J.E. (1993). *The reading teacher book of lists* (3rd ed.). Englewood Cliffs, NJ: Prentice Hall.

Gaab, N., Tallal, P., Kim, H., Lakshminarayanan, K., Archie, J. J., Glover, G. H., & Gabrielli, J. D. E. (2005), Neural Correlates of Rapid Spectrotemporal Processing in Musicians and Nonmusicians. *Annals of the New York Academy of Sciences, 60*, 82–88. doi: 10.1196/annals.1360.

Gambrell, L.B., Palmer, B.M., Codling, R.M., & Mozzoni, S.A. (1996). Assessing motivation to read. *The Reading Teacher, 49*, 518–533.

Gaskins, I.W. (2005). *Success with struggling readers: The Benchmark School approach.* New York, NY: Guilford Press.

Gaskins, I. W. (1996). *Benchmark extended word identification program.* Media, Pennsylvania.

Gaskins, I.W., Anderson, R.C., Pressley, M., Cunicelli, E.A., & Satlow, E. (1993). Six teachers' dialogue during cognitive process instruction. *The Elementary School Journal, 93*, 277–304.

Gaskins, I., Ehri, L., Cress, C., O'Hara, C., & Donnelly, K. (1996–97). Procedures for word learning: Making discoveries about words. *The Reading Teacher, 50*(4), 312–327.

Gentry, R. (2004). *The science of spelling: the explicit specifics that make great reading and writers (and spellers!).* Portsmouth, NH: Hienemann.

Gersten, R., Fuchs, S.L., Williams, P.J., & Baker, S. (2001). Teaching reading comprehension strategies to students with learning disabilities: A review of research. *Review of Educational Research, 71*, 279–320.

Gillett, J., & Temple, C. (2000). Understanding reading problems: Assessment and instruction. (5th ed.). New York, NY: Longman.

Goodman, K. (1996). *On reading: A common sense look at the nature of language and the science of reading.* Portsmouth, NH: Heinemann.

Gough, P.B., Juel, C., and Griffith, P.L. (1992). Reading, spelling, and theorthographic cipher. In P.B. Gough, L.C. Ehri, and R. Treiman (Eds.), *Reading Acquisition*, (pp. 35–48). Hillsdale, NJ: Lawrence Erlbaum Associates.

Graves, M.F. (1986). Vocabulary learning and instruction. *Review of Research in Education, 13*, 91–128.

Graves, M. & Watts-Taffe, S. (2008). For the love of words: Fostering word consciousness in young readers. *The Reading Teacher.* 62(3), 185–193.

Graves, M., Juel, C., Graves, B., & Dewitz, P. (2011). *Teaching reading in the 21st century: Motivating all learners.* Boston, MA: Pearson.

Guerin, W., Labor, E. Morgan, Reesman, J., & Willingham, J. (1992, 2010). *A handbook of critical approaches to literature* (6th ed.), Oxford University Press.

Guthrie, J.T., Hoa, L., Wigfield, A., Tonks, S., Humenick, N., & Littles, E. (2007). Reading motivation and reading comprehension growth in the later elementary years. *Coontemporary Educational Psychology, 32*, 282–313.

Guthrie, J.T., & Wigfield, A. (2000). Engagement and motivation in reading. In M.L. Kamil, P.B. Mosenthal, P.D. Pearson, & R. Barr (Eds.), *Handbook of reading research Volume III* (pp. 403–422). New York, NY: Erlbaum.

Hancock, M. R. (2004). *Celebration of literature and response: Children, books, and teachers in k-8 classrooms* (2nd ed.). Upper Saddle River, NJ: Pearson/Merrill/Prentice Hall.

Harmon, J.M., Wood, K. D., Hedrick, W. B., Vintinner, J. & Willeford, T. W. (2009). Word walls: More than just writing on the walls. *The Journal of Adolescent and Adult Literacy.* 52(5), 398–408.

Harris, T.L., & Hodges, R.E. (1995). *The literacy dictionary: The vocabulary of reading and writing.* Newark, DE: International Reading Association.

Hart, B., & Risling, R. R. (1995). *Meaningful differences in the everday experiences of young American children.* Baltimore, MD: Brookes Publishing Co.

Harvey, S., and Goodvis, A. (2007). *Strategies that work: Teaching comprehension for understanding and engagement.* Portland, ME: Stenhouse Publishers.

Hoffman, J. (1987). Rethinking the role of oral reading. *Elementary School Journal, 87*, 367–373.

Huttenlocher, J., Vasilyeva, M., & Cymerman, E. (2002). Language input at home and at school: Relation to child syntax. *Cognitive Psychology, 45*, 337–374.

Hyerle, D. (1995). *Thinking maps: Tools for learning.* Corwin Press.

International Reading Association and National Association for the Education of Young Children, (1998). *Using multiple methods of beginning reading instruction. A Position Statement of the International Reading Association.* Newark, DE: International Reading Association

International Reading Association (2010). *Standards for Reading Professionals-Revised 2010.* Newark, DE: International Reading Association.

Ivey, G., Baumann, J.F., & Jarrard, D. (2000). Exploring literacy balance: Iterations in a second-grade and sixth-grade classroom. *Reading Research & Instruction, 39*, 291–309.

Jenkins, H. (2006). *Convergence Culture: Where Old and New Media Collide.* New York, NY: New York University.

Jitendra, A. K., Cole, C. L., Hoppes, M. K., & Wilson, B. (1998). Effects of a direct instruction main idea summarization program and self-monitoring on reading comprehension of middle school students with learning disabilities. *Reading & Writing Quarterly: Overcoming Learning Difficulties, 14*, 379–396.

Johns, J. (2008). *Basic Reading Inventory: Pre-Primer through Grade Twelve and Early Literacy Assessments.* Dubuque, IA: Kendall Hunt.

Johns, J., & Lenski, S. (2009). *Improving reading: Strategies and resources.* Dubuque, IA: Kendall Hunt.

Johnson, D.J., & Myklebust, H. R.(1967). *Learning disabilities: Educational principles and practices.* New York, NY: Grune & Stratton.

Johnson, B., & Lehnert, L. (1984). Learning Phonics Naturally: A Model for Instruction. *Reading Horizons, 24*(2), 90–98.

Juel, C., Minden-Cupp, C. (2000). Learning to read words: Linguistic units and instructional strategies. *Reading Research Quarterly, 35,* 458–492.

Juel, C., Hebard, H., Park-Haubner, J., & Moran, M. (2010). Reading through a disciplinary lens. *Educational Leadership, 67,* 13–17.

Karther, D. (2002). Fathers with low literacy and their young children. *Reading Teacher, 56*(2), 184–193.

Kear, D.J., Coffman, G.A., McKenna, M.C., & Ambrosio, A.L. (2000). Measuring attitude for writing: A new tool for teachers, *The Reading Teacher, 54*(1), 10–23.

Keene, E. (2007). The mosaic of thought: The power of comprehension strategy instruction. (2nd ed.). New York, NY: Heineman.

Klinger, J.K., Vaughn, S., & Schumm, J.S. (1998). Collaborative strategic reading during social studies in heterogeneous fourth-grade classrooms. *Elementary School Journal, 99,* 3–22.

Kozlow, M., & Bellamy, P. (2004). *Experimental study on the impact of the 6 + 1 trait writing model on student achievement in writing.* Portland, OR: Northwest Regional Educational Laboratory.

Kucer, S. (2005). *Dimensions of literacy: A conceptual base for teaching reading and writing in school settings.* Mahwah, NJ: Lawrence Erlbaum Associates.

Kuhn, M., & Stahl, S. (1998). Teaching children to learn word meanings from context: A synthesis and some questions. *Journal of Literacy Research, 30,* 119–138.

Kuhn, M.R. & Stahl, S. (2000). *Fluency: A review of developmental and remedial strategies.* Ann Arbor, MI: Center for the Improvement of Early Reading Achievement.

Lane, H.B., & Arriaza-Allen, S. (2010). The vocabulary-rich classroom: Modeling sophisticated word use to promote word consciousness and vocabulary growth. *The Reading Teacher 63*(5), 362–370.

Langer, J.A. (1981). *From theory to practice: A pre-reading plan, Journal of Reading, 25, 2,* 152–156.

Lemke, J.L. (2002). Discursive technologies and the social organization of meaning. *Folias Linguistica 35 (1–2):* 79–96.

Leslie, L., Caldwell, J. (2011). *Qualitative reading inventory-5.* New York, NY: Allyn & Bacon.

Leu, D.J., Jr. (2000). Our children's future: Changing the focus of literacy and literacy instruction. *ReadingTeacher, 53,* 424–429. Retrieved from www.readingonline.org/electronic/elec_index. asp?HREF=/electronic/rt/focus/index.htmlBack

Lipson, M., & Wixson, K. (1997). *Assessment and instruction of reading and writing disability: An interactive approach.* New York, NY: Addison-Wesley.

Lipson, M., & Wixson, K. (2009). *Assessment and instruction of reading and writing difficulties: An interactive approach* (4th ed.). Boston, MA: Allyn & Bacon.

Lundberg, I., Frost, J., & Petersen, O. (1988). Effects of extensive program for stimulating phonological awareness in preschool children. *Reading Research Quarterly, 23,* 263–284.

Mandeville, T. F. (1994). K-W-LA: Linking the affective and cognitive domains. *The Reading Teacher, 47*(8), 679–80.

Mason, J., Herman, P., & Au, K.H. (1991). Children's developing knowledge of words. In J. Flood, J. M. Jensen, D. Lapp, & J.R. Squire (Eds.), *Handbook of research on teaching the English language arts* (286–302). New York, NY: Macmillan Publishing Company.

McAndrews, S.L. (2008). *Diagnostic literacy assessment and instructional strategies: A literacy specialist's resource.* Newark, DE: International Reading Association.

McCrudden, M. T., Perkins, P. G., & Putney, L. G. (2005). Self-efficacy and interest in the use of reading strategies. *Journal of Research in Childhood Education, 20 (2).*

McIntyre, C.W. & Pickering, J.S. (1995). Clinical studies of multisensory structured language education. Dallas, TX: International Multisensory Structured Language Education Council.

McKenna, M.C., & Kear, D.J. (1990, May). Measuring attitude toward reading: A new tool for teachers. *The Reading Teacher, 43(8),* 626–639.

McKeown, M. G., Beck, I. L., Omanson, R. C., & Pople, M. T. (1985). Some effects of the nature and frequency of vocabulary instruction on the knowledge and use of words. *Reading Research Quarterly, 20,* 522–535.

McKnight, M.W. (2000). In B. J. Ehren & P. G. Gildroy (Eds.), *Basic principles in reading comprehension* [Online]. Lawrence, KS: The University of Kansas, Center for Research on Learning. Retrieved from Onlineacademy.org

Metsala,j., & Ehri, L. (1998), *Word recognition in beginning literacy.* Mahwah, NJ: Erlbaum.

Moats, L.C. (1994). The missing foundation in teacher education: Knowledge of the Structure of spoken and written language. *Annuals of Dyslexia, 44,* 81–101.

Moats, L. C., & Farrell, M. L. (1999). Multisensory instruction. In J. R. Birsh (Ed.), *Multisensory teaching of basic language skills* (pp. 1–17). Baltimore, MD: Paul H. Brookes Publishing.

Moats, L.C. (2000). *Speech to print: Language essentials for teachers.* Paul H. Brookes.

Montessori, M. (1912). *The Montessori Method by Maria Montessori* (1870–1952). Translated by Anne Everett George (1882). New York, NY: Frederick A. Stokes Company.

Morrow, L.M. (1993). *Literacy development in the early years: Helping children read and write* (2nd ed.). Boston, MA: Allyn & Bacon.

Moustafa, M. (1997). *Beyond traditional phonics.* Portsmouth, NH: Heinemann.

Nagy, W., Anderson, P.C., Schommer, M., Scott, J.A. & Stallman, A.C. (1989). Morphological families in the intentional lexicon. *Reading Research Quarterly, 24,* 262–282.

Nagy, W. E., Diakidoy, I. & Anderson, R. C. (1993). The acquisition of morphology: Learning the contribution of suffixes to the meanings of derivatives. *Journal of Reading Behavior, 25,* 155–170.

National Reading Panel (2000). Teaching children to read: An evidence based scientific literature on reading and its implications for reading instruction. Bethesda: MD. National Institute of Child Health and Human Development.

National Institute of Child Health and Human Development Research Program (1997). Washington, DC: U.S. Department of Health and Human Services.

Neuman, S.B. & Roskos, K. (1997) Literacy knowledge in practice: Contexts of participation for young writers and readers. *Reading Research Quarterly, 32,* 10–32

Neuman, S., Pikulski, J., & Roskos, K.(1998). Continuum of children's development. *Of Primary Interest, 5,* 4–12.

Nilsen, A.P., & Nilsen, D.L. (2003). Vocabulary development: Teaching vs. testing. *English Journal 92(3),* 31–37.

Nolan, C. (Director/Producer), Roven, D., Thomas, E. (Producers). (2008). *The Dark Knight* [Motion picture]. United States: Warner Brothers Pictures.

Ogle, D. & Carr, E. (1987). KWL-Plus: A strategy for comprehension and summarization. *Journal of Reading, 30,* 626–631.

O'Shaughnessy, T. E., & Swanson, H. L. (2000). A comparison of two reading interventions for children with reading disabilities. *Journal of Learning Disabilities, 33*, 257–277.

Páez, M. (2009). Predictors of English language proficiency among immigrant youth. *Bilingual Research Journal, 32*, 168–187.

Palincsar, A. S. & Brown, A. L. (1984). Reciprocal teaching of comprehension-fostering and comprehension-monitoring activities. *Cognition and Instruction, 1* (2), 117–175.

Palincsar, A.S. (1998). Keeping the metaphor of scaffolding fresh—A response to C. Addison Stone's "The metaphor of scaffolding: It's utility for the field of learning disabilities." *Journal of Learning Disabilities, 31*, 370–373.

Paris, S.G., Lipson, M.Y., & Wixson, K. (1983). Becoming a strategic reader. *Contemporary Educational Psychology, 8*, 293–316.

Perfetti, C.A. (1985). *Reading ability.* New York, NY: Oxford University Press.

Persky, H. R.,Daane, M.C., & Jim, Y. (with Davis, S., Jenkins, F., Liu, H., et al). (2003). *The nations report card: Writing 2002.* Washington, DC: U.S. Department of Education. National Center for Education Statistics. Retrieved from http://nces.ed.gov/nationsreportcard/pdf/main2002/2003529.pdf

Place, N.A. (2002). Policy in action: The influence of mandated early reading assessment on teachers' thinking and practice. In D.L. Schallert, C.M. Fairbanks, J. Worthy, B. Malock, & J.V. Hoffman (Eds.), *Fiftieth Yearbook of the National Reading Conference* (pp. 45–58). Oak Creek, WI: National Reading Conference.

Pearson, P., & Raphael, T. (1999). Toward an ecologically balanced literacy curriculum. In Linda Gambrell, et al (Eds.), *Best Practices in Literacy Instruction* (pp.22–45). New York, NY: Guilford.

Pollock, J., & Ford, S. (2009). *Improving student learning one principal at a time.* Alexandria, VA: Association for Supervision and Curriculum Development.

Pontecorvo, C. (1993). Developing literacy skills through cooperative computer use: Issues for learning and instruction. In Duffy, T, Lowyck, J., Jonassen, D. (Eds.), *Designing environments for constructive learning* (pp. 139–160). New York, NY: Springer.

Pressley, M. (1998). *Reading instruction that works: The case for balanced reading.* NY: Guilford Press.

Pressley, M. Brown, R., El-Dinary, P. & Afflerbach, P. (1995). The comprehension instruction that students need: Instruction fostering constructively responsive learning, *Learning Disabiltiy Research & Practice, 10*(4), 215–224.

Pressley, M. (2000). Comprehension Instruction: What makes sense now, what might make sense soon. In M.L. Kamil, P.B. Mosenthal, P.D. Pearson, & R. Barr (Eds.), *Handbook of reading research*, Volume III (pp. 545–561). Mahwah, NJ: Erlbaum.

Pressley, M., Johnson, C.J., Symons, S., McGoldrick, J.A., & Kurita, J.A. (1989). Strategies that improve children's memory and comprehension of text. *Elementary School Journal, 90*, 3–32.

Pressley, M., Allington, R. L., Wharton-McDonald, R., Block, L. C., & Morrow, L. (2001). *Learning to read: Lessons from exemplary first-grade classrooms.* New York, NY: Guilford.

Pressley, M., Gaskins, I. W., Solic, K., Collins, S. (2006). A portrait of Benchmark School: How a school produces high achievement in students who previously failed. *Journal of Educational Psychology, 98*(2), 282–306.

Puckett, K., Shea, C., & Hansen, C. (2100). Discourse + technology/collaborative learning=fraction success. *Journal of Curriculum and Instruction, 5*(1), 68–84.

Purcell-Gates, V., E. McIntyre, and P.A. Freppon. 1995. Learning written storybook language in school: A comparison of low-SES children in skills-based and whole language classrooms. *American Educational Research Journal, 32*(3), 659–685.

Rasinski, T. (1985). *Assessing Reading Fluency. Honolulu, HA:*Pacific Resources for Education and Learning. Retrieved from www.prel.org/programs/rel/rel.asp.

Rasinski, T., Padak, N. (2000). *From phonics to fluency: Effective teaching of decoding and reading fluency in the elementary school.* New York, NY: Longman.

Rasinski, T. V. (2003). *The Fluent Reader: Oral Reading Strategies for Building Word Recognition, Fluency, and Comprehension.* Jefferson City, MO: Scholastic Professional Books.

Raphael, T. (1986) Teaching Question Answer Relationships, Revisited. *The Reading Teacher. 39,* 6, 516–522.

Reinking, D. (1997). Me and my hypertext: A multiple digression analysis of technology and literacy (sic). *The Reading Teacher, 50,* 626–643.

Reinking, D., McKenna, M., Labbo, L., & Kieffer, R. (Eds.) (1997). *Handbook of literacy and technology: Transformations in a post-typographic world* (pp. 269–281). Hillsdale, NJ: Lawrence Erlbaum Associates.

Resnick, L.B. (2004). Shared cognition: Thinking as social practice. In L.B. Resnick, J.M. Levine and S.D. Teasley (eds.), *Perspectives on socially shared cognition* (pp. 1–20). Washington, DC: American Psychological Association.

Resnick, L., & Snow, C. (2009). *Speaking and listening for preschool through third grade.* Newark, DE: International Reading Association.

Rhodes, L. K., & Shanklin, N.L. (1993). *Windows into literacy: Assessing learners K-8.* Portsmouth, NH: Heinemann.

Robinson, A. (2001). *Word Smart: Building an educated vocabulary.* Peachland Books.

Rosenblatt, L.M. (1938). *Literature as Exploration.* New York, NY: Noble and Noble.

Rosenblatt, L. M. (1994). *The reader, the text, the poem: The transactional theory of literary work.* Carbondale, IL: Southern Illinois University Press.

Rosenblatt, L. M., & Karolides, N. (2005). Theory and practice: *An interview with Louise Rosenblatt. Making meaning with texts: Selected essays* (pp. xv–xxxiv). Portsmouth, NH: Heinemann.

Routman, R. (1991). *Invitations: Changing as teachers and learners K-12.* Portsmouth, NH: Heinemann.

Routman, R. (2005). *Writing essentials: Raising expectations and results while simplifying teaching.* Portsmouth, NH: Heinemann.

Samuels, S. J. (1997). The method of repeated readings. *The Reading Teacher, 32,* 403–408.

Samuels, S. J. (2002). Reading fluency: Its development and assessment. In A. E. Farstrup & S. J. Samuels (Eds.), *What research has to say about reading instruction* (3rd ed., pp. 166–183). Newark, DE: International Reading Association.

Sawyer, D. J. (1991). Inquiry into the nature and function of auditory segmenting abilities: In search of the roots of reading. In D.J. Sawyer & B.J. Fox (Eds.), *Phonological awareness in reading: The evolution of current perspectives* (pp. 97–126). New York, NY: Springer-Verlag.

Shanahan, T., Callison, K., Carriere, C., Duke, N. K., Pearson, P. D., Schatschneider, C., & Torgesen, J. (2010). *Improving reading comprehension in kindergarten through 3rd grade: A practice guide* (NCEE 2010–4038). Washington, DC: National Center for Education Evaluation and Regional Assistance, Institute of Education Sciences, U.S. Department of Education. Retrieved from http://ies.ed.gov/ncee/wwc/publications_reviews.aspx

Share, D.L., & Stanovich,K.E. (1995). Cognitive processes in early reading development: Accommodating individual difference into a model of acquisition. *Issues in Education: Contributions from Educational Psychology, 1,* 57.

Smith, M. (1999). *Multi-sensory Teaching System (MTS) for Reading, United Kingdom Edition,* adapted by Mike Johnson, Sylvia Phillips, and Lindsay Peer. Manchester, England: MTS Publications.

Smith, M.T., & Hogan, E.A. (1991). *MTA: Teaching a process for comprehension and composition.* Forney, TX: MTS Publications.

Snow, C. (2002). *The RAND Reading Study Group. Reading for understanding: toward an R&D program in reading,* Washington, DC: Office of Educational Research and Improvement. 1465, Science and Technology Policy Institute (Rand Corporation), United States. Office of Educational Research and Improvement.

Snow, C. E., Porche, M. V., Tabors, P., & Harris, S. (2007). *Is literacy enough? Pathways to academic success for adolescents.* Baltimore, MD: Paul H. Brookes Publishing Co.

Stahl, S. (1997). Words, words, words. *Illinois Reading Council Journal, 25, 1,* pp. 28–62.

Spandel, V. (2007). *Creating writers through 6-trait writing assessment and instruction* (5th ed.). Boston, MA: Pearson Education, Inc.

Stanovich, K. (1991). Word recognition; Changing perspectives. In R. Barr, M.L. Kamil, P. Mosenthal, & P. D. Pearson (Eds.), *Handbook of Reading Research, Volume 2* (pp. 418–452). New York, NY; Longman.

Stanovich, K. E. (1986). Matthew effects in reading: Some consequences of individual differences in the acquisition of literacy. *Reading Research Quarterly, 21,* 360–407.

Suarez-Orozco & Paez. (2002). Latinos in the 21st century. *Harvard Journal of Hispanic Policy, 14,* 49–76.

Tabors, P. O. & Páez, M. (2008). One child, two languages: A study guide for early childhood educators of children learning English as a second language. In P. O. Tabors, *One child two languages* (2nd ed., pp. 223–244). Baltimore, MD: Brookes Publishing.

Taylor, B. M., Pearson, P. D., Clark, K., & Walpole, S. (2000). Effective schools and accomplished teachers: Lessons about primary grade reading instruction in low-income schools. *Elementary School Journal, 101,* 121–165.

Tierney, R., & Pearson, P.D. (1984). Toward a composing model of reading. In J.M. Jenson (Ed.). *Composing and comprehending* (p. 33–45). Urbana, IL: National Council of Teachers of English.

Torgeson, J.K. (1998). Catch them before they fall: Identification and assessment to prevent reading failure in young children. American Educator, Spring/Summer. Retrieved from http://www.ldonline .org/ld_indepth/reading/torgeson_catchthem.html.

Torgeson, J., Wagner, R., Rashotte, C., Rose, E., Lindamood, P., Conway, T. (1999). Preventing reading failure in young children with phonological processing disabilities: Group and individual responses to instruction. *Journal of Educational Psychology, 91,* 579–593.

Turner, J., & Paris, S. G. (1995). How literacy tasks influence children's motivation for literacy. *The Reading Teacher, 48, 8,* 662–673.

Valencia, S., & Riddle-Buly, M. (2004). Behind test scores: What struggling readers really need. *The Reading Teacher, 57,* 520–531.

Villaaume, S., & Brabham, E. (2002). Comprehension instruction: Beyond strategies. *The Reading Teacher, 55, (7),* 672–75.

Vygotsky, L. S. (1978). *Mind in society: The development of higher psychological processes.* Cambridge, MA: Harvard University Press.

Vygotsky, L. (1986). *Thought and language.* Cambridge, MA: The MIT Press.

Wagner, R.K., Torgeson, J.K., Rashotte, C.A., Hecht, S.A., Barker, T.A., Burgess, S.R., Donahue, J., & Garon, T. (1997). Changing relations between phonological processing abilities and word-level reading as children develop from beginning to skilled readers: A 5-year longitudinal study, *Developmental Psychology, 33,* 468–479.

Wagner, R. K., Torgesen, J. K., Laughon, P., Simmons, K., & Rashotte, C. A. (1993). Development of young readers' phonological processing abilities. *Journal of Educational Psychology, 85*, 83–103.

Walling, D., Warren, J., & McAlpine, G. (1997). *Reader-Response approaches to teaching literature.* Bloomington, IN: Phi Delta Kappa Educational Foundation.

Weaver, C. (1996). *Teaching grammar in context.* Portsmouth, NH: Boynton/Cook.

Wiesendanger, K. (2000). *Reading strategies.* Upper Saddle River, NJ: Prentice Hall.

White, T.G., Sowell, J., & Yanagihara, A. (1989). Teaching elementary students to use word-part clues. *The Reading Teacher, 42*, 302–308.

Yancy, P. (2002). *What's so amazing about grace?* Grand Rapids, MI: Zondervan Publishing.

Yopp, H., & Yopp, R. (2000). Supporting phonemic awareness development in the classroom, *The Reading Teacher, 54* (2), 130–143.

Yopp, H., & Yopp, R. (2002). *OO-pples and boo-noo-noos: Songs and activities for phonemic awareness* (2nd ed.). Orlando, FL: Harcourt Brace.

Yokota, J. (2009). Learning through literature that offers diverse perspectives: Multicultural and international literature. In D.A. Wooten, & B.E. Cullinan (Eds.), *Children's Literature in the Reading Program* (pp. 66–73). Newark, DE: International Reading Association.

Children's Literature Cited

Brett, J. (1989). *The mitten.* New York, NY: Scholastic Publishing.

Burnett, F. H. (2006/1911). *The secret garden.* New York, NY: W. W. Norton & Company.

Carle, E. *The very busy spider* (1995). New York, NY: The Penguin Group.

Cronin, D. (2003). *Diary of a worm.* New York, NY: HarperCollins Publishing.

Funke, C, (2004). *Dragon rider.* New York, NY: Scholastic.

Gibbons, G. (1988). *The seasons of Arnold's apple tree.* San Anselmo, CA: Sandpiper Publishing. Mooloolaba QLD: Sandpiper Publishing.

Henkes, K. (2007). *Chrysanthemum.* New York, NY: Scholastic.

Iasevoli, B. (2006). *Time for kids: Plants.* New York, NY: Harper Collins.

Jacques, B. (1998). *Redwall.* New York, NY: Ace Publishing.

Jordan, H. J. (1992). *How a seed grows.* New York, NY: Collins Publishing.

McCallum, A. (2006). *Beanstalk: The measure of a giant.* Watertown, MA: Charlesbridge Publishing.

Milne, A. A. (1996). *The complete takes and poems of Winnie-the-Pooh.* New York, NY: Dutton Children's Books.

Mitchell, L. (1999). *Different Just Like Me.* Watertown, MA: Charlesbridge.

Munoz-Ryan, P. (2004). *Becoming Naomi Leon.* New York, NY: Scholastic.

O'Connor, J. (2006). *Fancy Nancy: Bonjour butterfly.* New York, NY: Harper Collins.

Schaefer, L. (2006). *We need farmers.* Mankato, MN: Capstone Press.

Silverstein, S. (1999). *The giving tree.* New York, NY: Harper Collins.

Young, E. (1996). *Lon po po.* New York, NY: Puffin Books.

INDEX

Note: page numbers with the "f" appendix means the term is found within the figure on that page. Page numbers with the "t" appendix means the term is found within the table on that page.